Louis XIV and
Twenty Million Frenchmen

Louis XIV
and
Twenty Million Frenchmen

PIERRE GOUBERT

TRANSLATED FROM THE FRENCH
BY ANNE CARTER

PANTHEON BOOKS
A Division of Random House, New York

CONTENTS

6 *Contents*

PREFACE

YET another book about Louis XIV! This one lays no claim to provide new revelations or titillating information about the monarch's private life, and if that is what the reader is after, he had better turn to more specialized works. This Louis XIV is a popularization and at the same time something of an experiment.

Between the scholars, wrapped up in their special subjects, and the general public who are usually obliged to make do with historical gossip or political tracts, there exists a real and ever-widening gulf. This book is an attempt to bridge that gulf. The educated public has a right to information about the considerable new work accomplished during the past twenty years. Many accepted beliefs about the reign, if not about the king himself, are ripe for reappraisal.

Many people, unless they are particularly open-minded, will be shocked by some of the ideas put forward in this book. It is true that some interpretations appear as hypotheses, but they are free hypotheses providing food for thought and a spur to fresh work, and history, after all, is one of the refuges of liberty. It is no part of the historian's job to pander to existing beliefs and established methods.

Still less is it his task to pass judgement on any man, even a man like Louis XIV who invited the judgement of posterity and always proclaimed himself responsible for everything, great or small, that happened in his reign. The historian's role is to find out and try to understand, not to pass sentence.

Louis XIV by himself, enclosed in his majesty, is a purely literary figure. However strong and determined such a master may be, and however conscious of his responsibilities, he is as much dependent on his subjects and on the world in which he lives as his subjects are dependent on him and as that world bears his mark. The object of this book is rather to set Louis in relation to his kingdom and his time and ultimately to consider, yet again, the eternal problem of the great man in history.

There are bound to be criticisms of gaps in the narrative, an omission here, a cavalier dismissal or an unexpectedly protracted treatment there. But for those who want a complete account which will be didactic and, in the best sense, scholarly, there are admirable textbooks available and even the older of these are not to be despised. For those in search of fuller and more detailed information with evidence and academic arguments, there is a short bibliography at the end of the book.

Finally, it will be seen that this essay bears little resemblance to others, even recent works devoted principally to the king and to the king alone. I should like to make it clear that these differences are quite conscious and deliberate and that I accept full responsibility for them.

CHRONOLOGICAL ORDER OF EVENTS

I. LOUIS XIV UNDER MAZARIN

1638 (5 September): Birth of Louis-Dieudonné, Dauphin of France.

1643: Accession of Louis XIV. Regency of Anne of Austria.

1648: Beginning of the Fronde.
Peace of Westphalia: France acquires the greater part of Alsace.

1649 (6 January): Flight of the young king Louis XIV and the court to Saint-Germain.

1651 (September): The king's coming of age.

1652 (October): End of the Fronde. The king returns to Paris in triumph.

1653: The king, apparently acting on his own initiative, orders the arrest of Cardinal Retz at court.

1655: The king attends *Parlement* dressed for hunting.

1658: The king unwell outside Calais. Unrest throughout the country.

1658–1659–1660: Final European peace treaties: in the north (between Sweden, Denmark, Poland and Brandenburg), and between France and Spain (Treaty of the Pyrenees, November 1659. Acquisition of Roussillon and Cerdagne, most of Alsace. Condé pardoned. Marriage arranged between Louis XIV and the Infanta Maria-Theresa.)

1660 (9 June): Marriage of Louis XIV to Maria-Theresa.

1661 (9 March): Death of Mazarin.

II. TWELVE GLORIOUS YEARS 1661–72

At Home

1661: The king refuses to take a prime minister.

Colbert helps the king get rid of Fouquet and takes his place but not his title.

1662: Great tournament in Paris.

Widespread famine and revolt (especially in the Boulonnais). Bossuet's first great sermons.

1663: First of writers 'subsidized' by the Government. Foundation of (among others) the *Académie des Inscriptions et Belles-Lettres.*

1664: The 'pleasures of the Enchanted Isle' at Versailles. The king stands godfather to the child of Molière, who is engaged in writing *Tartuffe*, prepares to dissolve the *Compagnie du Saint-Sacrement* and expels the nuns of Port-Royal. Important foundations attributed to Colbert, including the East Indies Company and Beauvais tapestry works. Revolt in Béarn.

1665: Colbert finally appointed Controller General of Finance (but also the rise of Le Tellier's son, Louvois).

Troubles in Auvergne and attempt to restore order in the province.

Work begun on the great naval shipyards at Brest.

First issue of the *Journal des Savants.*

Title of *'cours souveraines'* reduced to *'cours supérieures'.*

1666: The (unofficial) *Académie des Sciences* brought under royal protection.

First detailed factory regulations.

1667: Ultra-protectionist customs tariff.

'Civil' Ordinance of Saint-Germain. The first of the reign's great ordinances.

La Reynie becomes lieutenant of police in Paris.

1668: 'The Peace of the Church': temporary solution of the Jansenist problem.

1669: Revival of legalized persecution of Protestants.

Colbert Secretary of State (for the Navy and the Royal Household).

Grande Ordonnance des Eaux et Forêts.

1670: Revolt in Vivarais.

1672: Louvois a member of the High Council (together with Arnauld and Pomponne).

Abroad

1661: Dispute over precedence in London.

1662: Spanish 'audience of apology', minor troubles in Rome (the Corsican guard).

1663: (Temporary) annexation of Avignon.
Seizure of the fortress of Marsal in Lorraine.

1664: Audience of apology of the Papal Legate.
Extension of the League of the Rhine (created by Mazarin).
Defeat of the Turks at Saint-Gotthard on the Raab, with French help.
Beginning of the war between England and Holland.

1665: Death of Philip IV of Spain and preparations for the War of Devolution.

1667: End of the Anglo-Dutch War (Treaty of Breda).
Beginning of the War of Devolution: invasion of Flanders.

1668: Invasion of Franche-Comté (Spanish).
Triple Alliance of The Hague (Holland, England and Sweden) against France: Louis XIV abandons Franche-Comté in return for a dozen Flemish strongpoints, including Lille.

1669: Crete falls to the Turks, in spite of French assistance.

1670: Treaty of Dover with England, against Holland.

III. THE DUTCH YEARS 1672–9

1672: Louis XIV declares war, crosses the Rhine and occupies part of Holland but the country is saved by the breaching of the dykes. William of Orange, Stadtholder.
For the first time national expenditure exceeds income.

1673: Coalition against Louis XIV: the Empire, Spain and Lorraine.
Trade ordinance. Increased financial deficit and first 'extraordinary' financial measures.

1674: England deserts Louis XIV (Treaty of Westminster); second occupation of Franche-Comté.
Victory of Seneffe (Condé).

Turenne saves Alsace and the realm (winter campaign end December).

New taxes help to provoke rebellion at home (especially in Guyenne).

Temporary loss of Martinique. Settlement at Pondicherry.

West Indies Company goes into liquidation.

1675: Death of Turenne and new campaign in Alsace (Condé).

Revolts in Brittany put down by armed forces.

Crushing defeat of Sweden by Brandenburg at Fehrbellin.

Birth of Saint-Simon, later historian of the reign.

1676: French fleet victorious off Sicily. Death of Ruyter.

Foundation of the *Caisse des conversions*.

Innocent XI becomes Pope.

1677: Capture of Valenciennes and Cambrai (Vauban).

Racine retires from the theatre after *Phèdre*.

Failure of the La Rochelle agency of the *Compagnie du Nord*.

1678: Treaty of Nymegen: annexation of Franche-Comté and parts of Flanders and Hainault: 1667 tariff rescinded.

Beginning of the affair of the *régale*.

Publication of Richard Simon's *Histoire critique du Vieux Testament*.

1679: Final treaties dissolving the coalition (in particular, peace in the north): beginning of the conflict with the Jansenists.

Legislation against the Protestants.

IV. THE TIME OF SCORN 1679–89

1680–1681: Progress of the affair of the *régale*; intensive persecution of Protestants and first *dragonnades*; first peacetime 'réunions': Strasbourg, September 1681; *Ordonnance de la Marine* 1681.

1682: The court moves to Versailles.

Declaration of the Four Articles and partial schism by Louis XIV.

Indies Company resigns its monopoly.

1683: Catholic victory at the Kahlenberg, forcing the Turks to raise the siege of Vienna.

Death of Queen Maria-Theresa. The king's secret remarriage. Colbert dies, largely out of favour.

1684: Short campaign against Spain concluded by the Truce of Ratisbon: the majority of *'réunions'* accepted even by the emperor.

Peacetime bombardment of Genoa.

1685: Edict of Fontainebleau: revocation of the Edict of Nantes. Publication of the *Code noir* (Colonies). Dispute over succession to the Palatinate.

1686: Formation of the League of Augsburg, led by the Emperor, against France.

French fleet off Cadiz. Catinat ravages the Vaudois.

Publication of Fontenelle's *L'Entretien sur la pluralité des mondes*.

1687: Clash with the Pope over the franchise (Rome): nomination to the see of Archbishop Elector of Cologne.

1688: Second revolution in England: William of Orange King of England.

Series of attacks by Louis XIV: on Liège and the Rhineland, the Palatinate and Avignon.

First edition of La Bruyère's *Caractères*.

Cost of living reaches exceptionally low level.

Creation of the militia (Louvois).

V. THE TIME OF TRIAL 1689–1715

1689: Sack of the Palatinate; landing of James II; war on all fronts.

Last appointment of provincial intendant at Rennes.

Soupirs de la France esclave qui aspire à sa Liberté (Jurieu?).

Death of Innocent XI.

1690: Victories at Fleurus (Luxembourg), Staffarde (Catinat) and Beachy Head (Tourville) but disaster at Drogheda (Battle of the Boyne).

1691: Death of Louvois.

1692: Victory of Steenkirk and naval disaster of La Hogue.

1693: Victory of Neerwinden (Luxembourg) and La Marsaille (Catinat).

Beginning of the great famine.

Louis XIV gives way in the conflict with Rome and becomes ultramontane.

1694: Spread of the greatest 'mortality' of the reign in most parts of the kingdom except the west and the Midi.

Foundation of the Bank of England.

Death of the great Arnuld. The Orator, Père Quesnel, author of *Réflexions morales*, becomes one of the moving spirits of Jansenist movement.

Denunciation of the 'quietest heresy' (Mme Guyon).

1695: Introduction of first capitation tax, theoretically affecting all alike.

Royal decree placing the minor clergy as a whole under the control of bishops and 'democratic' reactions of parish priests.

Boisguillebert's *Détail de la France*; Vauban's letter to the king (?).

1696: Duke of Savoy signs a separate peace with Louis XIV.

1697: Peace of Ryswick (only Strasbourg retained).

Beginning of the great inquiry into the state of the realm undertaken by the Duc de Beauvillier.

Bayle's *Dictionnaire historique et critique*; Fénelon *Explication des maximes des saints sur la vie intérieure*.

1698: Slight relaxation in persecution of Protestants.

First South Seas and China companies.

1699: Pontchartrain moves from Finance ministry to Chancellery.

Half-hearted condemnation of quietism by the Pope.

Fénelon's *Télémaque*.

1700: Revival of Trade Council including merchants.

Death of the King of Spain. Louis XIV accepts the will.

1701: William III initiates Grand Alliance of the Hague.

First clashes with imperial troops in Italy.

Reintroduction of capitation tax (suspended in 1698).

1702: Beginning of the War of the Spanish Succession.

Death of William III.

Beginning of the revolt of the Camisards.

Conscription of militia.

1703: Duke of Savoy rejoins the anti-French coalition.
Portugal likewise.

1704: Defeat of French at Battle of Blenheim. The English take Gibraltar.

1705: Death of Leopold I.
End of the violent revolt of the Camisards.
Heinsius makes peace offer to Louis XIV.
Papal Bull *Vineam domini* against Jansenists.

1706: Villeroy defeated at Ramillies. Loss of the Netherlands.
La Feuillade defeated before Turin. Loss of Italy. British enter Madrid but are driven out.

1707: Vauban's *Projet d'une dîme royale*.
Denis Papin builds a steamship.

1708: Defeat of Oudenarde and fall of Lille.
Desmarets Minister of Finance.

1709: The 'great winter' and start of famine.
Battle of Malplaquet, bloody but indecisive.
Louis strikes at Port-Royal.

1710: Famine and unrest in many provinces.
Failure of negotiations at Gertruydenberg.
Introduction of the *dixième*, theoretically universal.
Victory of Villaviciosa (December) restores Spain to Philip V.

1711: Death of the Emperor Charles III and half the heirs to the French throne.
England leaves the coalition and signs secret preliminary peace treaty with Louis XIV in London.
Final destruction of Port-Royal, including burial ground.

1712: Negotiations at Utrecht.
Victory of Denain.
More royal deaths: two-year-old Duc d'Anjou left sole heir.

1713: Treaty of Utrecht.
Papal Bull *Unigenitus* against Jansenists, varied reception.
More monetary manipulations.

1714: Treaty of Rastadt.
Clashes on the ratification of the Bull.
Terrible cattle plague.
Decree establishing right of succession to Louis' illegitimate

offspring (including the Duc du Maine), and Louis' will.

1715: Resumption of anti-Protestant persecution but pastor Court presides over a synod near Nîmes.

Death of Fénelon.

Death of Louis XIV (1 September). His will set aside and Philip d'Orléans regent.

December: temporary halt to devaluation of the *livre*.

PART ONE

The Inheritance:
France Under Mazarin

At long last, on 9 March 1661, the event took place to which the young Louis XIV had looked forward with a mixture of eagerness and dread. The all-powerful cardinal Giulio Mazarini, sole distributor of favours and positions, the king's godfather and the queen regent's lover, whose life had been despaired of weeks before by everyone except his physicians, finally passed away in the presence of his Italian confessor, Father Angelo. He had given a last audience to his trusted confidant, Ondedei, and to his intendant Colbert, made some small alterations to his will, taken notice of his weeping godson, listened to a Spanish priest who spoke to him 'gently' of death and had further permitted a Parisian *curé*, Father Joly, to visit him. His last moments have been variously reported but we have Father Angelo's word that they were very pious. More important, however, was what took place next morning.

Louis XIV summoned his council at daybreak. In a very few words he declared his intention of governing alone, with no prime minister, assisted by his councillors when he should call upon them. Ministerial rule was at an end. There would be no 'Third Eminence'. Louis XIV was assuming full responsibility for the control of his kingdom.

Ten years later, in his memoirs, written for the Dauphin, the king described the state of his inheritance – or permitted it to be described – in two concise phrases. At home, 'chaos reigned'; abroad, 'all was quiet on all fronts'.

Is this a fair description of the kingdom which Mazarin bequeathed to his royal godson?

The hexagonal shape of modern France had been built up slowly, its boundaries fixed for two years at the Pyrenees, at the Alps for two hundred and at the Saône for a further fifteen. Now, after twenty-five years of war, it had finally overstepped the old Carolingian frontiers of the Somme and the Meuse by the annexation of the greater part of Artois and Alsace and the strengthening of French strongholds in Lorraine. Within these bounds lived the eighteen million or so subjects who made up the most populous kingdom in Europe. We know that the vast majority of them were Catholic peasants. What of the less familiar aspects of their lives?

I

DEMOGRAPHY

In 1969, the average expectation of life is something over
seventy years. In 1661 it was probably under twenty-five.
These brutal figures show how, in those days, death was at
the centre of life, just as the graveyard was at the centre of
the village. Out of every hundred children born, twenty-five
died before they were one year old, another twenty-five
never reached twenty and a further twenty-five perished
between the ages of twenty and forty-five. Only about ten
ever made their sixties. The triumphant octogenarian, surrounded by an aura of legend that made him seem at least a
hundred, was regarded with the superstitious awe spon-
taneously accorded to champions. His sons and daughters,
nephews and nieces long dead, as well as a good half of his
grandchildren, the sage lived on to become an oracle for his
entire village. His death was a major event for the whole
region.

In normal times other deaths were part of the ordinary
fabric of existence. New-born babies died, followed or preceded by their young mothers, the victims, as like as not, of
an ignorant midwife or incompetent surgeon. The widower
consoled himself quickly, remarried – anything from a few
months to two years after – and forgot. At certain times, in
August and September especially, parish priests, dominies
and grave-diggers would perform cut-price funerals for the
'small corpses' of children. The family was not unduly concerned and the lost infant would be replaced within a year
or two. These were day to day events, of less moment than
a bad storm, a freak tempest or the death of a horse.

There were certain places – marshy or low-lying areas,

coastal regions and even the industrial outskirts of some towns or cities – where death struck with a peculiar relish, but this did not prevent the people flocking there because there was rarely any shortage of work for their distaffs, spinning wheels or looms, and because land, wood and water were plentiful and, if not actually free, at least available.

At certain times of the year, and in some years more than others, the familiar face of the countryside underwent an appalling transformation. At such times the apocalyptic figure of Death took on three terrible faces, sometimes distinct but more often confused. The three immemorial scourges of mankind, war, pestilence and famine fell upon King Louis' subjects. From war, which had claimed countless German victims in the second quarter of the century, the people of Picardy and Champagne had learned to protect themselves to some extent by retreating into walled towns, taking with them their cattle and their goods, by fleeing into the interior of the country, or by taking refuge in the astonishing networks of caves and underground tunnels which lay behind many of their villages. But the armies, which ravaged more than they killed, often left hunger and disease in their wake. France in those days was still a prey to that most dreaded of all disease, bubonic plague. Its symptoms, all too familiar to doctors, seemed, in the past thirty years or so, to have developed an even more virulent strain. One summer or the next, towns or provinces in every part of Europe might lose a quarter or a third of their entire populations within the space of a few weeks in a single, devastating outbreak. Then the disease would seem to lie dormant for a while, only to break out again without warning to the north, south or west. Its appearance was followed by panic, the wholesale flight of all who could afford it, isolation and quarantine. In 1661 mild outbreaks occurred in one or two places, although these may have been due to some other disease since every epidemic of any magnitude was invariably ascribed to the plague. The French were to suffer further visitations before long, and so, on an even worse scale, were the English.

Periods of scarcity or famine, *cherté* as it was euphemistically and accurately called, occurred with fair regularity. They were the inevitable result of persistent bad weather, an economy relying too heavily on cereal crops and of a particular type of society and attitude of mind. Except in the mountains and the south, the huge majority of the French people subsisted chiefly, if not entirely, on porridge, soup, and bread and dripping. Cereals – in this case rye with a leavening of wheat – were far and away the cheapest and most traditional form of nourishment. But it was also a fact that the varieties of grain used for making flour came from the Near East and did not adapt easily to a maritime climate with the cold wet summers so common in France and its rarer bitter winters. Over at least half the country, therefore, harvests were no longer sufficient to meet the immediate needs of the population. News and transport moved so slowly that swift relief was impossible. Rumours of famine spread quickly and made the situation worse. By May or June the price of grain would have risen sharply in the numerous markets, most of which were very small.

Society was organized in such a way that more than half the people of France, peasants included, were in the habit of buying their corn. Prices at twice or even three times their normal level put it out of their reach and sent half of them in search of other sources of food, much of it unfit for human consumption. People put their children to beg by the wayside, or fell back on private charity or theft, and tempers rose to the point where hoarders were threatened or actually beaten up.

Very soon infection appeared, spread by swarms of vermin and the constant movement of beggars, troops and pedlars.

Much of the sickness was due to malnutrition, various deficiency diseases and in many cases to starvation. People in 1661 had not yet forgotten the famines of the 1630s, still less the horrors of the years 1649–52: four years of rotten summers and bad harvests, four years of mounting famine made worse by bands of vagabond soldiers, rebels or not, and by the insecurity of the roads. Cases of cannibalism are known to have occurred and letters addressed to Monsieur Vincent at this time reveal still greater wretchedness. All this was still fresh in men's minds, even down to the names of the victims, one or two in every family over and above the normal toll. And ever since 1658, the times were out of joint again and the price of corn was rising steadily. By March 1661 the time for surmise was past, leaving only fear of the imminent reality. The major event of this year was to be not the death of the Italian cardinal, but one of the worst famines of the century. We shall have more to say about this.

Struggling to combat this obsession with death there was an extraordinary force of sheer, undisciplined animal life. The cult of Our Lady, the holy mother of God, was in many places simply a perpetuation of the cults of countless, half-forgotten goddesses of fertility. Mankind reproduced itself fast enough to keep pace with the appetite of death and still preserve the race. Except among courtesans and a sprinkling of great ladies, notably the burghers' wives of Geneva, nature was given free rein to produce all the births biologically possible – a child every twenty-five to thirty months was the regular pattern in regions where prolonged breast-feeding was the custom. Forty babies were born each year for every thousand or so of the population.

This natural fecundity was somewhat curtailed by custom and religious observance. There were not many illegitimate births, not nearly as many as in the twentieth century, and very few children arrived too promptly after the wedding. On the whole, people married late: boys marrying for the first time seem to have been from twenty-six to twenty-eight and girls from twenty-three to twenty-five on average. Numbers of bachelors and widowers who did not remarry were no greater than they are today. Contrary to popular belief, very large families were rare. Girls married too late in life and death soon undid too many marriages. The average was not more than five children for each household, only two or three of whom might reach maturity. No historian of the period has unearthed a family of more than twenty children among the rural population and even twelve was rare enough.

Nevertheless, in the never-ending battle marked by advances and withdrawals of the plague, by sudden attacks of famine, followed by equally sudden retreats, the forces of life and fertility tended on the whole to combat death in all its aspects. Such reliable information as we have, though this concerns only a very few parishes, suggests that in the first half of the seventeenth century, in spite of terrible but short-lived plagues and famines, the forces of life were almost uniformly victorious. It is possible that France in 1640 had reached an exceptionally high level of population. There is little doubt that the natural, political and economic disasters which occurred during the period of the Fronde dealt a severe blow to the kingdom's population everywhere except in the south; but after a few years, as always after a period of crisis, the time of multiple deaths had passed, to be followed by a spate of marriages and a triumphant increase in the number of christenings. Not all mourning was yet a thing of the past, and the generation which had suffered remained inevitably much reduced, but there were masses of young children to pave the way for future generations twice the size of any that had gone before. Even so, no one in March 1661 could have said for sure whether the forces of life and growth would carry the day and mark the real beginning of the reign of Louis XIV.

All this formed part of the natural rhythm of the land, of which every man and woman in the kingdom was to some extent aware. It belonged to the half-unconsciously accepted fabric of daily life. There was no point in dwelling on it. Makers of almanacs, writers of books and memoirs were content with the casual mention of a plague more virulent than usual, with much exaggerated stories of an amazingly fertile woman or a man who lived to exceptional old age. The unusual and exceptional were noted. Kings and their counsellors thought it a good thing for the people to multiply. An increase in population led to greater power: more subjects meant more work and more taxes which would of course bring in more money. They were also concerned to protect themselves from disease by ruthless isolation of stricken homes, and striving to contain the infection, and in this direction their efforts were not far from success. For the rest of the people it was simply a matter of good or bad fortune, the blessing of Heaven or a punishment for sin. Kings were to all intents unaffected by demographic considerations. The physical existence of their thousands of subjects did not constitute one of the objects of government.

Economic life concerned them rather more. 'Mercantilism' was of course a word quite foreign to the times, like corporation, capitalism, and a host of catch words we have learned to abuse so freely in the last century. All the same, the kings and their ministers were well aware that a nation's wealth was a considerable factor in its power.

2

ECONOMY

Looked at objectively, France at this period could be described very simply as a rich and varied agricultural country, extremely backward technically, with large but unexploited national resources.

No amount of national bias, whether unconscious or deliberate, on the part of the admirers of the France of the Grand Siècle, can disguise the basic fact that throughout the seventeenth and even a good deal of the eighteenth centuries the Dutch were the dominant economic power in the world. The Bank of Amsterdam, an impressive copy of the banks of Venice and Genoa, of unparalleled size and stability, sustained and directed the economy of the United Provinces even through its worst moments. The Amsterdam stock exchange was the Wall Street of the seventeenth century. Prices were quoted there for most of the world's goods and printed and circulated weekly to the major European centres to form the basis of current world prices. Antwerp and the southern banks grew gradually sleepier as the bulk of international trade moved away to carry on its business at Amsterdam. Before very long Parisian bills of exchange would find their way to Amsterdam, in particular to the famous private banking concern of the Pels family. The stability of the florin became a legend, and with good reason. Without paying too much attention to the jealous exaggerations of Jean-Baptiste Colbert, it may be said that the Dutch fleet of anything from eight to nine thousand vessels represented – with the exception of China – at least half of the world's shipping. This busy, enterprising fleet, kept at the peak of condition by continual rebuilding, was constantly at sea carrying

Nordic herrings, salt from Brittany and Portugal, wine from the Loire and Aquitaine, grain, flax, timber and tar from Muscovy and the Scandinavian countries, as well as all the treasures of the Indies: ebony, sugar, molasses and tobacco. The ships and sailors on which Dutch supremacy was based were to be met with everywhere in French ports and along her navigable rivers, filling the great gap left by the absence of an adequate merchant service.

Amsterdam was the market and warehouse of the world. French merchants and politicians went there for everything from Baltic corn in time of famine, Swedish artillery and gunpowder from Liège in time of war, to Lenten herrings and wool from Spain. And, last but not least, the city existed for the moneylenders.

The two India Companies, especially the East, were the most powerful in the world. The huge dividends they paid – an average of more than 25 per cent per annum – roused much jealous enmity and clumsy attempts at imitation. Between 1660 and 1670, Leyden reached its apogee as the world's foremost centre of the clothworking industry, manufacturing millions of yards of cloth in over a hundred different textures. Dutch agriculture remained a model unequalled but for Flanders and Brabant. The English, who studied their methods closely, paid just tribute to their achievements in the art of cultivation. For a century or more the Dutch had been familiar with all the discoveries, many of them borrowed from the Flemish, which were to be hailed as an agricultural revolution in France two hundred years later, including the importance of root, fodder and leguminous crops and the complete disappearance of fallow periods. They had perfected a complex system of crop rotation, as well as the selection and manufacture of a variety of fertilizers suited to different types of soil and cultivation, and the selective breeding of livestock. Dutch cows were already giving the best milk yields in Europe, and Dutch butter and cheese were being exported even to France. Flower growing, and 'tulipomania' in particular, completed the picture.

The additional fact that these achievements were the work of a bourgeois and nominally Calvinist republic, even though the majority of the inhabitants were in fact Catholics, made Dutch supremacy in these fields a natural object for Colbert's envy and spite, as well as a source of irritation to King Louis. Anti-Dutch policies were a basic and inevitable part of the personal rule on which Louis now embarked, superbly allied to a somewhat naïve attempt to remould the French economy on Dutch lines.

Needless to say, there was a vast gulf between the small, well-organized merchant republic and the great but still almost medieval kingdom.

France had never possessed a national bank, or even any really permanent and stable private ones. The title of banker was accorded to a few of the most substantial merchants who handled the business of exchange, lent money at interest and participated in certain dark and complicated dealings whose principal object was to profit from the financial infantilism of a state which had never had such a thing as a budget, let alone any regular system of accounts. There was nothing in France remotely resembling a stock exchange. Paris, comparatively new as the political capital, could scarcely be called the economic capital of the country. Rouen, Saint-Malo, Bordeaux, the growing port of Marseilles and the possibly already declining city of Lyons, could all lay some claim to this title. The French monetary system may not have experienced such a variety of troubles as the Spanish, but its stability could not be compared with that of the florin, or even of sterling. The basic unit of exchange, the *livre tournois*, had no monetary reality. From time to time, in a belated and ineffectual attempt to counteract market fluctuations, the name, weight and face value of the various coins would be altered by royal decree. A variety of foreign coinage circulated in the realm, Spanish in particular, as well as an abundance of notes and a good deal of counterfeit coin. All this, though prohibited in theory, was tolerated in practice. But the good gold and silver coins went underground, to be turned into gold and silver plate, vessels and church ornaments and lie dormant in the coffers of the wealthy. There were constant complaints about the shortage of coin, especially good coin, and even the king himself soon experienced the shame of being able to complete the purchase of Dunkirk only after a great deal of difficulty. The waterways which were the kingdom's best roads were impassable six months in the year through flood or drought, and cluttered at all times with a host of tax collectors levying, especially on the Loire, a mass of dues which no one nowadays has succeeded in unravelling correctly. The main roads were still worse. With practically no maintenance, they had a disheartening effect on the length of journeys and the cost of transport. A few hundred vessels, a few big ship-owners and a handful of brave captains were not enough to cover the great slump in French shipping in both east and west. In the fifteenth and sixteenth centuries, daring fishermen and enterprising privateers of Dieppe, Brittany and the Basque country had scoured the Atlantic and were to be found in every port from Labrador to la Plata and from Guinea to the Levant. By 1661 their fame had diminished considerably and their voyages were fewer and further between. All the splendid trading companies dreamed up in the days of Louis XIII were dead or dying. None were left in Madagascar or the East Indies and only a few sporadic descents were made on the gold or slave coasts of Africa, now dominated, after the Portuguese, by the ubiquitous Dutchmen and occasionally disputed by the English. There were a few hundred men in Canada and the beginnings of a more serious settlement in the West Indies where much later under Louis XV French fortunes were to be made from the sugar plantations. All this made a poor showing beside the vast empires of Castille, Portugal, the Netherlands and even England. Once again it was the inevitable Dutch who maintained the bulk of trade with the French West Indies.

The French coalfields lay dormant, unknown and unexploited except by a few peasants and a handful of Lyonnais, while the Walloons and the British were working theirs. The British Isles indeed had already experienced a century of what an American historian, John U. Nef, has called the 'first industrial revolution', based on a 500 per cent increase in coal production. The iron foundries of Germany, Liège, Britain and Sweden were at the height of their prosperity: the first for quality, the second for age, the third for recent expansion and the fourth for a combination of all these things, fostered by Dutch capital. French ironworks were scattered at random by woods and riversides close to the mines and, after a real step forward in the sixteenth century, no longer produced anything but small, irregular quantities of expensive, poor quality metal manufactured according to antiquated techniques, the majority of these, even, borrowed from neighbouring countries. Except at Rives, the manufacture of steel was unknown in France. Canon, balls and powder had to be purchased from Liège, Lorraine, Denmark or from the inevitable Amsterdam merchants. Side-arms and cutlery came from Spain or more frequently from central and south Germany. Scythes came from Styria. The farriers of Picardy forged their ploughshares, horseshoes and spades with metal from Hainault, transported all the way to Amiens. Even pewter, the basic material for most of the common people's household utensils, came from England. Copper, in increasing use for coinage, came from Sweden and Japan, in both cases naturally by way of Amsterdam. A degree of inverted snobbery attached to this preponderance of foreign goods. Even in those days people would say that English thread and cloth were the best (in earlier centuries it had been Florentine), and the best linen cloth was Dutch, and it was true that the bleaching trade of Haarlem could work miracles.

Where the land was concerned, the most surprising thing is the lack of reference books and the complete technical stagnation. Leaving aside the arts of gardening, hunting and preserving, not one single work dealing with agricultural matters was written by a Frenchman between 1601 and 1750. They were satisfied with reprinting or cribbing from Estienne de Liébault's *Maison rustique*, while the *Théâtre d'Agriculture* was all too quickly forgotten. In England in the same period books on farming were proliferating, encouraged by experiments with enclosures on the Flemish model. The Dutch and Flemings, while less voluble, were continually experimenting successfully in a way which found no echo in France. Except in two or three specially favoured regions, such as Aquitaine for maize, the Midi for small-scale irrigation, Poitou for re-allocation of estates, and the Île-de-France for market gardening, vines and lucerne, the French peasantry persisted in their wasteful habits of allowing fields to lie fallow, of sowing quantities of poor quality seed, of poor cultivation using wooden implements drawn by undernourished beasts, coupled with the wholesale exhaustion of fields and forest by general petty and haphazard farming methods, the best products of which were so-called fat bullocks weighing little over eight hundred pounds. One year in two, the grapes failed to ripen. One year in eight or ten, the harvest was poor, and even in the good years the yield was not above four hundredweight to the acre. Not one peasant in two owned a cow, fewer than one in four had his own plough and the team to pull it. Tools were made from wood and withy, even spades being merely clad in a metal sheath, while, possibly for lack of scythes, people still used a sickle for reaping. Except in the Midi, where there were land surveys and property tax, they did not even know the precise acreage of their land or the geographical contours of the region.

Nevertheless, there was a general belief which found expression in the writings of those approximating to the economists of the period and in the words of orators and public speakers, that this was the richest and most diverse of all possible realms, that it abounded in commodities of all kinds, especially in corn, salt, wine and textiles, and that it was able to be completely self-supporting, with no recourse to imports from abroad. It remains to be seen whether this old economic patriotism, strongly coloured by a classic autarchy, was based on anything other than the most beatific optimism.

Louis' kingdom had just endured twenty-five years of open war, with a further ten years of covert hostilities before that. Simultaneously, there had been as many years of more or less violent internal rebellions and civil wars. Now the internal troubles had been temporarily smoothed over and the wars with Spain and the Empire had been settled by victories, hard-won, but victories nonetheless. These successes are not to be explained simply by the talents of two ministers and a few commanders. Generals cannot win victories without plenty of well-fed and well-armed troops. The supply corps has the last word and there are no great generals or great ministers without material resources to back them. It may well be argued that Richelieu and Mazarin borrowed all over Europe at exorbitant rates in order to pay their armies and their allies but credit of this kind is based, not on words or ideas but on substantial guarantees. The guarantee in this case, realized by dint of endless taxes pledged in advance to the financiers, was the wealth of France. In the end all these creditors, in and out of the country, were paid by a drain on her resources. Had France been a really poor country, she could never have recovered from her wars at home or abroad.

Of what did the wealth of France consist? Not in brilliantly successful business enterprises such as the New England or India Companies, the armaments factories of the Bishop of Liège or the Swedish/Dutch canon of Louis de Geer and Gustavus Adolphus. Nor had she anything to compare with the American silver being unloaded at Seville or the world-wide trade of the Dutch. Her wealth lay simply in the happy combination of a fertile and varied land and a large, spirited and able population.

France at this time was a sprawling agricultural country in which the practical problems facing the bulk of the peasant population were threefold: to scrape a living, pay their taxes, tithes and other local and seigneurial dues and, if possible, enlarge their holdings and improve the social status of their families. Obviously, this triple objective was rarely attained, even in its most immediate part, but the means employed in the effort to achieve it may well explain the wealth of France. In order to meet both the needs of the family and the necessary surplus for taxation, the French peasants engaged in many and varied activities. Specialization was the exception, and often a dangerous exception since the vast cornfields were more liable to failure than anything else. As a general rule, the French peasant was a mixture of market gardener, mixed farmer, vine-grower, day labourer, spinner or weaver, clothworker or blacksmith, nail-smith or innkeeper, almost invariably poacher and if possible smuggler. In order to cope with his own work and that imposed on him by others, he became a jack-of-all-trades. It was his good fortune to find almost everywhere, except in a few dour regions, conditions of soil and climate so favourable that even his slight knowledge of farming methods was scarcely an impediment.

None of the statistics so beloved of modern minds, not even

approximate ones, are available for the year 1661. All that
can be said is that in spite of local shortages and widespread
regional famine, Louis' subjects made some kind of a living,
however poor and hard, and even managed, in spite of the
fragility of human life, to raise enough children to keep
the level of population roughly stable. In spite of the vast
expense of wars, rebellions, crooked ministers and officials
and unbelievable administrative chaos, the amount grudg-
ingly disgorged by the groaning and protesting people of
France had at least doubled in a quarter of a century. But the
triple burden of war, anarchy and the nation's creditors had
been borne. No other country could, or did, bear as much
and still emerge victorious after enduring for thirty years.

More than this, the 'bay' of Bourgneuf still supplied other
nations, and Holland in particular, with salt, despite Portuguese rivalry. Every other year or more, French grain went
to feed part of Europe. French wine and brandy, handled
again by the ubiquitous Dutch, went down the throats of all
the people of northern Europe, although the old markets
in England and the Netherlands showed signs of a decline.
The English consuls in the commercial ports of the Levant
and at Constantinople were complaining bitterly of competition from French textiles carried by vessels out of Marseilles which had a damaging effect on the heavy English
broadcloth and virtually superseded sales of Venetian
fabrics. The authorities in the Spanish Netherlands too had
reason to bewail a drop in exports to France of Hondschoot
serge, woollens from Lille and in particular linen fabrics, a
drop attributable in part to the war but also to the considerable advances made in French textiles, especially in the
manufacture of hempen and linen cloth from the valley of
the Oise, Maine, Brittany and the Vendée. Lapeyre has
shown that by the end of the sixteenth century these textiles
were already supplying Spain and her Empire. By the mid-
seventeenth, as Albert Girard has shown, they were reaching

Spain in large quantities ever finer and more closely woven, and better bleached and dressed. These in all probability constituted France's main item of export and yet they were made entirely by countless peasant workers scattered over the countryside.

There are some indications of the overall scale of French agricultural produce to be found in the contents of the barns, granaries and cellars of the various religious houses during those weeks in which they were the repository of all the collective tithes, dues and rents sent in by farmers of a particular region. In addition, there are the barns, granaries, and cellars of the collectors on behalf of great estates, wealthy peasant farmers and bourgeois middlemen.

Still more impressive are the amounts of cloth of all kinds in the possession of the merchants of Amiens and Laval, and the great variety of shops found in Paris, Rouen, Troyes, Lyons, Marseilles and all the major commercial towns and ports. With this evidence, the examination of such an intense concentration of rural industry, coupled with such widespread trade and distribution, begins to make it clear that expertise in commercial and financial methods is not the infallible mark of economic prosperity. In France in 1661, few people were at all familiar with the common practice of employing bills of exchange, about which the rules were vague and little in demand, although the Italians and Flemish had long been accustomed to all the refinements of accounting and money-changing techniques. Book-keeping was still in its most elementary stages. There was no shame in bartering one item in exchange for another, or in the circulation of small scraps of paper, signed and dated ious, memos and notes of hand which, though they went by a confusing variety of names like *cédules* or *obligations*, constituted the real hard cash of the times, even when not registered before a notary or confirmed by a court of law. And failing an exchange or a note of hand, men carried their moneybags with them when they went to make a purchase, just as in centuries past.

This was a strong but still traditional economy, thrifty and careful with little use for adventure on the high seas but instead firmly rooted in the generous earth like a centuries-old oak tree. It was varied, cautious and thriving and, with all its faults, drawbacks and unsatisfactoriness, ultimately capable of bearing, groaning but unflinching, not only a formidable and never-ending burden of social and political parasites but also whatever storms might blow from any quarter, and it had proved as much over a quarter of a century. It rested entirely on the hard, unceasing, intelligent and multifarious labours of a people who, in numbers and virtues, deserved to be the foremost in Europe.

3

SOCIETY

THERE was in the kingdom of France a traditional distinction between those who prayed, those who fought and those who toiled. The last of these were useful and consequently base. For a long time, at least since Loyseau, the Third Estate had been held to comprise officials, tradesmen and bourgeois, while right at the bottom were the most contemptible of all, the 'rude mechanicals' who worked with their hands: artisans, some tens of thousands of urban workers and the vast mass of the peasantry.

Society, like the State and the economy, rested on the most numerous, dependent and eminently productive section of the community: the peasantry. The peasants were less a social class than a complex group. What they had in common was their habitat, their occupations, the framework of dependency within which they were held and the fact of enabling the three real estates of the realm to live and prosper.

The working of the land was wholly in the hands of the peasantry which − allowing for a good deal of regional variation − owned less than half of it. Except for the very few remaining freeholds, peasant property was not of the 'Roman' type but manorial, that is to say that it was never independent. It is fashionable among royalist historians to assert the peasant's right to sell, lease, exchange, give or bequeath his land and this was true up to a point, but only with the consent of his overlord and after payment of what were frequently crippling dues and bearing in mind the fact that the *seigneur* always could, and often did, withdraw his consent. (It was quite within his rights to substitute himself as purchaser and at the same price.) It is further maintained nowadays that the peasants' feudal dues, which had been fixed for a long time, had dwindled into insignificance with the decline in the value of money. This is true of the old financial payments made in direct rents but false as regards all other dues which were often levied in kind and in particular of *rentes* and *champarts*; the last alone currently amounted to a tenth and sometimes a third of the crop. The feudal nature of his holding was to the peasant at the same time an annoyance and a burden, aggravated by the amazing variation in local conditions.

It seems probable that the small part of French territory which did belong to four-fifths of its inhabitants was divided extremely unfairly. The few serious studies which have been made of some provinces lead to the following conclusions. Not many peasants were altogether landless. About a tenth possessed the few hectares (varying from one region to the next) which meant economic security for their families. The vast majority had only a few scattered plots, often the poorest land in the district, and were compelled to find other means of livelihood. The peasants who were really rich and powerful were those who farmed great estates and manors who were to some extent the overseers and agents of the great landowners. These conclusions are valid at least for the Île-de-France and Picardy, though they have still to be confirmed elsewhere. A village of a hundred families would include one or two big farmers whose ploughs, teams, holdings and credit made them powerful men in the locality, a dozen or so more or less independent labouring men and the same number of poor souls whose only possessions were their hovel, their patch of ground or their ewe or who were frankly beggars. The remainder, farm hands, casual labourers, vineyard workers, woodmen and weavers were all humble folk scraping a meagre living from tiny holdings and turning their hands to any trade that came their way.

The tools, livestock and employment on which the entire village depended for a livelihood, at least in good years, were in the hands of the dozen or so 'big men' and even, in some cases, of a single 'cock' of the village. Nothing could have been less egalitarian than a French village community. 'Jacques Bonhomme' never existed except in the minds of novelists and pamphleteers. Village administration, which was more energetic and effective than that of our modern councils, was naturally in the hands of the farmers and labouring men who formed the 'better part' of the local assemblies. The village community levied taxes from all its members towards the upkeep of the church, priest's house, graveyard, schoolhouse and teacher, and for the communal shepherd, or shepherds, and wardens and keepers to watch over the crops or vineyards. In many cases the local village community was combined with the religious one of the parish to form a basic administrative unit of the kingdom in matters concerning *bailliages*, elections, salt stores and control of woods and forests and so forth. More rarely it was identified with the *seigneurie*.

This, with the village and the parish, constituted the third social group to which the peasant belonged. As we know, the *seigneur*, whether individual or collective, nobleman or *roturier*, clergy or layman, enjoyed a great many rights, honorary or otherwise, which varied endlessly from place to place and were persistently confused with the privileges of nobility. (A fact extremely convenient for the *faux nobles, seigneurs* of long standing who probably formed the bulk of the French nobility.) These seigneurial dues might be slight or they might be ruinous and were generally substantial but they were invariably a burden, the extent of which varied according to the region, the *seigneur* and his collector. In the long sequence of peasant revolts which go to make up the history of rural France in the seventeenth century it is as common to find the peasants allied with the *seigneur* against the king – as, for instance, in Auvergne – as it is the opposite – notably in Brittany and Picardy. Even an absentee *seigneur* often made his authority felt through the severity and unlimited powers of his collectors, intendants, judges, bailiffs, seneschals, clerks and fiscal attorneys, who were not always remarkable for their honesty. Insufficient study has been devoted to the seigneurial courts which were numerous, busy and basic to an understanding of rural life. They clearly served a useful purpose to their clients but sometimes at the cost of substantial fees and the imposition of large fines for trivial offences.

The parish priest was an inseparable part of rural life in 1661. He played an important, although variable role and he, too, took his share of the country's resources, for his own support and for the maintenance of church buildings and furniture. This was rarely in the form of major tithes (on corn etc.) which went to more powerful men than himself, but for the most part in small levies which were not easy to collect and in casual sums for the various offices of his calling.

This meant that there were four interested parties preying on the labour and income of the peasants: the local community, the Church, the *seigneur* and the king. The last of these was the most diverse and also the most oppressive, varying from simple, direct methods such as the *taille*, the *gabelle* and a number of additional taxes, to the more complex and equally burdensome host of indirect levies, the most loathed of which were the *aides* on liquor. In theory these were an extraordinary and purely temporary measure, as were the dues paid for the food and lodging of military personnel, although even these were not so harsh as the actual billeting of a swaggering, thieving soldiery which was dreaded almost as much as the plague and had turned up all too often in the past twenty-five years.

The levies raised in kind, whether they were collected or required to be delivered, difficult as they were, were the easiest to manage. For the rest, money had to be found somehow by dint of piece work, day labouring and the marketing of small items such as a calf, a few fleeces, some lambs or a clutch of eggs or chickens if these could be raised. The poorer peasants borrowed to raise the money, always from the same people: the better-off labourer, the tax collector or any scrivener, court official or tradesman prepared to advance the price of a piece of cloth or a few dozen nails. The debt remained to be paid, entered on a scrap of paper, with interest added in advance, and registered officially in the presence of a notary or before a court of law. The debtor did his best to pay it back in kind and the partial or complete repayment of these small ious was often his chief reward. One bad harvest, a visitation by the soldiers, an epidemic or the death of a cow or a few sheep could mean a swift rise in the amount of the debt and eventual foreclosure. Anyone who has gone through the inventories compiled after the deaths of labourers of the time finds the monotonous repetition of the same lists of liabilities, cutting into or even wiping out the assets, becoming an obsession. In order to satisfy the collectors of rents and taxes, the peasants fell victim to a host of creditors, some local but more often townsmen, a few in the church but the majority belonging to the *bourgeoisie*. When times were particularly hard, as they were during the Frondes, this system resulted in the wholesale dispossession of country folk by their creditors and in the passage of numerous smallholdings into wealthy hands to form the basis of large estates, especially in the vicinity of prosperous towns and abbeys. In this way a considerable portion of the income earned by the peasants of the kingdom was swallowed up simply in paying back loans. A number of attempts have been made to calculate exactly how large this portion was, but the results vary according to place, the attitudes of those engaged in the calculation and, above all, the year. Setting aside the possibility of vast discrepancies in time and place, it may be put forward as a general rule that the poorer French peasants hardly ever kept more than half the gross product of their labours for themselves. This was not in fact so very little if we think for a moment of the Spanish peasants, of the serfs of Prussia or Muscovy, of the incredible toll of four fifths of the total produce customarily exacted from tenant farmers in Muslim lands, of the appalling conditions of Chinese and Japanese peasants as revealed in recent studies, or of the North American Indians, driven from their own lands at gunpoint by their god-fearing conquerors.

The life of the small minority of urban workers, whom the peasants outnumbered by twenty to one, seems to have been much closer to the social conditions with which we are familiar. These were typical of the traditional type of the proletariat, owning neither land nor houses, living in rented accommodation and with practically no furniture or linen to their names. They lived entirely on their earnings, paid on a piece work rate, though sometimes by the day and occasionally including some food. The money, like the job itself, was always uncertain. In practice, a system of advances on the part of the employers turned these workers of the Grand Siècle into a class — for that is what they were — of permanent debtors, entirely at the mercy of their masters. They might or might not belong to the so-called corporative institutions (the word corporation is an English one and a good deal later than Louis XIV), but these were more like religious brotherhoods in appearance, or occasionally a means of self-protection : in general they were dominated by the employers and without any real influence. There are known to have been none in rural areas and we must therefore disabuse ourselves of the twentieth-century idea that society in the seventeenth century was made up of corporations. This urban proletariat suffered from a very real degree of exploitation which often took the form of a subtle cheating in the matter of goods, hours of work or the nature of remuneration – workers were paid with lengths of unsaleable cloth, in bad coin which was not easy to get rid of, in false measures of flour and so forth. More often than not they worked from home or were employed by the day. Workshops employing labour on a large scale were the exception and there is little reliable evidence of the so-called patriarchal care of a 'good master'. The profits earned by these methods did not often go to those who supervised the work, who were themselves simply links in the chain of an industrial hierarchy at the top of which were usually the powerful merchants who were the chief beneficiaries of the system.

In practice, although the poverty of the urban working class was frequently striking and better known than the sufferings of the peasants, it may well have been less dire. On the one hand, the workers in the cities had the advantage of organized charities of long standing which had been substantially improved by the recent expansion of the hospitals (first in Lyons, then in Beauvais, in 1653 and Paris in 1655) while on the other, the workers themselves possessed some means of putting pressure on their employers through the spontaneous formation of their own secret societies, many of which were very powerful. This was especially true in times when there was a heavy demand coupled with a shortage of skilled labour, such as occurred as a sequel to various demographic and economic crises. Finally, at this period townsmen were privileged in paying substantially fewer taxes than the peasants. Naturally they were not liable to tithes and generally got off more lightly in the matter of seigneurial dues. The worst troubles of the urban poor, shortages and unemployment, generally came together. In spite of some valiant efforts, private and public charity was unable to cope with really desperate crises in employment and rising prices and the workers, huddled in their wretched dwellings, eating what scraps they could and abandoned by all save a handful of doctors and priests, died like flies. This in itself, however, helped to solve the problems of shortage of food and work. The survivors could look forward to a few easy years before the next crisis occurred. And so, in 1661, the poor people of the towns were beginning to forget the recent troubles of the Frondes and were once more able to make an honest living while they waited for what new disaster should lie in wait for them.

Fifteen million peasants, therefore, together with a tenth or a twentieth of that number of workers (the title of journeyman had fallen into disuse) made up the productive force of the realm and made some kind of a living, mostly rather poor but occasionally quite good, punctuated every now and then by appalling periods of crisis. Taking into account time, place and attitude of mind, they should probably be regarded as among the more fortunate of the world's populations. If they did sometimes complain or resort here and there to active rebellion triggered off by a new tax, an unexpected shortage, a false rumour or some more or less well-founded apprehension, these revolts were never more than local or regional affairs, with little or no organization, and only became at all serious when some other sector of society – usually the nobility – began to take a positive interest.

These popular risings, the existence, duration and gravity of which is no longer in dispute, were regularly concluded by the triumph of order as symbolized by the king's army. They had no serious effect on the comparatively simple basis of society.

If, for the sake of brevity, we discount the middle class which was still very small although showing signs of development among the small shopkeepers, craftsmen and minor tradespeople, it would be fair to say that, as a general rule, nine out of ten of King Louis' subjects worked hard and thanklessly with their hands in order to permit the tenth to devote himself comfortably to the life of bourgeois, nobleman or mere idler. Directly or indirectly, this tenth of the population lived to a greater or lesser extent on the vast revenues of the land, scraped from the soil of the kingdom by the inhabitants of the countryside and swelled and transformed by their labour and those of the workers in the towns. To one of these numerous classes of *rentier* belonged nearly all the nobility, most of the clergy and the whole of the bourgeoisie, all those privileged persons in fact who also enjoyed the benefits of their own special legal system, the *leges privatae*.

This landed income reached them in a variety of ways. Members of the nobility, whatever their title, acquired their income from the land through divers channels: directly in the case of the less well-off country gentlemen who sometimes worked the land themselves in so far as regional custom – which was particularly lax in Brittany – permitted; indirectly in the case of large or scattered estates by means of intendants, tax-farmers, and share-croppers. The recent study (by M. Merle) of the reclamation of the Gâtine area of Poitou by the creation of prosperous *métairies* in wooded countryside developed absolutely from scratch affords startling proof of the rapacity of the resident nobility in the west of the kingdom. In this way a third of the landed income of the entire realm might be swallowed up by a hundred thousand families. The same nobles were also *seigneurs* of at least another third, and drew from it, generally by means of tax farmers, the dues which the Revolution was to call feudal but which were really seigneurial. We have already seen how widespread these dues were and how onerous they could be, varying from the nominal rent of an obol to the vast levies of Quercy, by way of innumerable fees and minor exactions, rents, levies on sales and so forth. Even more indirect ways of raising money from the land were the gifts and pensions bestowed by the king on his favourites and most loyal servants. In practice, these consisted of benefices, offices, governorships and the revenue from taxation, all of which fell heavily on the people, especially the rural population. Whether or not the nobility repaid what they took from the resources of the kingdom in civil and military benefits is a matter for argument on a political or even a moral plane: it does nothing to alter the economic and social facts of the case.

The bourgeoisie, made up of officials on the road to ennoblement, of state pensioners (especially in Paris) and those with private incomes, and even of certain trade and manufacturing elements, took a similar toll of a scarcely smaller share of the national income. The bourgeois, like the nobility, were landed gentry. They simply owned less land, except in the vicinity of the towns, and still fewer *seigneuries*, but it is common knowledge that they often ran what they had more attentively, with a closer eye to detail and altogether more for profit than the nobility. To a much greater extent than the nobles, they held notes of hand, bonds, and ious, sometimes by the thousand, which gave them claims on the land amounting virtually to a guarantee of future possession, in many cases from the nobility itself and much more often from the peasantry. The system of making advances of seed-corn, tools, materials and wages gave them further claims to annexation and kept the urban poor very much at their mercy. In addition, many of them became intendants supervising estates belonging to the nobility and clergy, and once installed in these lucrative positions did not fail to make them a new source of wringing an income from the land.

They also formed companies and associations for the purpose of farming the king's dues and taxes, advancing him the estimated revenues beforehand and then recouping themselves mercilessly from the usual sources. The landed income of the bourgeoisie, going as it did to men who often avoided any display, did not always appear very splendid. On the other hand it was easily confused with the income of the nobility since it was the ambition of every prosperous bourgeois to either buy or acquire some title of nobility.

The clergy, leaving aside its religious functions, was recruited largely from members of the nobility and the bourgeoisie. Bishoprics and the best religious houses were filled by the younger sons of the various ranks of the nobility who lived off the revenues and seigneurial dues attached to their offices without, except in the case of the regular clergy, forfeiting their inheritances. To these was added the income belonging to the Church such as the universal tithe, the actual amount of which varied and was in many cases less than a tenth. The wealthiest merchants and officials installed their children in the numerous city canonries, comfortable chapters which were generally extremely prosperous and particularly careful of their worldly goods. Except for such small fry as vicars and unbeneficed priests, both town and country *curés* enjoyed a fairly comfortable living and recent research has pieced together evidence which has considerably shaken the legend of the universal poverty of the minor clergy. This was in fact recruited from the middle ranks of the bourgeoisie and the richer peasantry and exercised a good deal of influence in country districts. This was some years after the establishment of the first seminaries, although a hundred years after the end of the Council of Trent, which had decreed their foundation, and that neither the private conduct of these priests, nor their apostolic functions could be called beyond reproach is proved by the actions of the authorities in the more responsible sees. Parish priests lived partly on the tithes, on irregular fees for their services, the produce of their gardens and of the land belonging to the parish church and on the income they received from the many local endowments made over to them by parish councils. These endowments were bequests of money or land made over to the parish by people who, on their deathbeds, were anxious to ensure the saying of masses for their souls in perpetuity. In rich and pious regions these might amount to an annual sum of several hundred *livres*. In poor parishes it was up to the major tithe-owners to guarantee a minimum three hundred *livres* according to circumstances. This was enough to provide a modest living, free from serious financial worries, but it seemed very small to the priests when they compared it with certain episcopal and conventual revenues. As yet, however, grievances of this kind were rare within the Church where rivalries were generally due to other causes.

The key to the social structure of the country could be described as a kind of landed capitalism which in some of its forms, such as the seigneurie and the tithes, was very ancient while others, derived from the ever-present money-lending, took the legal form of ground rent and, still more, of annuities (a loan agreed between two parties with an annual interest in law of 5.55 per cent, with in theory the option of repayment and a formal security in land accompanied by a mortgage). The richest families in the kingdom, those of the *noblesse d'epée* and *parlementaires*, were those of the greatest landowners and *seigneurs* but *rente* certificates – on the king or on private citizens – were beginning to figure increasingly in marriage contracts and in inventories of estates left after death. Even the fortunes of the merchant families often included a substantial amount of investments and landed income.

It was, however, in the world of commerce that men

found other sources and forms of income. A good many, and these not among the least prominent, even held the better part of their wealth in movable form: work in progress, goods in stock or in transit or even in the hands of factors, correspondents, clients, and not yet paid for but represented by different forms of credit. These fluctuating assets were continually in danger from any sudden crisis, a glut on the market, accidents in transit or the failure of an important client and understandably after a generation or two their owners frequently opted for the purchase of a safe office and a firm investment in land while they looked forward to ennoblement. There were some who persisted and, from simple merchants, became contractors for manufactured goods, and these merchant-industrialists at the head of a number of concerns, mostly rural and generally in textiles or possibly metalworking, were a faint foreshadowing of the industrial capitalists of the future, although there was nothing at all revolutionary about their activities and similar were to be found in Douai in the twelfth century. Nor were the companies of revenue farmers who handled the king's business – taxes, munitions, buying and selling – anything new in the way of businessmen. It was simply that Frenchmen were increasingly taking the place of the numerous Italians who had for so long been prominent in such matters. Although necessary to the state, they were universally loathed and served to some extent as scapegoats. In almost every case, their descendants rose to swell the ranks of the nobility and higher clergy, purchased landed estates and were, in short, assimilated.

Before 1661, the kings and their ministers had endeavoured to dominate this society which although simple enough in theory was extremely complex in its gradations and forms. They had not been very successful in this, as was shown by the recent history of rebellion among the nobility and the rural, urban and regional communities, and the five years of anarchy brought about by the Fronde. Could Louis XIV do any better? Would he even attempt to alter the social structure of his kingdom? Everything pointed to the difficulties of any such attempt, and especially the revolt of Marseilles while Mazarin lay on his deathbed, when the unrest among the sabot-makers of the Sologne was barely over.

4

THE GOVERNING INSTITUTIONS

For no less than four centuries, the Capetian kings had tried to cover their ever-growing kingdom with a close mesh of agents, commissaries and officials who would carry their will and their commands to every corner of the realm. This has been somewhat prematurely and not altogether accurately called royal 'absolutism'. In fact, it was a desire to bring about the unification of laws and customs, an attempt to ensure the obedience of each province, each town and each individual subject, a move in the direction of unity and centralized government. These royal aims were, it must be admitted, only fully achieved with the revolution and the Empire. Meanwhile that admirable constitutional historian Roger Doucet's description of France in the sixteenth century is still not far out for the France of Mazarin.

'The kingdom ... was very far from being a homogeneous unit with all its parts subject to the same laws and administered in an identical fashion ... (this) assimilation was still uncompleted right up to the end of the *Ancien Régime*.' In practice the monarchy rested on a series of contracts made with the different units of which France was composed: provinces, cities, ecclesiastical foundations, social classes and even economic groups such as the trade guilds. All these contracts left to each group its own liberties and privileges and no one saw anything out of the way in their existence side by side with submission to the king. Provinces, cities, foundations, groups, orders and states were all faithful subjects of the king, but with their own privileges.

Taking the provinces as an example, as soon as the old Capetian domains of the Île-de-France, Picardy, Champagne and the Loire were left behind, the traveller penetrated into provinces where the king's authority was limited. Brittany and Provence, where union was less than two hundred years old, each had its own *parlement*, fiscal court and Estates which gave their consent to taxation – never heavy, their own military privileges, and of course their own customs which had the force of law. Right up until 1661, Louis had been simply Count of Provence and Duke of Brittany. Even the rich province of Normandy, which had been joined to France since the thirteenth century, remained a duchy (though without a duke), with its own Estates, *parlement* and laws, which were like no others, especially in matters of succession, mortgages, marriage settlements and even rates of interest, and its own peculiar sub-divisions. Further afield, Languedoc, which had also been part of France since very early days, still preserved its original institutions, its powerful Estates which controlled taxation, its civil dioceses, existing alongside the ecclesiastical ones, and property tax based on quite remarkable surveys which were checked and brought up to date from time to time. Even in the Pyrenees, certain valleys were very nearly independent, like small pastoral republics. In spite of a great many efforts, such as the reduction of Béarn, the hard-won extension of the royal fiscal system into a part of Guyenne and the suppression of the Estates of Normandy after the Fronde, the king was not equally powerful in all parts of his kingdom.

Ever since the days of charters and oaths of fealty, nearly all walled cities had done their best to keep their 'franchises and liberties' and bargained for their confirmation with offers of money at the accession of each new monarch. These towns had their assemblies, councils, magistrates, mayors, consuls, and aldermen. There was, even in Provence, a kind of periodical congress of urban communities which was still causing Mazarin a good many headaches at the time of his death. All these municipal authorities were elected, in many cases by representatives of the guilds and other bodies. They had their own domains, tolls, their special duties and their own financial arrangements, even their own militia and arms, and sometimes their own customs and even courts. It is true that the king frequently intervened in the elections, at least in major cities and places of military importance, but a good many of the ancient privileges survived. Plenty of cities, like Paris and Rouen, were exempt from the *tailles*, or very well indemnified, or were released from the obligation to feed and house troops. And each one would fight tooth and nail in defence of its rights and charters.

As for the old feudal system, the chain of mutual dependence linking one man to the next, vassal and overlord, homage and fealty, fief and benefice, can this be said to have survived only as a legal form? To be sure, homage and fealty were no longer much more than a matter of written statement deposited at the door of the suzerain and, to be sure, the word 'fief' generally meant no more than a noble domain, possession of which was still not enough to ennoble the man who held it. But the greatest nobles still had their little courts of humble or impoverished gentlemen to swear loyalty to them and follow them, serve them and fight for them even in rebellion. These bands of loyal retainers, domestics in the old sense of the word, dependents and supporters, proved their usefulness in any number of rebellions, both seigneurial and provincial, the Fronde included. The ties of kinship, patronage and service binding one man to another extended into the *roturier* class. A peasant who was a copyholder or tenant farmer was regarded to some extent as the vassal of his *seigneur*. Even as late as 1664, the Pompadours of the Limousin could rely on the support of their peasants and fought vigorously to defend them against the claims of the king's tax collectors which conflicted with their own, in the face of officials, intendants and even troops. In certain provinces, the most remote or where unification with

France was most recent, the inhabitants, whether noble or *roturier*, belonged first and foremost to the familiar and effective local overlord before they were the humble subjects of the distant Bourbon with his commissioners, his *gabeleurs* and his regiments.

There was no single law for the whole country, for all the jurists' claims that the king was the source of law and that all justice came from him. Even after the tremendous labours undertaken in the formulation of customary laws in the preceding century, there were still sixty general and almost as many local customs, as well as the Roman law of the Midi and a thousand cantonal variations. All told, this amounted to several hundred 'codes', about which there was no geographical agreement and in some cases a hopeless confusion as to where exactly they applied. Eminent jurists such as Brisson and Loisel had endeavoured to extract from this a 'French' law which should be a synthesis of the major customary laws and from the sixteenth century onwards royal legists had produced innumerable statutes containing a great many articles on a variety of subjects but their very quantity is proof of their ineffectiveness. Moreover, the king's judges were certainly not the only ones. Deep in the countryside and even in some of the towns, the seigneurial courts were as much in demand as ever. They were handy, familiar and in many cases not unduly costly. The consular jurisdiction, theoretically reserved for merchants, was becoming increasingly widespread. It was quick, comparatively fair and cost practically nothing, while any man could claim to be a merchant simply by the sale of a fleece or a sack of corn. In spite of all the king's efforts, the clergy, too, still retained their own legal machinery in a good many cases. The most common was the diocesan council which was also the authority regarding marriage laws and even certain matters of conduct. All this meant that the king's officers sitting (for example) in bailliages and presidial seats were far from possessing a monopoly of justice in a country which was not even ruled by a unified legal code.

By establishing the companies of officers, the monarchs had added new rights, privileges and franchises to those already existing in the kingdom. Long before the seventeenth century, kings had been in the habit of selling the offices of judges, assessors and tax-collectors to private individuals, and by the beginning of the century such purchasable posts had become practically hereditary, involving simply an annual payment to the king of a sixtieth of the value of the office concerned. The king lost in authority as much as he gained in cash. The different groups of officers formed themselves into companies and defended their privileges with such determination that the king was obliged periodically to send further confidential servants into the provinces as 'commissaries' invested with extensive powers in order to keep an eye on the successors of the first. The struggle between the officers' companies and the king's commissaries and intendants was one cause and aspect of the Fronde, an aspect which was decidedly reactionary in the strictest sense of the word. The most powerful companies, those of the revenue officers, the *Élus et Trésoriers de France*, had even formed themselves into organized syndicates with their own funds and news sheet, and openly resisted royal attempts to reduce them to obedience.

True, the Frondes were over; the intendants were re-established after their temporary partial suppression; officers, *parlementaires*, great landowners, rebellious cities and troubled countryside had made their humble submission, a few privileges had been abolished but others confirmed, and the chief rebels had been mollified with pensions and places. But for all the genuine, universally felt respect for the king and all the fine vows of loyalty, not one province or social group, not a single major city or high-ranking noble had abandoned one jot of their liberties, franchises or privileges.

By 1656, a Spanish victory at Valenciennes was already tempting the old soldiers and *parlementaires* of the Fronde to fresh conspiracy. In the following year, the *dévots* were busy spreading false rumours about the conditions of the treaty between France and England, while in Anjou, Poitou, Angoumois and even in Champagne popular risings were breaking out once more against the revenue men and the soldiers who were there to reinforce them. In 1658 Sologne and the Vendée were in a state of open rebellion, and when the young king fell ill before Calais it was the signal for a fresh round of plots and conspiracies, serious enough for the garrisons around Paris to be strengthened to deal with any trouble. 1659 was the year of the great conspiracy among the nobility of Normandy, supported once again by that of Anjou and Poitou. Three nobles were arrested, a great many fled and the Sieur de Bonnesson lost his head. A journey made by the king into the Midi (1659–60) was more like a military expedition and work was speeded up on the royal forts of St Jean, St Nicolas and Château-Trompette, dominating the cities of Bordeaux and Marseilles, whose loyalty was not to be depended on.

Louis XIV's words in his memoirs for the year 1661 ring all too true : 'Chaos reigned throughout.'

This then was the kingdom to which Louis acceded. Economically it was rich, if somewhat backward. Socially, administratively and in the state of its provinces, it was complex in the extreme. We shall deal further on with religious and intellectual differences.

But how did the king himself see his kingdom? What was his conception of his task? Had he already laid his plans?

PART TWO

The Time of Action
(1661–79)

5

1661: THE YOUNG KING IN QUEST OF GLORY

THE KING

To show Louis in his twenty-third year is an intimidating task. So much has been said already, both by his admirers and his detractors. The best way is to let him speak for himself. In his *Mémoires* for the years 1661, 1662, 1666, 1667 and 1668, intended for the 'education of the Dauphin', he either composed, revised or at any rate approved what was written for him by such excellent secretaries as president Périgny. And since he announced, a few hours after Mazarin's death, that it was his 'will never to take a prime minister' and 'to combine all the powers of a ruler in his own person', let us watch him in action and hear his own account of his conduct during the first year of his reign.

Four words crop up constantly in his writings. These are: 'my dignity, my glory, my greatness, my reputation'. The last is the most frequent. When, in 1670 or thereabouts, the king looked back on his early days, he saw the quest for 'reputation' as the supreme goal of all his acts, past, present and certainly future as well; reputation at home, by reducing his kingdom to obedience and doing away with the 'chaos' which reigned there; reputation among the Christian Princes of Europe (with the rest he was not concerned), at that time his peaceful neighbours, none of whom made any great impression on him. But 'they did not know him yet' and he burned to confront them 'at the head of his armies'. At twenty-two years old, 'preferring in his heart, a high reputation above all things, even life itself', the king was very conscious that he would have to 'render an account of all his actions to the whole world and to all times'. Already, he was preparing himself to do so. But what qualities had he in himself to ensure his success in achieving 'that dominant and ruling passion of kings ... their own advancement, greatness and glory'?

To begin with, there was his magnificent health. For all the small stature, which explains his high heels, his great perruque and upright bearing, he evidently inherited the powerful vitality of his grandfather, Henri IV. Like him, he was an indefatigable huntsman, warrior, dancer, gormandizer and lover and yet this dashing sportsman, with no time to spare for the weak or the nervous, resigned himself to spending hours every day shut up in an office, alone or with a few colleagues. Before he was twenty he had shown his amazing courage, in battle, in sickness, and in action against the Spaniards. He continued to go his own way obstinately in the face of several generations of physicians, working sixteen to eighteen hours a day studying papers, hearing reports, giving audiences and public appearances, riding on horseback and making love.

Of a far from bookish education, the lessons which seem to have stuck in his mind were chiefly those he learned from a Spaniard and an Italian, and even more those of the tempestuous years of his minority. From his mother, from whom he inherited the many Spanish traits in his character – there was a good deal of Philip II in Louis XIV with his fondness for secrecy, his concentration on his work, his taste for splendour and formality – he seems to have acquired a regular and meticulous devotion in the exercises of his faith and that cold, exquisite courtesy which never deserted him. From his godfather, the cardinal, who had finally admitted him as a silent spectator to the Council, he had learned to know Europe, with all its intrigues, the details of its princely marriages and the consciences that were for sale.

Hustled out of Paris at the age of ten and shuttled from one town to the next in the midst of wars, rebellions, dangers and epidemics of disease, he had learned the hard way that no one, or hardly anyone, was consistently loyal, not even an archbishop or the first prince of the blood. In later years he could urge his son to forgive those who injured him, but for all that he never forgot that 'in wise and able kings, resentment and anger towards their subjects is only prudence and justice' and that 'a little harshness was the greatest kindness I could do my subjects'. None were above suspicion, the clergy, the nobility with its 'thousands of petty tyrants', the *parlements*, the supposedly sovereign courts, officers, governors, or towns, since 'there is scarcely any order of the realm, Church, nobility or Third Estate that has not at some time fallen into fearful error'. The highest tribute he could pay his dead mother was to note 'how fully she had yielded up the sovereign power' and that he had 'nothing to fear from her ambition'. Fond as he was of his brother, he denied him any post of responsibility or command in which to distinguish himself: the memory of his uncle and fear of the very name of Orléans made him state firmly that 'the sons of France should never have any other retreat than the court or any place of safety but in their brother's heart'.

This universal distrust, born of experience, was the root of his reserve, of his utter self-command in affairs of state, and of his passion for secrecy which he tried to pass on to the dauphin. Louis learned to overcome the displays of emotion and the tendency to burst into tears which had marked his early manhood, or at least to keep them for the discharge of his private feelings. We may ask ourselves how many of the tears he shed for the death of Mazarin, the Queen Mother, and later on for his own queen and Monsieur, were really genuine. His real feelings were, after all, well known. Even of Mazarin, whom he professed to love, he could write in the same breath that he meant to abolish 'the very name' of prime minister in France and stress how far 'his (Mazarin's) methods and ideas differed from mine'. Controlled tears, a studied courtesy, calculated silence, the art of evasiveness (his invariable answer to all unforeseen questions was 'I'll see'), all the consummate skill of royal stage-craft – the first stroke of which, the arrest of de Retz at the end of 1652, came as a complete shock to everyone – all this became second nature to him and was undoubtedly one of his greatest assets. Based on education, experience, suspicion and a deep determination to be, in all things, the 'master', the king's ability to act in secret was essentially a triumph of the one great virtue of the age, the will.

With it went a self-confidence that was clear from the first and which is displayed with disarming frankness in the *Mémoires*: what Lavisse has called 'the pride of a Pharaoh'. Given the political, social and judicial climate in which he lived, Louis could not help but identify himself with France and believe, as Bossuet wrote later, that 'he was the whole State, and the will of all the people was locked in his'. He prepared to instruct his grandson in the axiom that 'The body of the nation resides not in France. It dwells wholly in the person of the King'. It seemed quite natural to him that the greater part of the court, the clergy and the kingdom should proclaim him God's lieutenant upon earth, and later cry with Bossuet: 'Oh kings, you are as gods!' He was early convinced that on some occasions he was directly inspired by 'I know not what blind instincts or intuitions above reason, which seem to come straight from heaven'. The king's pride was natural, even inevitable, and could be a most useful instrument in ruling. In 1661 it was at least balanced by thought and by hard work.

AT HOME

In 1670, his 'tenth year of going forward ... quite steadily along the same road', Louis XIV, at the age of thirty-two, looked back and meditated on the course of his first year of personal rule. The things he remembered, those he left out, even his way of describing and stressing events, all these offer an unequalled portrait of the intrepid gallant and imperious master, his Most Christian yet libertine Majesty, the magnificent monarch whose will it was to command the admiration of all Europe.

His first job was the complete reorganization of his system of government. He completely and utterly abolished the office of prime minister on the grounds that 'there is nothing more shameful than the sight of all the practical authority on the one side and nothing but the title of king on the other': a curious tribute to his father, mother and two cardinals. This was undoubtedly the most important act of the young ruler who has been called, somewhat grandly, 'the great revolutionary of the seventeenth century'. The King's Council was a crowded affair, overfull of clerks and persons of noble birth. Louis dismissed nearly all of them, including his mother, and retained only three men: Le Tellier, Lionne and Fouquet, the latter already watched and soon to be replaced by Colbert. These were the only ministers. Not a single prelate, great nobleman or even prince of the blood, not even the wise and illustrious Turenne, had access to what was soon known as the 'High Council' at which all important matters of state were decided.

All three men were of humble birth, wide experience and proven loyalty. All three had been Mazarin's men and all three were to owe their fortune and their advancement to the king. No one of them was dominant and none put their signature to anything at all without the king's authority. 'It was not in my interest,' Louis declared, 'to take subjects of a

higher degree . . . it was not my intention to share my power
with them. It was necessary that they should entertain no
higher hopes for themselves than I might be pleased to
gratify.' As for the rest, whether too exalted, like the Chancellor, too illustrious, like Turenne or Condé, too old, too
young or too dim-witted like Brienne, la Vrillière or
Guénégaud, they were fobbed off with administrative posts
and given no hand in the government of the realm. Thus,
after the arrest of Fouquet who was too rich, too splendid
and too presumptuous but no more knave than many others,
there came into being the famous 'Triad': the reign of the
king, what Saint-Simon was to call the *'règne de vile bourgeoisie'* had begun.

Every day, the king dutifully presided over the High
Council. He attended regular meetings of the *Conseil des
Dépêches*, held twice a week with the Chancellor and the
four secretaries of State, ministers or not, to hear the news
from the provinces and watch the young masters of requests,
the up-and-coming administrators, making their reports. In
September he set up the *Conseil des Finances* at which, in
the presence of the Chancellor, two financial intendants and
Colbert, the king acted as his own financial secretary, signing
accounts, endeavouring to fix a budget and make some sense
of the country's finances. He was not even above occasionally
taking the chair, which was always ready for him, at what
he called the *'Conseil des Parties'*, although he considered
this of minor importance since 'it dealt only with cases between private individuals on matters of jurisdiction'. He also
found time to receive petitions and read a great many of
them himself, to keep himself fully informed on all matters
and in particular on the state of his troops, on income and
expenditure and foreign news, to distribute places, favours,
pensions and benefices and in short to perform a tireless job
of patient inquiry, often going into minute detail. At the
same time, his trusted ministers were beginning, under his

supervision, to lay the basis of the immense task of reorganization and codification which historians have too often
attributed to Colbert alone.

In addition to this everyday business, there were sudden,
unexpected 'masterstrokes' aimed at reducing the remnants
of the Fronde, the corps, companies, orders and privileged
individuals and all those responsible for the chaos which
reigned at home. The first object of this general reduction to
obedience was to 'cut down the power of the principal companies which, on the pretext that there is no appeal from
their judgements . . . had gradually assumed the name of
sovereign courts and looked on themselves as so many
separate and independent authorities'. Tough words and
harsh methods produced a frightened submission: the king
exiled several officers of the *Cour des Aides*, silenced the
Paris *Parlement* in the matter of registering royal edicts, cut
the remuneration of officers by a quarter and compelled the
courts, which had previously refused to do so, to acknow-
ledge all royal decisions taken in council and not merely
those ordinances and decrees which had been ratified. In
short the king had, in his own words, deliberately 'mortified'
his administrators of justice. But he kept his best strokes for
the *parlements* whose 'overweening arrogance . . . had put
the whole realm in jeopardy during [his] minority. It was
necessary to humble them, less for the harm which they had
done than for that which they might do in the future.' Louis
did not resort to drastic measures yet. For the moment he
was content to silence them and destroy in a few words their
'false picture of themselves as champions of the so-called
interests of the people as against those of their prince'. 'For
subjects, peace lies only in obedience: it is always less harm-
ful for the people to endure even the bad government of
kings who are judged by God alone than to attempt to check
it . . . ; the reason of State which is the first of all laws (is)
. . . the most difficult and incomprehensible to all those not

concerned in government.' But the complete subjection of the *parlements* of the kingdom had only just begun.

The first order of the realm had already felt the weight of the king's will. Let Louis XIV speak for himself:

'The Assembly of the Clergy [this met every five years], which had been going on for a long time in Paris, was putting off the moment of breaking up, against my expressed wish. . . .' In fact the assembly claimed to be waiting for certain edicts which it had called for to be signed, sealed and delivered first. Nothing could have annoyed the young king more than this kind of bargaining. 'I let them understand that nothing more was to be gained by these kinds of methods,' he says roundly. The assembly dispersed and only then were the edicts dispatched.

Days of reckoning were also at hand for the second order of the land but, in the meantime, this was attacked indirectly. The duc d'Épernon, who had been colonel-in-chief of the infantry, had just died. His post carried with it 'unlimited' powers, including the appointment of a great many officers of lower rank who formed a reliable court of his own 'creatures . . . by whose means he was more master of the chief forces of the State than the king himself'. This post was abolished and taken over by the king himself. In a subtler, but more far-reaching reform, the powers of military governors were gradually reduced on the grounds that they were 'subject to great abuse'. Louis relieved them of the power to levy funds 'which made them too powerful and too absolute'. Then, by a quiet rearrangement of garrisons, he took away those 'troops who were their own men' and replaced them with 'others who, on the contrary, served only myself'. Before long, in certain provinces at least, the king would be putting an end to the 'tyranny' exercised by too many of the nobility with exemplary rigour and severity. But most urgent of all was to foresee and forestall any *émotions* in the kingdom such as those which had filled the century so far.

With this object in view the Third Estate – the bourgeoisie – needed to be similarly threatened. The fortifications at Bordeaux, the most obstinate and determined of the cities of the Fronde, and at Marseilles, which had given the king such a bad reception two years earlier, were kept up 'for future safety and as an example to all the rest'. Even so, some unrest did occur, 'coming close to disobedience', in Normandy, the south-west and Provence, regions with a tradition of revolt about which the king says very little. They were 'put down and punished' by the troops which Louis had resolved to 'maintain in substantial numbers' in spite of the peace.

This severity, he states, 'was the greatest kindness I could do my people'. From the first year of his reign, the armed repression of any hint of sedition became an absolute rule. It was a rule applied on very many occasions with a ferocity which only a few sensitive souls could consider barbarous. This was the price of order, obedience, reputation, glory and greatness. More masterstrokes would follow.

The king's memoirs for the year 1661 make little mention of the people of the towns or countryside. The king merely observes that in March they were 'heavily taxed, oppressed by poverty in a number of places and by their own idleness [which we should nowadays call unemployment] in others and in need, above all else of occupation and relief'. Otherwise 'no unrest or the fear or appearance of unrest' had appeared in the kingdom at that time. For the relief of 'the people', the king reduced taxation by three million in 1662, saying that the peace enabled him to do so, asserting that he found work for the 'idle', and repeated that in 1661 there was 'no unrest in the kingdom' but added that 'anything at all approaching disobedience, such as occurred on a few occasions at Montauban, Dieppe, in Provence and at La Rochelle was at once put down and punished' by troops. In plain terms this means that the troubles were not over but were immediately suppressed by the army. The king, who had lived through the Fronde and the rebellion of half the kingdom, asked no more. There is no mention of the cost of this tranquillity, of the 'rotten' summer, the disastrous harvest of 1661, of the unusually severe famine which followed almost at once, except for a few belated remarks (in 1662) recalling his own generosity. Glory and reputation marched on regardless of such incidents. Besides, the king was in a hurry to go on and tell the dauphin of more important matters : the great and brilliant masterstrokes abroad to which the bulk of his memoirs is devoted.

ABROAD

Louis XIV's view of Europe was of a society made up of more or less powerful princes belonging to more or less ancient houses, served by more or less venal ministers. In this time of peace, relations between the States came down to the family business of marriages and inheritances, money matters such as the price of a foreign minister or ally and, above all, the affairs of precedence abounding in any aristocracy.

'The kings of France, as hereditary kings ... may boast that there is without exception in the world today no greater house than theirs, no monarchy as ancient, no greater or more absolute power.' From this dogmatic pronouncement it is clear that, in any event, precedence and predominance rightly belonged to the monarchy of the Lilies. From 1661 onwards, any occasion would serve to demonstrate this fact to the rest of Europe.

One example is the claim made by the ambassadors of the republic of Genoa to be treated as royalty at the court of France and 'always to be given audience on the same day that this was granted to some royal ambassador so that, entering the Louvre immediately after him and to the same roll of drums, it could not be distinguished whether these honours belonged to them or not'. This undeserved fanfare reminded King Louis that for a long time Genoa had been a possession of his own ancestors and had rebelled, and that 'legitimately by several titles' it belonged to the house of France. Louis XIV therefore made it clear to the Genoese that he would not endure their 'absurd pretensions' any longer which made them 'quake with fear'. This was, admittedly, an impressive gesture involving no great risk. It was another matter to impress the emperor with the superiority of the French crown.

Louis XIV therefore took pains to explain at length 'how far the emperors of today are from the greatness of titles (of Caesar and Roman Emperors) to which they aspire' and how they had unlawfully taken on themselves the succession of Charlemagne who was, in reality, the forbear of the kings of France alone. Moreover they were only elected rulers and 'in being elected must submit to whatever conditions are imposed on them'. As a result they had little authority, small revenues and, unless they had anywhere of their own, 'only the town of Bamberg' to live in. All this was not, it should be stressed, entirely disinterested because the emperor had thought it beneath his dignity to write first inviting Louis to attend his election but had waited to receive some letter of congratulation. Louis not only refused to write the slightest note, he actually made the emperor remove the titles of comte de Ferette and landgrave of Alsace, regions ceded by the Treaty of Munster, from the powers of his ministers and, more important still, to resign the title he had assumed in a projected league against the Turks of 'head of Christendom'.

Such victories in subtle points of European precedence were particularly dear to the young king. They prepared the ground for others still more remarkable. They might also have inspired a more cautious man with some fear of future retaliation. But in 1661, young Leopold and the timid Genoese could only bow and bide their time.

Louis XIV was busy in a more practical way, getting the last ounce of advantage from application of treaties so as to cover his northern and eastern borders which he knew to be weak and too close to Paris. On the Flemish frontier, in the marches of Lorraine and Alsace, he gained moral, territorial and financial concessions, repaired his fortresses, put them in a state of defence and equipped them with everything necessary for the conduct of a war. Finally he turned his attention to those he was already thinking of as his future enemies as they had been his father's, the emperor and the crown of Spain. He used the classic means to achieve this. He got the Elector of Trèves into the League of the Rhine, that is, as he somewhat blatantly put it (the idea was originally Mazarin's), 'into a powerful and extensive union I had formed in the middle of the Empire, upon pretext of safeguarding the Treaty of Munster and the peace of Germany'. By the Florentine marriage of an Orléans princess he strengthened his ties with the Medicis in the heart of a half-Spanish Italy.

He cemented the English alliance which had made possible the victory over Spain in 1659 by the marriage of 'Monsieur'. That both these princely, and therefore diplomatic unions had been concluded by Mazarin is a fact which Louis omits to mention. Finally he congratulates himself on bringing about the marriage of Charles II of England with Catherine of Braganza, the infanta of Portugal, even though this alliance brought the English a great deal of gold, the town of Bombay, the gateway to the Indian Empire, and the beginnings of an economic and political protectorate whose dangers France was only later to appreciate. But at this period Louis XIV regarded England as a weak, pro-French country, 'barely recovered from her past troubles and concerned only to stabilize her government under a newly restored king and moreover, naturally inclined to favour

France'. This judgement was permissible in 1661: it was unfortunate that Louis pronounced it in 1670. For him, the Portuguese marriage presented the considerable advantage of dealing a blow to Spain by giving Portugal, then struggling hard for independence, an effective protector. For King Louis the constant enmity between the two thrones of France and Spain was a basic fact, borne out by a hundred years of history. 'One cannot be raised except by lowering the other,' he wrote, their 'jealousy' was 'fundamental' and everlasting. It even excused acting 'notwithstanding the Treaty of the Pyrenees', in other words of violating it, although it went somewhat against the grain for the king to do so. However, he forgave himself by proving to his satisfaction that 'a great many "words" of the treaty were not to be taken "literally" and that in any case the Spaniards had broken the Pyrenean Treaty first "in a thousand different ways" '. If Louis meant to enhance his 'reputation' and his glory, he would have to bring down Spain and this meant going to war with her, with or without an excuse.

This obsession with Spain, like his jealous contempt for the emperor, was the result of both recent and centuries-old events and it led Louis XIV to underestimate not only the English but also the Dutch. All their policies, he declared, were directed at two things only: maintaining their trade and humbling the House of Orange; 'the smallest war would do them great harm ... and their chief support was in my friendship'. Merchants, republicans, and in some sense his own protégés: all three reasons for displaying his royal condescension towards them. Of course, Louis XIV could not have guessed the future in store for the infant William of Orange. But he might have noticed that the United Provinces had grown stronger during the wars, and because of them, paid rather more attention (in 1670, with Colbert at his side) to the material might of a merchant republic. He was above wasting his displays of grandeur on the Dutch.

Only real kings were worthy of his attention, and it was these alone he bothered to impress with his youthful power.

GOD

It remained for Louis XIV to face up to the one person he had ever desired to serve, or to thank 'with real gratitude for the favours which daily he received from him'. And so he concludes his survey of the first year of his reign with an inventory of all that he has done for God.

Any young prince eager for glory and brought up a Catholic is bound at some time to feel the breath of the crusading spirit. Louis, in addition, could not bear to see the King of Spain calling himself by his traditional title of 'Catholic Majesty' and taking on himself 'the status of outstanding Catholic'. What he found still harder to endure was that the emperor, who was merely the 'head and captain-general of a German Republic', should claim to be the 'head of Christendom, as if he had truly possessed the same Empire and the same rights as Charlemagne' from whom only Louis himself could claim direct descent ... 'when he had defended the faith against the Saxons, the Huns and the Saracens'. Consequently, on his accession he offered '100,000 *écus* to the Venetians for their war in Candie' and a great many promises of assistance in 'driving the infidel' from Crete. He offered the emperor 20,000 men, and gave him 6,000 in 1664. He 'empowered' his representatives in Rome to 'form a league against the Turk', to which he would contribute 'much more than any other Christian prince'. All dreams, as we shall see.

Instead of actually taking the cross himself, Louis took up the cause of Catholic minorities in Protestant countries. He interceded 'with the Dutch on behalf of the Guelder Catholics'. At Dunkirk, held by the English, he disbursed 'considerable sums in alms to the poor ... for fear that their wretchedness might tempt them to follow the religion of the English ...'. Defending the Roman Catholic faith abroad enhanced Louis' reputation; he boasts of it to God; in future nothing shall prevent him from making many more such interventions; it is inconceivable to him that they should make him enemies, except for heretics and infidels who do not matter.

Louis had his own heretics too. He had some significant things to say about the Jansenists. This Most Christian King frankly despised theological argument, 'long disputes on academic subjects, no knowledge of which, it was admitted, was necessary for anyone's salvation'. He was much more worried about the threat of a schism, which was to be feared from the 'warmth of feeling' involved, from the quality of the opposition, 'very meritorious if only they had themselves been less convinced of it', and the intervention of bishops 'of high reputation and a piety truly worthy of respect'. Jansenism, 'the newborn sect' which had introduced a spirit of 'innovation' and of division which was bound to be unwelcome to the king, was made a still graver threat because of the 'human interests' it aroused and by its partial connexion with that former figure of the Fronde and escaped prisoner, Cardinal de Retz. 'Matters of State' were involved here, and it was for political reasons that Louis continued in 1661 to persecute the followers of St Augustine. He had already ordered the burning of the *Provinciales*; next he dispersed the 'Messieurs' and their pupils, while waiting his chance to set an Archbishop of Paris who shared his views against the daughters of Port-Royal and strike at the recalcitrant bishops and religious communities.

It was a matter of policy, too, that Louis, in a long and remarkable speech, turned his attention to 'that great number of my subjects adhering to the so-called reformed religion'. More than once, in words which are hardly ever quoted, he outlines what was to be said in favour of the Protestant religion :

The ignorance of churchmen in the last century, their luxury and debauchery, the bad examples they set and those they were obliged to suffer ... and all the abuses which they permitted in the conduct of individuals against the rules and public sentiments of the Church. . . . The new reformers were clearly telling the truth in many things of this kind ... [although] on the other hand [they] were guilty of falsehood in all those concerned not with facts but with belief.

As a result the people found it hard to pick out the Huguenots' well-disguised deceit from many obvious truths. Moreover when the people saw all these heretics dying for their faith they 'were still more inclined to believe that [their] religion must be good, if they would face such perils for it'. The king's first advice to his bishops is therefore to offer only good examples and 'avert scandals' which would put off the Protestants so as to 'bring back those whom birth, education and often a great but untaught zeal maintained in all good faith in these pernicious errors'. This is not the language of the 'new Constantine, the new Theodosius' hailed by Bossuet in 1685 .... He does not fulminate with the Church Assembly against 'the fatal liberty of conscience'. He accepts the Edict of Nantes, confirmed several times over since 1643. But he does wish to see the Huguenots brought by slow degrees back into the true faith. He puts forward his own methods for achieving this, involving no persecution, no 'harshness', but merely the strict observance of the Edict, the suppression of everything not permitted by it, the denial of any favours to the members of the reformed religion, and the offer of a reward to 'those who yielded meekly'. In dealing with heretics, Louis put his faith in the power of money to buy consciences.

After this summing up of all the services he had rendered

God 'out of real gratitude for the favours' he received 'daily', not forgetting certain decrees against 'swearing' or duelling, Louis goes on to provide his son with a few important rules about the way a king should conduct himself towards God. First, it is proper to practise the devotional exercises 'regularly' and in public and in particular to enlighten the people by making 'the stations of the cross on foot, with [his] whole household on festivals'. 'The public reverence we do to this invisible power may in short be justly called the first and most important part of our political duty since, after all, our own submission to [God] is the rule and example of that which is owed to ourselves by the people.' Louis goes even further: 'Armies, councils and all human industry would be feeble instruments to maintain us on the throne, if each man ... did not honour a higher power of which our own is a part.' This concept of the king's public piety as a model and guarantee of the loyalty of his own subjects, is a political attitude to religion not perhaps altogether unrealistic. True, Louis does add that a certain 'inner disposition' towards religion is 'nobler and more disinterested', and that 'this selfish point of view' is 'very bad when it is the only one' and 'the outside is nothing at all without the inside'. But all the same, neither his ideas nor his expression suggest a very deep or heartfelt faith. Louis' religion, in the first decade or so of his reign, was a mixture of studied policy and a well-taught conformity. The time of his inner conversion was still a long way off. In 1661, Louis was prepared to dissolve the Company of the Holy Sacrament, to support Molière against the 'tartufes' and dare to stand godfather to his first child. His life was happily compounded of myths and gallantry, and he had already become the joyous libertine who made the glorification of adultery the fashion in both Court and City. Bossuet's next Lenten sermons were to call down his first disgrace on the head of the audacious young priest. With his clergy, the devout party, and even with God himself, Louis XIV kept his distance. As yet the Most Christian King was thinking only of his glory, not of his salvation.

The thirty-year-old king who thus described the first year of his reign for the benefit of his son, was confident that he had fulfilled his 'great, noble and delicious profession of kingship' very well indeed. For twelve years, faced with no unduly tiresome obstacle or serious setback, he went his way, 'quite steadily along the same road, relaxing none of his concentration' in order to show 'to the whole world and for all time' how a great king could achieve the triumph of his ruling passion for glory.

6

TWELVE GREAT YEARS
1661–72

FROM his twenty-third until his thirty-fifth year, Louis encountered no obstacle to his pursuit of glory that he could not either overcome, circumvent or ignore. The early years of a great reign unfolded in majestic succession before the dazzled eyes of the kingdom and of Europe. This phase of youthful ascendancy was intended, often successfully, to be one of Splendour, Obedience, Victory and perhaps of Wealth.

SPLENDOUR (1661–72)

At this time the king and his court presented none of the solemn, grandiose spectacle of Versailles as propagated in textbook and legend. The court was essentially nomadic, moving from one château to the next escorted by an army of coaches and carriages bearing furniture, candlesticks, wardrobes, penholders, the Great Seal, records, boots, ministers and grooms. There was as yet no clear idea of distances, and promiscuity and licence gave to these caravans an air of fantasy. From time to time the king resided in the old palace of the Louvre, half of it still unfinished, the other falling down, surrounded by an atmosphere of reeking damp that defied description. For fresh air he went out to Vincennes or Fontainebleau or sometimes to Louis XIII's little hunting lodge near the hamlet of Versailles; more rarely he went to Chambord or, more often, to Saint-Germain, his birthplace, between the river and the forest. The hunt, the need for some basic spring cleaning or the whim of a favourite dictated these removals. The cavalcade camped here or there for a tournament, a firework display, a ballet or a water picnic. The court, like the city, often knew little of the long hard hours of work, remembering only the *dolce vita* with its wonderful *fêtes*: the summer of 1661 at Fontainebleau, with its water sports and *fêtes champêtres*; the tournament of 1662, held between the Louvre and the Tuileries, and led by the king ablaze with jewels in the presence of three queens and fifteen thousand distinguished personnages from every corner of Europe; the 'Pleasures of the Enchanted Isle' in 1664 at Versailles, where the gardens and fountains had already been laid out, with its ballets, '*machineries*', entertainments and mythological scenes, Lully's musicians and three comedies by Molière, including *Tartufe*, all done for Louise de la Vallière; the '*grand divertissement*' on the night of 18 July 1668 for Montespan, still with Molière, Lully, the fireworks and the machines but set in an enlarged Versailles to which Louis was becoming increasingly attached. From time to time the court would visit Achères or Moret to watch the finest regiments manoeuvring, or see the king take a Flemish town . . .

However, the young king had not as yet made any definite choice of his favourite place. He was building, enlarging and making alterations nearly everywhere, even in Paris which he had never liked since the Fronde. It was his firm belief that glory and reputation were also to be gained by magnificent buildings. In January 1664 he made his Intendant of Finance, Jean-Baptiste Colbert, Superintendent of Buildings as well. But as early as 1661, he had already acquired the unrivalled team of men who had built Vaux for Fouquet: Le Nôtre, Le Vau, Lebrun, the 'engineers' of the waterworks and even the orange trees. Very soon he had repairs, enlargements and new buildings going on practically everywhere: at Fontainebleau, Vincennes, Chambord and Saint-Germain with its marvellous terrace. With the Pope's permission he brought Bernini from Rome to complete the Louvre in the

Italian style but then changed his mind and chose Claude
Perrault whose colonnade was begun in 1667. Also in Paris,
the *portes* Saint-Denis and Saint-Martin, the Collège Mazarin, the Observatory and the Invalides were gradually
taking shape. Versailles to begin with had been turned from
a hunting lodge into a park and pleasure gardens. Groves, a
labyrinth, grottos, a lake and waterways, the first orna-
mental and allegorical statues, the first fleets of boats and the
first menageries were all designed by Le Nôtre. The house
itself was scarcely touched. Le Vau, who wanted to pull it
down, was obliged to be satisfied with padding it out a little
while one of the earliest follies in the shape of a Chinese
pavilion, the porcelain Trianon, was built at a little distance.
In 1670, much against Colbert's wishes, Louis decided to
move in. In 1671 it was decided to transform the neighbouring hamlet into a royal town. But Le Vau was dead, leaving
countless plans behind him, and others were to build the
Versailles of the king's mature years. Le Nôtre, too, rede-
signed his park.

Like Colbert and the learned Chapelain, Louis considered
that buildings alone were not enough for his glory. All the
arts, letters and sciences must come together, as in the time
of Augustus, to glorify his person and his reign, and all
naturally, in perfect order and obedience.

The first to be brought to heel were the painters and sculptors among whom there had been a good deal of disagree-
ment. Faced with the old '*maîtrise ès arts*', most of the
king's painters and sculptors, whether they lodged in the
Louvre or not, had been anxious to form an Academy, as in
the days of Alexander, to distinguish themselves from such
'rude mechanicals' as mere daubers and marble polishers.
They obtained this privilege in Mazarin's time and even the
promise of a monopoly of teaching. Protected by Mazarin
and afterwards by Séguier and Colbert, the Academy became,
in the two years from 1662 to 1664, an institution in the

king's service, with a chancellor, rector, director (Le Brun, for life) and forty chairs. Given lodging, material rewards and strong protection against any freelancer who attempted to open a school or even pose as a model, the Academy had a firm grip on the realm of Beauty on his majesty's behalf. Two years later it had extended its influence to Rome, where a director took charge of twelve boarding pupils each year: this was Le Brun again, but somewhat later. The students' timetable, lectures and meals were all arranged and there was even a prize given each year on the feast of St Louis to the most deserving. Since two architectural students were to go to Rome, there had to be an Academy of Architecture as well and this was established in 1671, but was to consist of only ten chairs, with a school attached. In 1667, the old firm of Gobelins which had been purchased in 1662 simply for the manufacture of tapestries, became the 'Royal Makers of Furniture to the Crown' with, of course, Le Brun as its director. Several hundred artists and craftsmen, with some dozens more apprentices, many Flemings and Italians imported for their talent, worked in wool, silk, gold wire, marble, precious woods, bronze and silver. The exquisite results of their labours went to adorn palaces or were presented to ambassadors so that the wonders of French artistry and the magnificence of the king might be carried as far afield as Muscovy and Siam. There was even an Academy for the violin. Louis XIV was passionately fond of music and dancing and very early distinguished the young Lully whose 'little violins' followed him on his travels and even into battle. Lully composed his first ballet as early as 1658 and his first comedy-ballet in collaboration with Molière in 1661. By 1665 he was Master of all the King's Music and cut down the overwhelming influence of the 'king of violins'. Shortly afterwards he purchased from a certain Abbé Perrin, who was in prison for debt, the privilege of establishing 'academies of opera'. In 1672, the king extended this privilege by making Baptiste the only man entitled to present Italian opera which had become fashionable since Mazarin, to found an Academy of Music in Paris and 'establish music schools wherever he might think fit for the good and advantage of the Academy'. And so all the arts were brought into line and independent spirits firmly desired, on pain of a fine, not to take in pupils.

In the same way, the Academy of Science, a private assembly of scientists with twenty-one members, found itself presented with Colbert's library as a meeting place and later in 1666 with that of the king in the rue Vivienne. It was not 'regularized' and installed in the Louvre until the end of the century. The *Académie Française*, a private society under the 'protection' of the two cardinals and later of Séguier, passed under royal control in 1671. It was then installed in the Louvre and subsidized to some extent before being endowed with tokens of attendance which produced a great increase in its activities, and led to the decision to go ahead more seriously with the *Dictionary*. By 1663 the *Académie des Inscriptions et des Médailles* began the history of the coinage of the reign, with a great deal of art and Latin : *Felicitas temporum* and *Nec pluribus impar* distinguished the year 1663.

Those that were not made into academies, even those that were not altogether 'regular', or even strictly national, were subsidized. At least as late as 1673, illustrious foreigners, Dutch and Florentine especially, were handed letters of credit and the compliments of Colbert in the king's name. Flemish lacemakers, glass-workers of Murano, Hyghens, Van Robais, Cassini and Caffieri, were offered a real 'golden bridge' to come and work in France. For a long time the king and his superintendent allowed Chapelain a free hand with the 'pensions sheet'. He inscribed his own name at the head of the list for the largest sum and subsidized friends, such as the Abbé Cotin and Desmarets de Saint-Sorlin, whose names are remembered now only as objects of raillery from Boileau, who was left out of the earliest lists, while Molière had to be content with 1,000 *livres* and Racine with 800. Chapelain was following the fashion of the times which took little notice of those we now call the great classics. Louis XIV, whose unerring taste astonished even his detractors (Lavisse was petty enough to write that Molière was 'kept short by the king' when he owed nearly everything to him), to his great credit, imposed his own very liberal likes even on *Parlement*, the Church, and the *salons* of the précieuses or romantics. The king's own personality cannot have been a negligible factor in the accumulation of masterpieces which enhanced the early years of his reign: all of Molière, most of Racine, La Rochefoucauld, the first sermons and the first funeral orations of Bossuet, the first satires and the first fables, owed much to his early encouragement, which culminated in Jean de la Fontaine whom he finally received into the *Académie Française*, as he had taken his fables to adorn Versailles.

Surrounded by his courtiers, his mistresses, his academicians and his polishers, his musicians and his bronzeworkers, his savants and engravers, patronizing some and pensioning others so long as they pleased him or had taste, the young king was unlike all who had gone before him – *nec pluribus impar* – and shone like the sun which he took as his emblem in 1662. It was his good fortune in the early years of his reign to have about him the best legacy bequeathed to him by Mazarin, a group of men of talent or even genius. It is to his own credit that he kept them. Upon examination it is these twelve years, or perhaps a further five if we include *Phèdre*, that contained all that was best in the age of Louis XIV. After this, the wave of creativity declined, building was not so widespread, pensions, subsidies and patronage dropped off and virtually disappeared and writers moved gradually into another sphere. But this regal splendour, however dazzling, does not give a complete picture of the king and his reign at the height of his youth and vigour.

ORDER AND OBEDIENCE (1661–72)

Louis XIV entrusted the business of hastening the details of those measures which were to pull France out of her chronic state of disorder and disobedience chiefly to two men. Both had been trusted associates of Mazarin, one as a minister, the other as intendant and private secretary. They were also related, the sister of one having married the cousin of the other, Colbert de Saint-Pouange.

Le Tellier was the only man the king addressed as 'Monsieur'. He was a contemporary of Louis XIII and none had better deserved the nickname of the 'Faithful' bestowed on him by Mazarin and Queen Anne in their coded correspondence. He knew almost everything there was to know about the law, about military affairs which he controlled for thirty-four years, and even about foreign affairs and major State secrets. He was respected, and occasionally feared, for his modesty, his knowledge and his calm. Had Louis XIV taken a prime minister, the post would certainly have been his, and in 1661 it was expected to be.

His son, Chaville, whom people were beginning to call Louvois – both titles taken from family lands – grew up in his shadow and under his stern authority: a Councillor of State at fourteen and promised the reversion of the Secretaryship of State for War. In his father's office and beneath his eye, he dispatched letters and began signing them himself in 1662. The king took to him at once and made him a member of the Council on the death of Lionne in 1672.

Colbert had grown up in the offices of his cousin, Le Tellier's brother-in-law, Saint-Pouange. His own family were of plain merchant stock. Singled out by Mazarin at an early age, he stuck to him as Mazarin had done to Richelieu and served him indefatigably, even in such menial tasks as supervising his dinner. He was in an admirable position to know all the affairs of Mazarin and the State, and to further his own. He had great perseverance, an immense capacity for work, a liking for order, administrative experience, some clear, if occasionally wrongheaded ideas, and inordinate greed. Only this last trait was at all typical of his time.

The cardinal bequeathed him to the king. The two men worked together to some extent in arranging the arrest and condemnation of Fouquet and later on Colbert and his wife also took charge of the royal mistresses and bastards. This universal factotum had to wait until 1665 to be made *contrôleur général* (he was then Superintendent of Buildings and Intendant of Finance) and until 1669 before becoming Secretary of State for the Navy and for the King's Household. His devotion was absolute and the king knew it. His most amazing years were from 1664 to 1672 when, alone, he did the work of six ministers and even took over some of the responsibilities of the old Chancellor Séguier. Only military and foreign affairs, the province of Le Tellier and Lionne respectively, lay outside his sphere, and even here he was kept informed by means of the High Council.

And so for twelve years we find these men, assisted by a handful of councillors of state and masters of requests, a few dozen clerks and fewer than thirty intendants with virtually no administrative organization, striving to restore France to a state of order and obedience. Most of what we know about their work concerns its official aspect: legislative documents, reports and administrative correspondence. We can see its quantity, its general tenor and its style, but its real effects are not easy to assess. But even if all this administrative business did amount to no more than a collection of intentions, at least these intentions were the king's own, and some of them were not without results.

Among the measures that did have an effect were those

aimed at eliminating from the country the 'remnants of the Fronde' and in particular the companies of officers. In 1665, the king decreed that the *'cours souveraines'* should in future be called *'supérieures'*. Adding insult to injury, in 1673 the *parlements* received letters patent to the effect that they were to register immediately, without modification, such edicts as were presented to them. If they then felt it proper to submit their respectful remonstrances to the king, Parisians were to do so within a week and provincials within six weeks. The king would say yea or nay and that would be the end of the matter. This stern decree and the culmination of a number of others, succeeded very well. Thenceforth the members of the Paris *Parlement* ratified whatever the king desired, including legitimizing the illegitimate issue of twofold adultery, without a murmur, not even bothering to take a vote on it. Some of those in the provinces were less compliant. The Bordelais who failed to prevent a rising in 1675 were sent into dreary exile at Condom. The members of the Rennes *parlement* suffered fifteen years of retirement at Vannes for daring to permit a revolt in Brittany. The eclipse of the *parlements* was so complete that Colbert was able to write in 1679: 'Parlementary troubles are out of date. So much so that they are quite forgotten. . . .' There was, however, one danger in a debasement of this kind, assisted by the largesse handed out to the more servile magistrates, which the king and his colleagues failed to perceive, and this was the danger of a revival and recrudescence under a weaker regime.

Other companies of officers, not belonging to the *noblesse de robe* but still hereditary and extremely powerful, had played a major part in the Fronde, notably the officers of finance and, in particular, the *trésoriers de France*. These were an obvious target. Their societies were dissolved in 1662 and measures taken to prohibit the creation of anything remotely similar in the future. In a financial memo for 1661, Colbert wrote: 'Take firm action in suppressing the *trésoriers de France*.' Short of suppressing them by force, he aimed at securing at least the redemption of their offices. Since the king could not bring himself to adopt the first, the *Chambre de Justice* managed to release a hundred million, recovered from the less able financiers, which were used to buy out a good many offices. But ten times as much was needed. Colbert and Le Tellier had to be satisfied with reducing the *élus et trésoriers de France* to a representative or secondary role by means of the intendants who almost entirely superseded them in all matters concerned with the establishment and assessment of the *taille*. E. Esmonin has shown that in Normandy their exclusion was completed by 1666. Before very long the *élus* were reduced to judging minor tax offences and the *trésoriers de France* no longer took the trouble to become resident. They were wealthy men: they busied themselves with their lands, their revenues and their mansions in Paris and turned to speculation instead. The conspiracy of the officers against the commissioners, which had been partly responsible for the Fronde, was avenged and at the same time the conditions which might have produced a recurrence were removed.

The way in which Louis set about silencing the great order of the nobility, which had also taken part in the Fronde, is well known. The king contributed to his brother's degradation by restoring to him, after a short period of exile, his minion, the Chevalier de Lorraine, to whom he also gave the title of *maréchal de camp*. To the princes of the blood he distributed great offices of the crown: splendid-sounding posts conferring no actual power. Countless posts were created, connected with the king's military and civil households, his table, lodging, stables and hunting, and were distributed among the greatest names in the kingdom. Those with provincial governorships found these cut to three years with no permission to reside there. The manna of ecclesiastical benefices and pensions was confined to the nobility. But it was necessary to appear at court in order to obtain such 'favours' and the hectic and brilliant life of the court was calculated to bring crippling debts on courtiers who could not or would not keep a close eye on the intendants of their estates at a time when, as we shall see, the land was bringing in less and less. Those of the nobility who stayed at home were subject to 'searches' into their titles which were at the same time an indirect method of taxation and a calculated irritant. In Brittany, where 2,500 families were dealt with in this way from 1668 onwards, genuine members of the nobility were demoted because they could not produce documents to prove that their families had the necessary three quarterings which were the only proof of nobility in that province. Certain sharp *roturiers*, on the other hand, were recognized or 'maintained' simply in return for substantial sweeteners offered to the examining commissioners, over and above the legal costs. The detection of these false titles offered the king an excuse for reopening the inquiries from time to time : a new source of revenue and a further irritant.

The younger members of the nobility, with the exception of the Bretons who rarely served even in the navy, were eager to go to war and had to equip themselves to do so at their own expense. The king was to provide them with ample opportunity for shedding their blood and they did so with such a will that whole families were decimated as a result. But no one of the nobility – or hardly anyone, for after 1674 the convocation of vassals revealed the presence of a good many far from warlike gentlemen – complained of this toll of bloodshed. What the old nobility must have found much harder to understand was how its king came to create so many more new titles of nobility than any of his predecessors and to accept so many false claims on pretext of 'courtesy' or for reasons of state. But at this period, although he introduced so many '*petits marquis*' that the title finally became a joke, the king did not create too many titles by purchase, or too many dukes 'by royal warrant'. However, the time would come when Louis sold titles and coats of arms in order to replenish his coffers and, quite apart from the financial necessity involved, his action was a clear expression of the royal will. For all his lavish praises, Louis wanted not merely the subjection of the Second Estate but also its degradation.

In and around the heart of the First Estate, there had been and still was a 'devout party' which had resisted Mazarin as it had fought Richelieu. From 1630 onwards, these *dévots* had formed a secret society, called the Company of the Holy Sacrament, and had been responsible for a great many moral and charitable works. They had also attempted to impose a minister of their own choice on Louis XIII and Anne of Austria and this had cost one of their brethren, Monsieur Vincent, the nomination to benefices withdrawn by the victorious Mazarin. Ardent members of the brotherhood had included Gaston d'Orléans, the prince de Conti, great *parlementaires* such as the Lamoignons and the Fouquets, a good many Jansenists and celebrated churchmen like Olier, Vincent de Paul and Bossuet. During the Fronde, most of them, and Olier and Vincent de Paul in particular, had supported the party of Condé or of 'Monsieur' and circulated copious attacks on Mazarin throughout the country inserted in religious tracts. The shrewdest had become reconciled in time. There can be no doubt that the king's outward piety, his harsh treatment of the Church Assembly of 1661, his support of Molière at the very time when the Company was attacked and officially disbanded (1665), possibly the trial of Fouquet and certainly his relentless persecution of the Jansenists were all comparable aspects of the same hostility towards the excessive influence of the *dévots* who had dared to form a secret sect whose members included too many doctors, *parlementaires* and form fondeurs for comfort. Louis, generally so punctilious in other respects, had no scruples about en-

listing the help of the Pope and the Nuncio in bringing to
heel the most stubborn of the remaining Jansenist bishops,
the pious Pavillon, Bishop of Alet and three others who conscientiously refused, despite the edict of April 1664, to sign
the pontifical formulary condemning the five propositions of
Jansenius. The result was the 'Peace of the Church' of 1668,
an adroit and somewhat precarious achievement which the
king celebrated as a victory over the threat of impending
schism, and the Academy struck a medal to commemorate
it. The nuns of Port-Royal were permitted to return to their
convent and the 'Messieurs' likewise. Here, as elsewhere,
the spirit of meekness had, at least temporarily, prevailed.

It seems to have been the Protestants who suffered for
this reconcilation between the various sects within the
Catholic Church. A declaration published in 1669, immediately after the 'Peace of the Church' amounted virtually to
a kind of counter-Edict or charter of prohibitions. It consisted of forty-nine articles, listing every restriction that could
be imposed on the Huguenots which had not been covered
in the Edict of Nantes. Hitherto, although the heretics had
been kept under surveillance and there had been attempts
to convert them, notably by the distribution of tracts and
money, the law had not dealt harshly with them, except in
the case of converts who relapsed or of Catholic converts to
Protestantism who were liable to banishment for life. Now
with the introduction of measures concocted by such wily
legal minds as that of Bernard of Béziers, or by such astute
clerics as Père Meynier, the way was being made clear for
the Revocation. The Edict of Nantes was held to apply only
to the kingdom as it was in 1598: all Protestant places of
worship built after that date were to be destroyed; interments not accounted for in the Edict were to take place only
at night, in unconsecrated ground and with no public ceremony; Huguenot marriages were to be attended by no more
than twelve persons and members of the reformed faith were

obliged to respect Catholic feast days and religious processions.

There was nothing in these measures directly contrary to
the Edict of Nantes. They provided plenty of incentive to
'reconciled' Catholics but with only a faint foreshadowing
of the Revocation. The king was shocked and pained to see
so many heretics in his kingdom and continued to hope for
their conversion but, in his determination to be obeyed, he
was not averse to applying a certain amount of pressure in
order to achieve his ends.

In addition, Louis had persistent outbreaks of unrest
among the people to contend with. In 1662, trained bands
were formed all over the country to drive back the hordes of
beggars from the rural areas who besieged city gates and
charitable institutions demanding bread. In a number of
towns the citizen militia had to be called out against the
people. When rioting broke out in the region of Boulogne,
in protest against a new tax, it took thirty-eight companies of
the king's troops to quell the thousands of demonstrators,
and a master of requests to preside at the ensuing trials. The
authorities were satisfied with hanging some and condemning four hundred more to the galleys for life. In the following year, troops were dispatched to Auvergne to enforce
payment of the *taille* and a number of people were killed.
In 1664, there was trouble in Poitou and Berry and a few
hangings, but the dragoons had to occupy Béarn in order to
introduce the *gabelle*, and even then the leader of the insur-
rection, a gentleman brigand by the name of Audijos, held
the country for ten years. In 1669 a woman and several men
were hanged at la Croix-Rousse for resisting the collector of
customs dues. During the disastrous winter of 1670, rumours
of fresh taxes to be imposed spread panic among the peasants
of the Vivarais and the king dispatched d'Artagnan and his
musketeers, the Swiss guards, a few squadrons of cavalry
and several infantry regiments to deal with the trouble. Once

again there were hangings, men sent into exile or to the galleys, refugees and hundreds of innocent casualties. Finally the leader, another gentleman by the name of Antoine du Roure, was cut to pieces. Roussillon, further south, was up in arms yearly. In the midst of the Dutch war a complete army had to be raised in order to put down rebellions in Bordeaux and Brittany. Order and obedience depended on the army and all outbursts of popular feeling were forcibly suppressed.

To ensure that the provinces were quieter still, if possible, it was necessary to do away with anything that could remind people of former privileges. The provincial Estates, where these were still in existence, were rendered powerless, even in Brittany and Languedoc. Deputies, presidents and the places where they were to meet were all named by the king, any discussion of the level of taxation was either rigged or suppressed altogether, and bribes and threats were handed out alternately. The major cities continued to see their franchises nibbled away little by little : one would lose the right to maintain its walls or its exemption from billeting troops or providing winter quarters for the army, another would have its magistrates, consuls or mayor nominated from above and all were obliged, at a very early date, to hand over their accounts to intendants on the pretext of 'reducing their debts'. Here and there at least a few privileges, honorary, financial or electoral, were left and the mayoralty was not yet sold to the highest bidder. The last remnants of the traditional liberties had not entirely disappeared. Those cities that were most prone to unrest were kept under constant military supervision. Every precaution was taken to prevent a possible recurrence of the Fronde in the cities.

Paris, especially, had to be closely watched : a city of four hundred thousand inhabitants, with forty thousand beggars in organized bands, the same number of domestics and irre-

sponsible lackeys, thousands of state pensioners in receipt
of irregular incomes, a floating host of craftsmen and tradespeople and a rabble of soldiery; a city of immensely wealthy
parlementaires and bourgeois, of a couple of dozen seigneuries and as many dens of thieves with an inadequate and
unreliable watch and the ever-present memory of the barri-
cades of 1648 and the troubles which had ensued. A provisional police council was set up and studied the problem for
several months. Then, in 1667, the king created the major
post of 'lieutenant general of police for the provost of Paris',
a post which Nicholas de la Reynie filled loyally for twenty
years.

La Reynie increased the numbers and efficiency of the
watch and the mounted sergeants and worked hard to confine the beggars to the General Hospital, regulate the
behaviour of lackeys and soldiers, see that the city was
cleaned up, lit, fed, watered, paved and protected against
flood and to keep a watchful eye on taverns, places of public
entertainment and meetings generally, as well as on the
tradesmen's guilds and on publications.

Paris was becoming the intellectual capital of the kingdom. Books, pamphlets, broadsheets and gossip had
flourished there in Mazarin's time. The king's council had
already cut down the number of printers and taken over the
charge of appointing new master printers. Fifteen were
appointed each year up to 1667 and only nine altogether in
the succeeding twelve years. Illicit presses, journals and bal-
lad sellers were prohibited or prosecuted. No book, even a
straightforward reprint, could be published without the royal
consent and letters patent signed and sealed with the great
seal. The chief of police, *parlement* and the king's council
were united in their efforts to control freedom of thought.
But independent minds were not to be satisfied with the
Gazette de France, the *Mercure Galant* or the new *Journal
des Savants* and the result was simply an increasingly vora-

cious demand for journals and broadsheets from Holland and Germany. The final result of all this censorship, prohibition and confiscation was simply to bring fame and fortune to Dutch printers and underground presses in France. Even so, the days of the *mazarinades* were well and truly over.

The days of Mazarin himself were over, also. It is scarcely an exaggeration to state that, internally, the twelve years leading up to the attack on Holland were a period of reaction against the weaknesses and disorderliness of Mazarin's regency. The passion for order and obedience extended even into spheres where individualism was strongly entrenched. An edict of 1673, laying down that 'all merchants, tradesmen, craftsmen and artisans are to be ordered into guilds and professional bodies', seems to have been designed to turn France into a collection of 'corporations'. Henri III and Henri IV had already decreed the same thing from the same fiscal motives, and had failed in the same way. After Colbert's time 'corporations' in France remained, as they had been before, a strictly urban phenomenon and even in the cities they were an institution to which only a minority of workers belonged.

In 1661, the king even imagined, like his forbears and like Cato of old, that he could control the way his subjects dressed and 'do away with all these fancy foreign ideas'. But even in his early days, French fashion declined to bow to Louis.

For all its naïvety and its inevitable failures, there are two things about this grand determination to take the kingdom firmly in hand which can never be too strongly emphasized. The first is that it was all thought out, decided and where possible put into practice in the space of ten years. These were the years during which Colbert was in power and generally supported by the king. They were also years during which the country was more often at peace than at war, when the national finances were once more on an even keel and people had time to think and make plans. After 1672, the most important thing was to keep the machine running, which amounted basically to supplying the war.

The second thing is how incredibly few people were actually responsible for it. A king and three ministers to make the decisions, thirty odd councillors of state and fewer than a hundred masters of requests to prepare the material; these with the minor scribes and ushers probably made up an administrative personnel of under a thousand persons: a thousand persons with their desks and files, all following their nomadic monarch and his court as best they could. Thirty masters of requests 'toured' the provinces. Initially, these were dispatched here or there for a particular purpose, as it might be to conduct a trial, govern a town, or to inquire into false titles of nobility or forests and estates belonging to the king. By 1670 or so, they had become resident in most areas (with the exception of Brittany and Béarn) as a kind of superior administrator combining the offices of *ex officio* judge of all courts, director of finance, governor of towns and villages, and officer in charge of all movements of troops, ships, grain, textiles and money. They were the direct representatives of the king and of his unlimited powers but they were virtually without an office in their town of residence, and had no official agents in the other towns and villages of their 'departments' other than such voluntary helpers, private correspondents and secretaries as they themselves might appoint. When, at the same time, we recall that the entire country boasted a mounted constabulary of only twenty-seven brigades, that is a police force of two thousand men at most, it is no longer astonishing that so much should have gone wrong with this vast undertaking, or that there should have been so many instances of persistent anarchy and law-breaking. On the contrary, what is astonishing is that with so few men, such limited powers of coercion and so few agents in the field, a scheme of this magnitude could ever have been conceived, formulated and even sometimes successfully carried out.

But there were some, Colbert among them, who dreamed of something far beyond simply taking the country in hand. They had visions of a France wholly unified under the monarchy, powerful by land and sea, rich in soldiers, merchants, artists and in far-flung provinces. They saw a kind of Augustan Rome transposed into the seventeenth century with all the Indies for Empire and all kings turned into good Catholics, gathered respectfully about King Louis' throne. Some of these visions of a new France actually took shape. Others remained a dream.

Colbert would have liked to see the country rid of the troublesome companies of officers and run instead by administrators who were strict and efficient servants of the king. In fact all he succeeded in doing was gradually establishing ill-equipped intendants above the traditional companies. He wanted to extract a unified French law from the mass of local customs. He had to be satisfied with setting commissions earnestly to work drawing up a number of individual codes. Even the great Ordinances, apart from such major creative measures as those dealing with woods, forests and with trade, were often merely codifications of existing customs. A host of regulations were devised to sort out the tangle of 'manufactures' – what we should call industry – but to little effect. Distant lands and seas were divided up and presented as monopolies to the great companies which, on paper, sounded almost as wonderful as those dreamed up by Richelieu: the two India Companies, and those of the North and the Levant, all between 1664 and 1670.

All these brilliant plans served to keep the king amused for a while, but his real dream was of military glory. Wealth and order were merely the material background or agreeable additions to that ultimate goal, which, for him, always consisted of magnificent victories in the field.

VICTORIES (1661–72)

Louis XIV's foreign policy has seemed to many historians to possess a profound unity. Mignet has asserted, with some justification, that the War of the Spanish Succession was the 'turning point' of the reign. Degrelle saw a 'lengthy policy of armed aggression', dating from the tangled treaties of Westphalia and the Pyrenees, but this is to confuse means and ends. Albert Sorel discerned a policy of 'natural frontiers', an opinion which others have disputed with somewhat unnecessary vigour, one insisting that the king was obsessed by the idea, which certainly occurred to him, of acquiring the imperial crown for himself; another portraying him as essentially a champion of Catholicism and the hammer of the heretics. George Pagès is more moderately inclined to show the great king as a kind of pragmatical opportunist. Gaston Zeller sees the psychological element, and the passion for glory in particular, as the key to the king's policies. All these theories, as well as a good many others, deserve some consideration. There is something in all of them but none provides a complete explanation.

No one will argue with the straightforward statement that it was the king, and the king alone who, after due consultation, made the final decision on matters of foreign policy whenever a decision had to be made. It can be said, also, that he was almost invariably moved by his love of glory and that he was much concerned with Spanish affairs. But the king changed a good deal in the course of his reign and Europe changed even more, nor did the king always perceive the extent to which Europe was changing. The weakened England and the degenerate Empire of 1661 bore no resemblance to the resurgent Empire of the victor of Kahlenberg and the England full of renewed energy under William of Orange, with its national bank, backed by the strength of the Dutch economy. Louis XIV's own dashing and youthful glory of the sixties held as yet no shadow of the unprovoked, peacetime aggression of the eighties, still less of the good sense, dignity and courage of his defensive last years. Moreover, a reign lasting for fifty-five years cannot be summed up in a single phrase. The one unifying factor was the royal control with its emphasis on greatness: all the rest was made up of change, whether slight or far-reaching, slow or rapid.

1662–7: Jockeying for position

The weakening of the European nations, the temporary peace of 1661, the magnificent designs of the young man who was truly king at last, the obsession with Spain: these were the starting points. They dominated the seven years until the rise of the Dutch problem.

These seven years are studded with brilliant moves and magnificent gestures. They have been written about over and over again. The squabble over precedence between the French and Spanish ambassadors in London as to who should walk in front which was settled by a grim affray between their respective followers; and disputes over precedence between French and English vessels as to which should fire the first salute – such problems are the time-honoured stuff of diplomacy but they were serious matters for the prestige-conscious minds of the times and a point of honour for the youthful king. After some months of shilly-shallying, Spain gave way and the subsequent 'audience of apology' which took place gave clear warning to the courts of Europe that Louis intended to be premier monarch. The naval pride of the English, however, was not to be overcome by six years of wrangling. In 1667 a compromise was reached: it was decided that both flags should salute at the same time or not at all and French and English ships were to be seen on the 'narrow seas' engaged in complicated manoeuvres in order to avoid the necessity of a salute.

The most startling and possibly the most ill-advised of all these preludes to greatness was the humiliation of the Pope. Skirmishes among drunken ruffians in the vicinity of the Farnese palace had resulted in the murder of a French page by Corsican troops belonging to Alexander VII. The incident was of little importance in itself but the two courts had been on bad terms since the time of Mazarin. In those days Louis XIV had no love for 'priests'. He found even the spiritual pre-eminence of the papacy hard to stomach and dreamed of 'mortifying' Rome 'in every way'. The Chigi family and its pope held out for two years. Unable to resist the annexation of Avignon and the Comtat, or the invasion of Italy by a force of three thousand troops, they were obliged to yield to all Louis' demands. The Corsican garrison was dismissed, a legate, the Pope's nephew, was sent to Fontaine-bleau for another audience of apology, and a pyramid set up in expiation in a prominent and well-guarded position to remind the Romans of the pontiff's errors and of the supremacy of the Most Christian King of France.

This did not, of course, prevent the said Most Christian King from aspiring to the title of ultimate defender of Christendom or finding it intolerable that the emperor or the King of Spain should lay claim to that honour purely out of what he was pleased to call their 'ridiculous vanity'.

Perhaps the attacks, bombardments, invasions and provisional treaties directed against the berbers of the Maghreb may really have seemed like some kind of crusade. But while others were thinking of the security of the maritime trade, Louis also had in mind the by no means insignificant 'Mediterranean empire'. All these operations, however, bore negative results: the pirates continued to capture vessels, ravage the Provençal coasts and incidentally provide Molière with plots.

The struggle against the Turks held out further opportunities of glory but further dangers also. The Ottoman

Empire, under the Vizirs of the Köprülü family, still retained the splendid vestiges of power. It had been an effective ally in the past and might be so again and it afforded excellent prospects to French trade. But once again the infidel was battering at the gates of the Empire, and hence of Christendom. Could the Emperor Leopold be left to bear all the burden of what was clearly going to be a stiff fight or, worse still, all the glory of halting the infidel alone? Louis XIV paid careful attention to the form, the timing and the strength of the assistance he sent. He incorporated it in the army of the League of the Rhine, an assembly of his German vassals which, by this means, he obliged the Empire to recognize, but he sent six thousand men instead of the two thousand four hundred for which he had been asked. This little army played a decisive part in the victory over the Turks which took place at the river Raab on the Hungarian border in August 1664 and bore the name of a nearby monastery dedicated to St Gotthard. Louis sent the Ottoman standards captured by the French back to Vienna but the ostentatious gesture had in it an element of contempt. He had heard that the imperial troops had scattered at the approach of the Turks and that the German princes were coarse and venal and the Emperor Leopold incompetent and irresponsible. Louis celebrated this latest exploit by striking more medals, one of them bearing the barefaced inscription *Germania servata*. At the same time he was engaged in negotiations with the sultan and pointing out to him that it was not France but the League of the Rhine which had halted him on the Raab.

While Louis indulged in a mixture of ostentation and Machiavellian cunning calculated to amaze a by no means appreciative Europe, his diplomatists were working assiduously behind the scenes. At the heart of it all lay the affair of the Spanish Succession.

The diplomatic corps of the period was a far cry from the Quai d'Orsay of the present day. Louis XIV's most trusted negotiator was Hugues de Lionne, a nephew of Abel Servien. The uncle was largely responsible for the Peace of Westphalia, the nephew for the Peace of the Pyrenees. The family hailed from Dauphiné, belonged to the *noblesse de robe* and was both loyal and hardworking. Lionne, who was probably the most intelligent and the most open-minded of the king's servants, remained always very much under his master's thumb. After his death in 1671, this was held against him, but was it in his power to do otherwise? Offices were inadequate and ill-equipped, staffed chiefly by mere clerks; ambassadors, whether noble or not, clerks or laymen, might be chosen for their merit or for their position at court and they, like residents, envoys on a particular mission, secret agents of French or other nationality, and the king's own special emissaries were without a fixed salary. There was no administrative organization, none of what was later to become 'career' diplomacy, though there were plenty of talented men like Grémonville and Courtin, like the two prelates Bonzi and Forbin-Janson and the two lords Estrades and Feuquières.

With talent and dedication, this remarkably disorganized diplomacy produced some admirable results: buying allies, negotiating royal marriages, intimidating the weak and keeping spies in its pay. Its object was to isolate Spain and to bring about in Europe the balance of collusion and neutrality needed in order to exploit the Treaty of the Pyrenees at the precise moment when the long-overdue death of King Philip IV, the French king's much indebted father-in-law, should finally occur.

Louis had already recruited English support for Portugal which had been struggling for twenty years to break the Spanish yoke. Now he sent money and men. In the end, one of the great captains of the period, the Huguenot Schomberg, achieved a decisive victory at Villaviciosa (1665). For the time being, Portugal became an ally and a weak spot on the Spanish flank.

Louis XIV believed he could count on the friendship of the 'maritime powers'. He thought himself certain of England because her king was his pensioner. Charles II, besides receiving regular subsidies, had sold back Dunkirk, which had been given as a reward to Cromwell in 1659. This was a triumph for the French which appalled even the English papists. But Charles II was bound to be under an obligation to Madame's rich brother-in-law. The States General of the United Provinces – Holland, in other words – had been an ally of the French since 1662. The Dutch were suspicious of the restored English monarchy, because it favoured the house of Orange which was feared by John de Witt, and also of the disquieting rise of English seapower. Louis XIV turned his attention to the Spanish Netherlands, covering the region roughly of modern Belgium. An offensive and defensive alliance was concluded, in principle, for twenty-five years. Of the two northern countries whose strength was ebbing fast, Sweden was still the traditional ally, in return for a hundred thousand *écus* a year plus a few additions, but was far from delighted that her Danish neighbour was also the ally of the king of France. The Scandinavians were not powerful and, despite financial inducements, by no means reliable, but at least they might give the emperor a few headaches, keep the Elector of Brandenburg – who was also to be bought – amused, and engage in intrigues in Poland.

It was essential to annoy the emperor. The Turks were doing this fairly well. On the Polish side, the duc d'Enghien was a claimant to the throne: a hopeless one, but the French continued to push him. To the south, the Swiss cantons became firm allies, providing troops in return for money (1663). A good half of the Italian princes were either allies or kindred and the rest were of small account. The basic task was to 'safeguard the liberties of the Germans' against the emperor. The League of the Rhine, initiated by Mazarin, was renewed in 1663 with the participation of new princes and at one point in 1665, even Brandenburg belonged. After some difficulties the vital positions in Lorraine, though not the whole duchy, were occupied. But Louis experienced great difficulty in governing the patchwork of Alsace and he made some serious mistakes. One of these was to lend military aid to the Elector of Mayence to quell a revolt at Erfürt in 1664. The German princes became uneasy and the League of the Rhine was weakened and not renewed in 1667. A contributory factor was the publication at this date, with the king's approval, of a strong pamphlet by the advocate Aubery proclaiming 'the king's just claim to the Empire' and maintaining the superiority of the French king's title to the dignity of the emperor, including references to Charlemagne as 'King of France' and master of Germany. There is some doubt as to whether the king was responsible for these excesses, but they certainly had an adverse effect on the patient work of the diplomats to isolate Spain and neutralize the Empire.

At last, in September 1665, the King of Spain died, leaving only a four-year-old son so sickly that he was not expected to survive. In accordance, as he claimed, with the treaty of 1659, the deceased had formally barred his daughter, the Queen of France, from the succession, but Maria-Theresa's dowry had never been paid which rendered this part of the treaty null and void. Now the whole efforts of French diplomacy were prepared to exploit to the full the celebrated conditions, actually introduced by Lionne at a time when he was simply one of Mazarin's advisers. Twenty different ways had been thought up and argued in order to lay hands on part of Philip IV's domains. They had even gone so far as to ask for a settlement in anticipation. They had considered

coming to an understanding with the Dutch over the Belgian
territories, without engaging in any actual negotiations.
They had sounded out Vienna with regard to the possibility
of an agreement between the potential heirs. As early as
1662, the lawyers had dug up in Brabant a law of 'devolution' by which the property of the father devolved solely
upon the children of the first marriage (Maria Theresa being
the only one). But this was a common law custom applying
to only a very small part of the Spanish inheritance. However, writers were paid to produce a massive 'Treatise on the
Rights of the Most Christian Queen' which clothed the royal
claims to part of the Netherlands and Franche-Comté in
some rags of legality. Counter-blasts were quick to follow.
In the most famous of these, Lisola, a native of Franche-
Comté in the service of the Empire, denounced the 'piracy
and brigandage' of the king of France and appealed, if not
to the conscience of the world, at least to the union of German and European princes. But in 1665, Louis XIV was not
yet ready to use his armies to back up the claims of his
lawyers. He was deeply involved in the second Anglo-Dutch
war.

There was keen rivalry between the English and the
Dutch, for the slave trade in Africa and the Antilles, on the
American mainland around New Amsterdam, on the Atlantic and in the narrow seas. In addition, Charles II was
actively supporting his young nephew William of Orange
who had been deprived of power by the Dutch republicans
under their leader John de Witt, and in so doing added a
strong political element to the conflict. Initiating what was
to become a favourite habit, the English, in 1664, began
launching peacetime attacks on Dutch colonies and trading
posts. Then, once war had been declared, the English fleet
patrolled the North Sea and Charles II acquired a continental infantry by purchasing the support of the bishop of
Munster, a *reiter* with 18,000 men at his back, all ready to

pillage the eastern United Provinces. As far as Louis XIV
was concerned, the bishop of Munster was a dependent, the
English king a debtor and the Dutch allies. On the other
hand, the King of Spain was a dying man and the inheritance would bring about a fatal split with the allies in the
Netherlands. Finally, English and French colonists had
come to blows in the Antilles . . .

In this extremely uncomfortable situation, Louis XIV and
Lionne favoured a 'compromise' solution. At first the belligerents would not hear of this. They were therefore obliged
to make up their minds to assist their allies, although they
were in no great hurry to do so. To begin with they took the
simplest way by sending six thousand French troops to
Maastricht, by way of the friendly neutral territories of the
Bishop of Liège, in order to protect the Dutch against the
ravages of the Bishop of Munster's army. The alternative
threat was that the Brandenburg forces, at that time active
supporters of the French and the Dutch, would act as a
further deterrent to the raiders. At the risk of offending the
Swedes, Louis XIV enlisted Danish aid on behalf of the
Dutch to close the Baltic to the English. The cost of this
was 120,000 *écus*, paid by France. In the end, however, it
became necessary to declare war on the English who were
beginning to hammer their opponents by sea. But this was
not until January 1666 and by then the King of Spain had
been dead for some months, Anne of Austria had died also
and the French army was preparing for war in the north of
the kingdom. The French position was becoming more
difficult than ever.

Louis had promised the Dutch the aid of his renascent
fleet of thirty ships but first these had to undergo repairs for
heavy damage inflicted by the Barbary pirates. This occupied
1665. At the end of April 1666, Beaufort sailed from Toulon
to join Ruyter. In June he was waiting near the Tagus for
the duchess of Nemours, betrothed by Louis XIV to the

King of Portugal. The bride failed to arrive and since the
Portuguese were unable to supply the squadron it returned
to the Mediterranean. The delay, though certainly unforeseen, proved a fortunate one. Enlarged by the addition of
some vessels out of La Rochelle, the fleet finally dropped
anchor at Brest at the end of August. Meanwhile, the English and the Dutch had each won a sea battle over the other.
Charles II, penniless, and under pressure in Scotland and
Ireland as well as in his own Parliament, hankered after
peace, urged on by the citizens of London who were suffering from the simultaneous effects of the plague, the fire and
the falling off of trade. John de Witt was likewise a prey to
opposition from the Orangists and Zeelanders and was
accusing Louis of failing to honour his obligations, which
was manifestly true, and of preparing to invade the Netherlands, which was quite certainly the case. After six months
of discussions, Sweden, a mediator, obtained theoretical
assent to the suggestion of a congress at Breda. This was in
the spring of 1667 and Louis XIV was already moving into
Flanders. The war which everyone had expected was beginning and the entire situation was altered.

The First War (1667–8)

Thorough preparations had been made for the war, both at
home and abroad, and the very excellence of the preparations
was in itself a remarkably new thing for the French
monarchy.

Six years of unremitting and still incomplete struggle
against disobedience, disorder and dishonesty had succeeded
in doubling the king's revenues. Louis was well aware that
there could be no glory without money but he left the details
of its acquisition largely in Colbert's hands. No other ruler
in Europe, Holland excepted, could even hope for more than
a quarter of Louis' income of sixty million *livres* a year. It
was Colbert, also, with some others, who had embarked on

the purchase of a navy from Sweden and Denmark : French, Scandinavian and Batavian labour was hard at work in a number of western ports building French ships from materials purchased from the Baltic by way of Holland. But even so, this was not yet a navy.

The young Louvois, duly trained by his father who may have done most of the work but remained in the background in order to advance his son, took the army firmly in hand. Discipline, inspections, manoeuvres were all reorganized from scratch or increased enormously. Staging posts were reconsidered; stores of arms, ammunition, grain and fodder carefully selected and liberally maintained; military positions in the north repaired and garrisoned while the morale of the army was kept up by a dozen public reviews in the presence of the king and of his court. The admirable Turenne was well to the fore and inspired great confidence. The great Condé was waiting eagerly for a fresh opportunity to serve. Vauban was already achieving notice with a small but remarkable troop of 'royal engineers'. Besides these, there were a great many humble but experienced commanders, many of them Huguenots, a youthful nobility panting to distinguish themselves for the king's glory and the love of their ladies, and some 25,000 mercenaries from Lorraine, Germany, Italy and, most numerous and reliable of all, the Swiss: in all, about 70,000 men, a good half of them French, and some 1,800 cannon, 800 of which were from Denmark. This was the King of France's army and there was no other to equal it, certainly not the Spanish army of the Netherlands: barely 20,000 men, ill-armed, ill-equipped and badly paid. The king's 'Flemish' campaign was beginning under the best possible auspices.

The diplomats had succeeded in helping matters considerably. The king of Portugal had pledged himself, in return for a few millions, to continue the war and keep the Spaniards busy at home. A quarter of the German princes of the Rhine, won over by like arguments, had promised not to allow a passage to the imperial troops if they should attempt to go to the aid of the Netherlands. The north, east and south of the Empire were either friendly, neutral or impotent. Leopold agreed to discuss the ultimate division of the Spanish inheritance with France and seemed to be paralysed and helpless in the face of events. Both the Dutch and the English, up to their necks in negotiations about their own war, were powerless to move. Better still, Charles II, in a secret agreement in April 1667, had agreed to leave Louis XIV a free hand for at least a year in return for a financial consideration and certain concessions in the Antilles. Hugues de Lionne and his agents had done their work well.

And so, after the usual legal-diplomatic comedy to deal with the Regent of Spain, three French armies under Turenne, Aumont and Créqui, marched into Flanders at the beginning of the campaigning season, in May, to claim the queen's rights. Far from walking straight into a defence-less country, they spent the summer laying siege to a dozen places, not all of which succumbed without a struggle. The king observed their progress from a distance. Unlike his father and grandfather, he was not fond of the smell of powder and believed that it was wrong to expose his royal person. He took some time off to fetch the queen and the court and show them the captured towns. In September, Turenne, who had reached the vicinity of Ghent and Brussels, declared the campaign over and on 1 November the troops settled calmly into their winter quarters, leaving the next move to the diplomats.

In the same year, 1667, de Witt tired of the prevarications of the English and sent a Dutch fleet up the Thames to bombard the Arsenal at Chatham, sink a number of ships and strike terror into the hearts of Londoners. There was nothing for it but to treat and agreement was reached at Breda at the end of July on a basis of mutual concessions. Now the two former enemies had their hands free. De Witt thought that the French were coming much too close to the Republic and the English suddenly found themselves appealed to as arbiters on all sides. The stage was set for interesting developments.

The French, however, gained in rapid succession an alliance with Brandenburg, the friendly neutrality of Bavaria and then, suddenly in January 1668, an agreement with the Emperor Leopold on the subject of a first partition, on paper, of the Spanish inheritance in return for which Leopold promised to employ himself in bringing about some 'arrangement' with France and Europe. But four days later, on 23 January, the maritime powers came to an agreement to make peace between Louis XIV and Spain by means of a plan previously suggested by Louis himself. This was to offer Spain an 'alternative', in other words a choice between the various strongholds captured by France. At about the same time, Condé, who had finally been recalled, invaded Franche-Comté which, short of troops, arms and morale, capitulated within twenty days. This extended the sphere of application of the alternative. De Witt was deeply involved. The treaty of The Hague which, with the inclusion of the Swedes who had been disappointed by France and were now in the pay of Spain, rapidly turned into a 'Triple Alliance', was largely the work of the Dutch. It came as a bad shock to the French diplomats who had been completely unprepared. Lionne put a good face on things and historians have even maintained that the Triple Alliance did nothing to halt Louis XIV and actually helped him to achieve his objects in the war. This astounding piece of sophistry takes little account of a secret clause providing for the entry of the three allies into the war if Louis rejected their mediation and furthermore it ignores anti-Dutch reaction which swept both court and country.

The generals, Louvois and even Louis himself believed

they could win through. But in February the Portuguese abandoned their struggle against Spain, the Swiss were uneasy at the proximity of Condé, the Duke of Lorraine was making up his mind to take a hand, while the Dutch were bribing the Germans and fitting out ships. Even the English Parliament was voting subsidies for war. Louis XIV was wise enough to see that if he persisted he would only strengthen and enlarge the coalition, whereas by treating he might easily dissolve it.

Peace was made on 15 April on the principle of the alternative. The real object of his policies being to keep the French at a safe distance, de Witt was hoping that Spain would choose to give up Franche-Comté. However, the reverse occurred and the kingdom of France was made the richer by a dozen enclaves, Lille among them, in the very heart of Spanish territory and a good way from the borders of Artois. These advanced positions strongly suggested an imminent rectification of the frontiers and the French withdrawal from Franche-Comté, after carefully disarming it beforehand, seemed a purely temporary measure. Even after peace had been signed at Aix-la-Chapelle in May 1668, no one believed otherwise, Louis himself least of all, indeed he boasts of it in his memoirs, written more or less at the time of these events.

The war had been magnificent, an affair of ordered well-deployed armies, sieges which, if they were a trifle hasty, unfolded like classic spectacles, a succession of admittedly not very hard-won victories, and all carried out before Louis' very eyes while the trumpets rang in his ears bearing far and wide the echoes of his fame. The 'queen's rights' had, in the end, been universally acknowledged. Twelve fine new strongholds covered a frontier which, though still too close to Paris, was destined to be pushed further before very long. Franche-Comté was within reach and of the two traditional rivals, Spain and the Empire, one was humbled and the other paralysed. The loss of men had been negligible and the cost to the nation's finances so small that Colbert, little as he liked the war, was able to avoid any deficit or any 'extraordinary levy'.

But the heart of the Triple Alliance which was at the centre of the coalition was Holland, and Holland, republican, Calvinist, a nation of 'cheese merchants' and 'sea peddlers', boasted with some justification in 1668 of being the arbiter of Europe and of having subdued five kings. She might actually have struck the alleged medal showing Joshua making the sun stand still. This was something neither Louis nor those close to him could endure. For once Louvois and Colbert were in agreement in their hatred of the 'jobbers of Europe', and the insults poured from their pens. Louis XIV thought of nothing but 'punishment'. He was 'cut to the quick', he wrote after the treaty of The Hague, and was merely putting off 'the punishment of this perfidy for another time'.

The four years between the peace of Aix-la-Chapelle and the crossing of the Rhine were occupied chiefly by his obsession with Holland.

The Dutch Obsession (1668–72)

Without going over them again in detail, it is sufficient to say that the activities of French diplomats and the preparations of her military leaders can be described under three headings. They were trying to break up the Triple Alliance, to neutralize possible future adversaries and to forge a still more powerful army.

To Pomponne, an able diplomat who succeeded Lionne as foreign secretary in 1672, fell the task of laying to rest Dutch fears of royal reprisals, and in this he succeeded very well. The Swedes were bought back, senator by senator, and in April 1672 they pledged themselves to an attack on the north German princes, Brandenburg in particular, who were likely to side against France. Charles II was also bought off, at a price, on 1 June 1670. The Treaty of Dover was his delightful sister's final achievement. It set the seal on the offensive alliance against Holland: Charles II offering his navy and 6,000 men in return for three million and a few islands. He was to have an additional two million and 6,000 French soldiers if he agreed, despite the English, to become reconciled to Rome. Money, fine words and the Catholic faith had each made an effective contribution towards breaking up, for a time, the Triple Alliance of the maritime powers.

It remained to harass the ultimate enemy, the Empire. Complicated manoeuvres in its rear (Poland, Hungary, Turkey) failed to produce the expected results. The Great Elector was unreliable, the rest were either flattered or subsidized. The three ecclesiastical electors were won over or neutral, the Saxon and the Palatine (whose daughter had reluctantly become the second Madame) at least neutral and a formal treaty was signed with the Bavarians in 1670 by which, in return for the promise of large chunks of Spain, they forbade all passage of troops to their own emperor. The emperor himself, impoverished and preoccupied with the Turkish threat, promised his neutrality on 1 November 1761 on condition that no fighting took place within the Empire. Finally, in 1670 the French armies marched into Lorraine in peacetime, cutting the Spanish route from Franche-Comté to the Netherlands. A few Germans protested but without enthusiasm. There were no protests when, in the same year, Louvois and Vauban set out as though on a simple provincial tour from Spanish Italy into Franche-Comté.

The military preparations were similar to those made before 1667 but on a larger scale. Vauban and the frontiers, Louvois and the army, Colbert and the navy, were all the outward symbols of this considerable effort. In 1672, Europe might well be impressed by a French army numbering 120,000 men, a good third of whom were Italians, Swiss, Germans and Irishmen. No one had seen anything to equal it in numbers, equipment, organization of stores and fortresses, or the fame of its leaders, the two most illustrious of whom were in the last, dying splendour of their careers.

Faced with such a situation, the United Provinces, ravaged by internal conflicts and half unconscious of what was coming to them, seemed doomed to the general complicity or indifference. The Great King saw the easy prospect of fresh triumphs lying before him and Boileau could sharpen his pen to hail the crossing of the Rhine.

But the attack on Holland was more than simply the monarch's revenge for the offences of the republican, Calvinist merchants. It was, for Colbert and a number of others, the longed for culmination of the task, undertaken more than ten years before, of increasing the wealth of France. For once economic dreams and interests were to coincide with political and military grudges and ambitions. The success of what has been, somewhat inaptly, dubbed Colbertism was narrowly dependent on the swift defeat of Holland. It is worth taking a short, retrospective look at this unity of all interests, appetites and illusions and perhaps, at the risk of heresy, revising our ideas on it a little.

WEALTH (1661–72)

The immense work of Jean-Baptiste Colbert has suffered from the distortions put upon it by more orthodox minds and sunk beneath mountains of fulsome praise. Jurists have manufactured 'isms' and numbered arguments about it. The *grands bourgeois* of the last century turned Jean-Baptiste into their own greatest progenitor, a magnificent prototype of all that is best in a ruling bourgeoisie. In a now famous passage, the great Lavisse, as a kind of official historian of the radical Republic, produced a quite brilliant but wholly imaginary picture of Colbert's contribution:

At this unique and transitory moment of time (1661), Colbert counselled a tremendous innovation, that France and her king should set themselves earnestly to the basic task of making money . . . . It was therefore by Colbert's will that France became a country whose wealth was based on commerce and industry . . .

He concludes still more impressively: 'How France and the king himself welcomed Colbert's contribution is the major question of the reign of Louis XIV.'

Put this way, the question naturally produced the answer that the proud and warlike monarch rejected the contribution of the brilliant and progressive bourgeois. By their very denials, even his shrewdest opponents have always fallen in unconsciously with the old historian's thesis. This view of the 'cloth merchant of Rheims', the 'bourgeois of genius' has always served to cloud men's judgement and thrown a thick veil over seventeenth-century France. The country has been studied through Colbert's writings when the only valuable course would have been to work in the opposite direction, studying the country first and then seeing how far Jean-Baptiste knew, understood and altered it.

This unconscious falsification of history has been carried to its extreme by the worthy Boissonade who raised Colbert to the level of a cult: before his hero there was nothing; after him, France was 'first among the first industrial powers of the world'. Boissonade might be guilty of muddled thinking, of contradicting himself from one page to the next, an accumulation of distortions, of errors of fact or judgement, but in France at least, this over simplification has too often remained current. In 1939, Charles Wesley Cole, a professor at Columbia, certainly published a *Colbert* that was moderate and conscientious but it was splendidly ignored. And since Hauser is no longer here to reflect, prove and cleave through all argument, people are at liberty to smile at certain of his ideas, especially those expressed in his last work, the *Pensée et Action économique du cardinal de Richelieu* which is the best introduction to an understanding of Colbert.

It is necessary to mention this dispute among experts, painful though it is, chiefly in order to 'demystify', in the modern phrase, the character of this good servant. We have to re-examine Hauser's thoughts and intuitions and, on the whole, accept them. Colbert was born into the cadet branch of a great merchant family. There can be little doubt that he owed his advancement to his undistinguished father's brilliant cousin, M. de Saint-Pouange, who had the wit to marry Le Tellier's sister and occupied an important position in the ministerial administration. Little is known of Colbert's youth and after an unremarkable student career he entered Saint-Pouange's office. His training there marked him for life. He loved files and detailed paperwork. In 1643 he was serving under Le Tellier in the war office, dealing with the commissariat. While there, he met Marie Charron, the daughter of a rich army paymaster with a dowry of a hundred thousand *livres*, and married her in 1648. He entered Mazarin's service early in 1651 and once in charge of the cardinal's affairs he set about putting to rights what was the most immense, scandalous and complicated private fortune of the times. Mazarin, as we have already seen, bequeathed him to his godson. In all this, the cloth merchants of Rheims played no part. The man was a bureaucrat, a major-domo, an intendant and a confidant: the true 'servant' in the best contemporary sense of the word. Incidentally he acquired wealth and nobility for himself, the latter probably by means of the councillorship of State conferred on his father in 1652.

Most of the ideas with which he has been credited had been current for a hundred years. It is more than thirty years since Hauser, studying 'Colbertism before Colbert' amused himself by drawing attention to the same basic principles outlined in a particular debate of the States General or the Assembly of Notables in 1614, 1596, 1588, 1576, 1538, even as far back as 1485 and 1471. His reading of the British historians also enabled Hauser to demonstrate without difficulty that the basic elements of Colbertism were to be found in the policies of Elizabeth's minister, William Cecil. Moreover Hauser was unacquainted with the pioneer work of the sixteenth-century Spanish economists and could not know the brilliant article in which the English historian Fisher has demonstrated that any national economy or protectionist attitude on the part of the state is primarily an indication of a disordered state of affairs, that the state does not intervene when matters are running smoothly and, as a corollary, that 'Colbertism' is in itself a sign of economic withdrawal, recession and decline.

In his concluding pages, Hauser has proved how far Colbert's most often quoted dicta were simply copied from the theories of Richelieu himself whose papers he had studied and whom he was never tired of quoting to the king as an example. 'Sire, the great cardinal....' Hauser went on to show that what Colbert had to add to Richelieu was mere foolishness, as for instance in his private law regarding the fixed amount of money circulating in Europe, the constant 'volume of trade' and the number of vessels handling it. Richelieu, on the contrary, believed in expansion and in economic growth: 'the distance between a perfect clerk and a statesman'.

In the last resort, as Cole wrote in 1939, what was original in Colbert was his indefatigable energy. He was devoted, body and soul, to the king's service and all his family with him. Besides a few ideas on economic policy, he had the broadest conception of the king's glory and therefore, since the kingdom was the king, of the glory of the kingdom also.

The king should have the finest palaces, the best generals, the best artists, dominion over land and sea and hegemony in the arts of war and peace alike. Priests and the Pope himself should bow before him. His God should be defended everywhere and false beliefs extirpated. France, herself superbly independent of all other nations, would deign to bestow on them the best products of her land, her industry and her ideas. Wealth and magnificence, splendour and opulence were Colbert's watch words, and in this Gallic recreation of Augustan Rome, governing the world, Colbert's own family should have its place. Wealth and honours should be heaped on it, as much and more as on other ministerial families, for who in those days could conceive of ministers who were poor and humble?

To these magnificent prospects, Jean-Baptiste sacrificed food and drink, sleep and enjoyment. A demon for work, the sworn enemy of weakness in any form, he harried unmercifully such useless people as *rentiers*, officers, beggars, monks and tavern-keepers. He was a tireless scribbler, a devourer of documents, avid for details and inquiries, liking nothing so much as a well-conducted ruling, and cursing when agriculture could not be reduced to a matter of ordinances, titles and articles. Everything was grist to his mill and he would borrow, buy or steal from abroad all that he thought necessary to enhance the glory of his king: men, machines, methods, or merchandise. He was meticulously attentive to justice, law, finance, buildings, customs, ports, ships, workshops and harvests, more to the conduct of artists than to art itself, and to the good behaviour of craftsmen and journeymen. Half of what we would call nowadays the 'ministries' were under his control and his influence was strong in the rest. On all these subjects and more he was forever writing lengthy memoranda, which from clear beginnings became lost in a mass of verbiage. Some sensible pronouncements floated to the top: Colbert's gleanings from more original minds. Generations of historians have handed them on, not troubling to study their dreary contents. Endlessly persistent, loading the king with papers and, consciously or unconsciously, managing to present plans as accomplished facts and decrees as being already in operation: such is the realistic portrait of the conscientious clerk as it emerges from the quantities of his published writings – never finished or revised – as they were collected by the scholars of the last century, Pierre Clément chief among them.

The circumstances which enabled Jean-Baptiste to provide the king with means to carry out his glorious designs were more propitious than any France had known since 1630: twelve years of peace, for the insignificant campaigns of the so-called War of Devolution and one or two expeditions of a trivial nature can be passed over.

His was no easy task. Thirty years of war had led to thirty years of high taxes, financial deficits and fiscal revolts. The *taille*, the *gabelle*, the deficit and the national debt had all doubled since the time of Richelieu and even Richelieu had not had much success when confronted with half the kingdom in a state of active or passive rebellion. The second cardinal had been obliged to turn for help to financiers, tax farmers, moneylenders and the most enterprising and unscrupulous businessmen, although without making matters noticeably worse, since under him the French economy and finances were in a much healthier state than is generally imagined. Moreover, like them, he involved his own considerable fortune in state affairs and recouped himself lavishly at the taxpayers' expense. In addition, he raised the 'unaccountable expenses' to the sum of a hundred millions, more than the gross revenue of the state. At his death, in fact, the revenue for 1661, 1662 and half of 1663 had already been pledged, in other words swallowed up in advance.

The exemplary and persevering work done by Colbert

and his associates, with its eminent good sense, is common knowledge. To substitute the 'principle of order' for the 'principle of confusion'. To put the king ahead of his commitments, and make him 'his own superintendent', presenting him with all financial papers for his perusal and signature, and obliging him to make frequent checks on the three new registers which were the A B C of a previously non-existent budget: the day-book, and the accounts of income and expenditure, checked and amplified by the monthly abstract, the king's private agenda, the treasury accounts, the provisional budget for the coming year, drawn up in October, and the actual accounts for the preceding year, made up in February. Colbert's aim, in fact, was to direct the affairs of France with all the thoroughness of a good private accountant.

The new regime owed it to public opinion, which was by and large very bitter against the financiers, to organize a good hunt for abuses. In 1661, a special court was set up, presided over first by Lamoignon and afterwards by Séguier, with Omer Talon as *procureur-général*, 'to investigate all malpractices committed later than 1635'. The court employed informers, frightened *rentiers* and small moneylenders, allowed the most notorious rogues to escape and made deals with some others. A few of the more unfortunate were put in prison and a few more, who were safely out of the way, condemned to death but altogether, in the course of eight years, the court succeeded in finding only the paltry sum of 110 millions, the equivalent of eighteen months' income for the State. Even this, however, was enough to enable Colbert to achieve in part one of his aims which was to reduce the amount of the national debt – more than half the gross receipts for 1661 – by paying back some of the substantial creditors with money recovered from the officers, as cheaply as possible, of course.

Colbert's work was, in fact, much more remarkable for

the reduction of the financial burden than by any increase in revenue or tightening up on expenses. His efficiency in this direction was formidable. Of the various annuities payable by the state (in many cases through the Paris Hôtel de Ville), half were quite simply abolished and the remainder cut by a half or a quarter. The recipients, most of whom were in Paris, grumbled, showed signs of rebellion and then gave in. The result was an annual saving of more than four millions. Thousands of new offices, nearly all of them unnecessary or absurd, had been created and sold since 1630 and payment of all these salaries was costing the budget more than eight million a year. Colbert would have liked to redeem all these unnecessary offices and a good many others as well. He did pay off a quarter of the principle, one hundred millions or thereabouts, which eased the budget of more than two million a year. The officers concerned, wailed and protested and offered 61 millions to keep their posts but to no avail. Altogether, in spite of delays, difficulties, schemes and protests from below, the permanent drain on the budget dropped in ten years from 52 millions to 14. This, for the period, was an astonishing achievement.

Colbert contemplated a reform of the fiscal system, which was antique, complicated, unpopular and inefficient, but he knew that this was beyond him. Nevertheless, he did put into practice here and there his project of a general land survey of France, but to no effect. The kingdom was old and set in its ways and reacted unfavourably to what it regarded as a dangerous innovation. The principal form of direct taxation in those provinces which had been French for the greatest length of time, the *taille personelle* of the *pays d'élections* (with the exception of the *généralité* of Montauban), had been raised by Richelieu from 1636 onwards to the unprecedented level of 40 millions. Any number of bailiffs, sergeants, collectors, intendants and troops could not compel the peasants to pay a tax out of all proportion to their traditions or their means. Moreover tax farmers, executors and law enforcement officers only added to the cost of recovery and decreased the net income. Colbert realized that the excessive taxes, delays in payment and costs of collection were as absurd as they were burdensome. Sparing the source of taxation, exhausted by seizures and executions, he gradually reduced the *taille personelle* until in ten years it had fallen from 42 to 34 millions. In the long run this 'relief for the people', amply compensated for in other directions, finished by bringing in more money to the coffers of the state. Rebates to collectors (for 'expenses' incurred in the execution of their duties) dropped suddenly from the scandalous figure of 25 per cent to 4 per cent. A rigorous hunt was instituted for all false claims to exemption: false titles of nobility, newly appointed officers, the bourgeois of the free cities and the privileged and bourgeois of Paris, the extent of whose exempt lands was limited to a few acres. Establishments were ameliorated in order to facilitate payment; and we find fewer elections, of parishes or individuals 'fixed' by the credit of some influential person. Most important of all, collection was speeded up and regulated according to a strict time schedule. Colbert would have liked to avoid the seizure and imprisonment of defaulters and collectors, which added more to the costs than to the revenue but in practice, in spite of all the fine-sounding decrees, goods, crops and cattle were seized just as they had been in the past. Ploughs and horses may have been spared but three-quarters of the peasants owned none.

Income from all other sources increased perceptibly. The *taille* in the *pays d'État* which was based on landed property and in many cases on sound surveys, went up on average by 50 per cent. These regions were well off and could afford to pay. The estates themselves were obliged to submit to the doubling of their *'don gratuit'* – except in Burgundy where they found it wiser to make an annual payment to Colbert himself and so got off more lightly. The clergy also were faced with an increase in their '*don gratuit*'. For thirty years the king had been leasing, transferring or simply letting go large parts of his domains: forests, land, mills, tolls, and rights of municipal boundaries, aids and excise. Colbert either repurchased cheaply or simply took back everything that had been parted with. By 1671, the royal estates, which had produced virtually nothing in 1661, were bringing in 5 millions, while the income paid in by the farmers rose from 37 to 60 millions.

In return for a reasonable commission, the king's tax farmers undertook to collect on his behalf the *gabelles*, town entry dues, the multitude of aids and the inextricable confusion of local, provincial and harbour dues as well as certain manorial rights, postal dues and a score of minor impositions. For a time, the people subject to the *gabelle* paid a little less for their salt but controls became much stricter. The tariff of aids remained stable but there was a notable increase in the amount they brought in. This was because both farmers and taxpayers were subject to much stricter supervision, simplified regulations and a much improved system of accounting. Even so, it seems unlikely that an increase of 60 per cent (23 millions) in the revenue from tax farmers could have come about without a substantial contribution from the French people as a whole.

For some years, even the king showed very willing, keeping a watch on his expenditures and drawing on average not much more than five or six millions on the exchequer for his personal expenses, much of it for political ends.

The results of these earnest efforts towards clarification, if not reform, can be seen in the estimates of the royal income and expenditure left to us by seventeenth-century administrators and studied at great length by learned scholars in the nineteenth. From 1661 to 1671, the king's *net* income easily doubled. From 1662 onwards, income exceeded expenditure and except during the War of Devolution when a slight check is discernible, a substantial surplus mounted up from year to year. Louis XIV was probably alone in Europe in possessing the financial resources to enable him to sustain a major military venture without anxiety. In the spring of 1672, everything seemed set for a swift and glorious campaign against the Dutch. Colbert had done his work well and although the French had certainly paid dearly, this was probably because they were able to do so.

Colbert was only too well aware that the best system of taxation in the world was totally useless without something to tax. More and more, the essential goal of what has been anachronistically called Colbert's 'economic policy' was to put the people in a position to finance the nation's glory. In order to achieve this, the people must obtain the necessary money since the king, unlike the clergy, had no use for a tithe payable in kind. Two conditions were therefore essential. One was for money to come into the country, since France produced no precious metals of her own. This had long been the business of the great merchants and businessmen of international standing who were at least as numerous in France as anywhere else. The second was for a good deal of this 'imported' money to filter down to the level of the ordinary taxpayers whose only way of earning it was by the sweat of their brow, which was 'industry' or by the sale of the small surplus from the produce of their own farms, which was 'commerce'. In the seventeenth century, the ideas of trade and industry were closely linked and included everything that brought in ready money which could then be sucked back into the fiscal machine. Everything else, which amounted basically to the necessities of life, was obtained practically without the use of money at all, by the time-honoured methods of barter and fair exchange whose products never reached the royal coffers and were only of concern to the Government in so far as they were a pre-requisite for 'trade'. This is the light in which Colbert's acts must be regarded. He was not aiming to enrich the kingdom for love of its subjects but to satisfy the needs of government.

There was a second motive which was particularly power-ful during the first decade of the reign. This, as we have seen, was an extension of the concept of magnificence. France must astonish the world by producing mirrors as fine as those of Venice, cloth as fine as that of Haarlem, serge as fine as that of Florence, tapestries as fine as those of Brabant, ironwork as good as that of Germany or Sweden, as many ships as heavily laden as those of the United Provinces, or all these things finer and better still. In this way glory and prosperity should come together, each supporting the other.

His methods of going about this task are only too well known: work and the necessity to work, organization and supervision, a frantic spate of minute regulations, copying or taking over all that was best from abroad, and the setting up of closely controlled and subsidized royal companies and manufactories. Admittedly, none of these methods was exactly new. Louis XIII, Henri IV, England and above all, Holland, had all employed them, with varying degrees of success. But never before had any single ten-year period wit-nessed such a concentration of effort and enterprise. More important still, never before had the national budget come to its aid in this way, frequently providing nearly a million to-wards commerce and industry, and rarely less than three million for the navy. Unkind critics may point out that these few millions amounted to only a few per cent of the total French budget compared with the much greater expenditure on the royal plate or stables but even so, what matters is the novelty and continuity of this 'investment' outlay. In fact the eight years from 1664 to 1671 were the high point of Colbert's administration and laid the foundations of a genuine economic boom, of which the following was only the beginning:

1664: Creation by royal decree of the Tapestry Manufactures of Beauvais, and of the East and West India Companies opening up distant sources of wealth to French trade. Introduction of so-called 'protectionist' customs tariffs, although protectionism as such had existed since the time of Mazarin.

1665: Reorganization of the *Conseil du Commerce*. Drive to keep down the Barbary pirates. Trial introduction of seaboard conscription for the navy, in Aunis and Saintonge. Letters patent granted to Riquet for preliminary work on the *Canal des Deux Mers*. Re-establishment of the national stud. Edict of the 'denier 20' within the province of the Paris *Parlement*.

1666: First regulations covering manufacturers.

1667: Introduction of new, ultra-protectionist and anti-Dutch tariff laws and, at the same time, the Gobelins tapestry works turned into a '*manufacture des meubles de la Couronne*'.

These were followed by the formation of the last companies, the great ordinances, a host of new regulations and subsidies for a score of industrial undertakings, as well as for the arsenal and the naval dockyards.

Set against this expansion on a scale unprecedented for any French monarch, was one ever-present obstacle against which Colbert fulminated incessantly. The 16,000 (actually 8,000) Dutch vessels which he innocently believed constituted fourth-fifths of the world's shipping, still carried the bulk of French and international trade. French cloth and textiles could not compete with the Dutch, even when they were manufactured 'in the Dutch style'. Arms, munitions, cannon, ships and military supplies continued to come from

Holland, or through Dutch middlemen and it was still Dutch ships that carried the trade in wine and brandy from the west of France. When, at great expense, he formed a *Compagnie du Nord* to rob them of the Baltic trade, his few ships either went astray, brought back nothing or failed to sell their goods because the Dutch were engaged in dumping French products themselves. Such French ships as did sail for the Indies – and there were a few lost on the way – either failed to keep hold on the markets that they captured or failed to buy the Asian merchandise cheaply enough. The Dutch answered the ultra-protectionist tariffs of 1667 with savage reprisals. The dividends of the Dutch Company were regularly over 25 per cent, while the French equivalent paid out nothing. By July 1670, Colbert was writing to the effect that His Majesty could not long endure 'the arrogance and insolence of this nation'. Powerless in the face of the economic superiority of the Netherlanders, Colbert could now see only one end to the situation: war. It was a short step to picturing the advantages to the kingdom to be gained by the annexation of the wealthy United Provinces. A famous memo of 8 July 1672 shows him already counting his chickens:

'If all the united provinces of the Netherlands were to become subject to the king then their trade being the trade of His Majesty's subjects would leave nothing more to be desired. . . .'

The king wanted his revenge and since it was also the desire of everyone of any importance – soldiers, nobles, Catholics, and ministers of home and foreign affairs – the attack on Holland was the first decisive action of the reign and perhaps its most crucial moment.

7

THE FIRST TURNING POINT
(1672–9)

THE ATTACK ON HOLLAND (1672)

HOSTILITIES were begun on 28 March by Charles II of England who was anxious to come into his own and rid himself of a Parliament which was becoming a nuisance. For once, England made a formal declaration of war. Louis XIV did not trouble to; he merely stuck up a notice explaining to his subjects that he had gone off to chastise the Dutch because they had failed to give him 'satisfaction'. In fact, Louis left Paris on 27 March and went to war on 6 April with 120,000 men, the English fleet, Condé, Turenne, Luxembourg and Vauban.

The Dutch had done nothing to lessen their chances of defeat. At the end of 1671, they still believed in the duration of a peace the continued existence of which was a constant source of surprise to the rest of Europe. Their army, some 30,000 ill-fed and ill-clothed men, was rotting away in dilapidated fortresses. It was only in January that the States General took the decision to conscript another 20,000 men, to reintroduce the urban militia and to appoint the young prince William of Orange Captain-General, with plenty of honest burghers on hand to keep an eye on him.

The two French armies advanced as calmly as if they were simply on manoeuvres from Charleroi (annexed in 1668) and Sedan to Maastricht and on towards the Electorate of Cologne. The king conducted some exemplary sieges, even as many as four at a time. With his allies from the Rhineland at his back, he met no difficulty in penetrating deep into Dutch territory. William of Orange waited for him behind the Ijsel with 20,000 men to defend Amsterdam. On 12 June, Louis crossed the Rhine at a ford by a custom's house, Tolhuis in Dutch, and took him by surprise. The Dutch offered some resistance, wounding Condé and killing his nephew, Longueville. The crossing of the Rhine became a legend in history, literature and art. The Dutch army, hopelessly outflanked, melted away. Condé urged that a few regiments of cavalry should be dispatched to seize Amsterdam. The king ignored his advice and there is no doubt that in doing so he made a terrible mistake. But he preferred more spectacular sieges. Utrecht surrendered at the sight of a few mounted men and the Dutch Catholics gave a fervent welcome to the conqueror who treated them very graciously in return. But on the same day that Utrecht was captured, the dikes were opened at Muiden. Three days later, Amsterdam was the capital of a small archipelago: all that remained of the province of Holland. The only way to conquer Holland now was by sea, but Ruyter had beaten the enemy fleet at Sole Bay.

The Dutch were making a quick recovery, levying troops, bringing Ruyter's seamen ashore to aid the defenders, throwing up fortifications, opening more sluices, especially in defence of Bois-le-Duc, forcing de Witt and William into cooperation, and electing the young prince stadtholder of five provinces and finally, on 8 July, of the republic as a whole. Their diplomats and their florins began to have an effect. Spain came to their assistance. On 23 June, in Berlin, the Elector of Brandenburg and the Emperor Leopold agreed to intervene against France and a month later both were negotiating openly with the Dutch. There was little practical help to be looked for in this direction but at least it was the beginning of a coalition. In the last days of June the States General sent envoys to Louis XIV with an offer of all the land south of the Meuse, all the towns he had conquered and ten millions in cash. Louis, drunk with success, demanded much more land, much more money, the restoration of the Catholic faith in all the provinces, unheard-of privileges for French trade and, as the final outrage, the dispatch of an annual embassy to Paris to present him with a gold medal in token of submission. The ambassadors departed, never to return.

But someone had to pay for the invasion, the desolation caused by the flooding and the terror suffered by the Dutch people. At last, on 20 August, they ran amok and murdered de Witt who had been the man of peace. William of Orange was undisputed master of the whole country. This sickly, taciturn young prince was to become the living symbol of the nation's resistance and spirit of revenge.

In spite of all this, Louis XIV went back to France to breath in fresh incense in the belief that such few Dutch strongholds as remained to be captured were not 'worth his presence'. The campaign was over. It was the universal opinion that no such wonders had ever been seen: the Rhine was crossed, so many towns had been taken and so many protestant temples returned to the Church. To be sure, the king of France was not yet altogether king of Holland or the Dutch fleet under Colbert's control but this was only a matter of time. France basked in glory. Monuments were raised in honour of Louis' conquests even while, in the words of Voltaire, 'the powers of Europe schemed to wrest them from him'.

For the time being, there may have been some grounds for this sublime disregard of the facts. But still, Turenne on the Rhine was forced to keep up a running battle against the Habsburg and Hohenzollern armies. Luxembourg's winter offensive against Amsterdam was defeated by the thaw. By 15 December, William was laying siege to the French stronghold of Charleroi and the invaded had become the invader. Horrified, Louis XIV hurried in person to Compiègne from where he hoped to be able to defend Saint-Quentin at least. Had the Great King 'ceased to be victorious'?

The attack on Holland was his first important failure – for it may justly be called a failure – to have dire consequences. Not one object of the war had been attained, neither Colbert's nor the king's. The cheese-merchants had not been chastised, in spite of their wretched army, and neither the Dutch fleet nor the Dutch Indies had been brought to heel. On the contrary, France had actually brought about the rise to power of the most ruthless and intelligent of all her enemies in the person of the twenty-two-year old stadtholder. Her northern frontier had been breached. A coalition was in the making, and there was the prospect of a lengthy war which would mean a call for more troops and more expenditure. Already, Colbert's financial work was threatened and his economic achievements endangered. The great administrator was to be reduced to the role of a provider of ready money and there was still the possibility that the country would respond by armed rebellion to the enormous demands that would certainly be made on it.

The sluices at Muiden and William's accession marked the end of the era of easy triumphs. Louis, now in his thirty-fifth year, was sometimes, though all too fleetingly, aware of it. Colbert was quicker to understand, but the mass of courtiers, intoxicated with the nation's glory, still had no suspicions. For us, three centuries later, it is only too easy to look back on the crucial year of 1672 as the great turning point of the reign and see the hard times that were coming, the era of coalitions, of small concessions that preceded the great epoch-making decisions of the king's maturer years.

THE FIRST COALITION (1672–9)

It took William of Orange less than two years to rouse almost the whole of Europe on behalf of the United

Provinces to form a coalition against her aggressor. On 30 August 1673, three treaties were signed, bringing Holland three new allies. The Duke of Lorraine would give 16,000 men in return for the restoration of his duchy, occupied by the French in time of peace. Spain promised to enter the war if her 1659 frontiers were guaranteed. The emperor sold 30,000 men for the sum of 45,000 *écus* a month and 100,000 in advance. Meanwhile first Condé and then Luxembourg, after waiting in vain for the Anglo-French fleet which had been defeated once again by Ruyter, were living off the land, burning some Dutch villages, much to the delight of Louvois, but by the end of the year had abandoned all but a few of their positions in Holland. The invading army had no choice but to beat an inglorious retreat. Louis, however, was pre-paring with great ceremony to witness the spectacle of the siege of Maastricht while Turenne, on the Rhine, was fight-ing and sacking as far as the Palatinate. In Cologne, the diplomats brought together by Sweden as mediator, began their talks. Louis XIV sensibly offered the same conditions for peace which he had rejected when put forward by the Dutch in June 1672. William of Orange felt himself in a position to offer only three cities, to be handed over to the Spaniards. At the same congress, the emperor was em-boldened to pick up one of the most active of France's agents, Fürstenburg. To these two affronts, which showed how times had changed, was added the desertion of England.

On 19 February 1674, at Westminster, Charles II signed a separate peace with William of Orange – and followed it up by giving him his niece Mary in marriage. All England had been calling for peace. The country had had enough of the king's pro-Catholic policies and the last straw had been the marriage of the Duke of York, the sole heir to the throne and a papist, to Mary of Modena, a niece of Mazarin and one of Louis XIV's dependents. Besides, the war was making no progress and the combined fleets of Spain and

Holland were providing a serious impediment to trade. All Louis XIV's subsidies were powerless in the face of a nation that no longer wished for war.

At the same time, most of the Empire, with the exception of Bavaria, was inclining to William's side. William was continually offering them his florins just at the very moment when the supply of French *écus* was drying up. He published fierce denunciations of the very real atrocities committed by French troops in Holland. The Germans, led by Lisola, clamoured for the German nation to awake to the ravages of the invader, and even the emperor himself, although still short of money and fully occupied in the east, leaned more and more towards war with the French. One by one the former members of the defunct League of the Rhine made up their minds. In January 1674, Denmark threw in her hand with the emperor. On 1 May, the Reichstag declared war in the name of the Empire as a whole. On 1 July, Brandenburg, after a temporary reconciliation with France, joined forces with the emperor.

Even at home, there were murmurs of revolt. Ever since the Fronde there had been a constant succession of petty rebellions, nearly always fiscal in origin. Now the kingdom was about to suffer a fresh burden of taxation in order to pay for the war: stamp duty, a new tax on pewter and a rise in the taxes on salt and tobacco. In 1674, Bordeaux was up in arms, soon followed by Guyenne. By 1675 the rumour of revolt was everywhere but was particularly serious in the south-west and in Britanny. The English and to an even greater extent the Dutch had ideas of turning this interesting new development to the advantage of the coalition but, unfortunately for them, these internal troubles came a year too late. Louis XIV's most dangerous year was 1674.

For all that, the year began magnificently. In the spring, the whole court had gone to see the king conquer the ruined and deserted strongholds of Franche-Comté. 'The sieur

Vauban,' Louis wrote, 'lays before me the plans which I have previously decided.' Franche-Comté was duly taken, to the accompaniment of suppers and gaming-parties. Meanwhile, Condé and Turenne were struggling to prepare against real dangers. The old marshal had done his best to prevent the juncture of the imperial armies near Philippsburg but was obliged to fall back, after ravaging the Palatinate, for lack of food and reinforcements. In spite of an attempt at resistance, he was forced to abandon Alsace to the imperial armies who then began pushing forward into Lorraine. By the end of the year, the kingdom was threatened with invasion from the east. An invasion from the north had been narrowly averted when, on 11 August, the great Condé halted three allied armies, Dutch, Spanish and Imperial, in a bloody battle at Seneffe. The members of the coalition, exhausted but not defeated, retired to lay siege to Audenarde and then, at the onset of the bad weather, withdrew separately to take up their winter quarters. As for Turenne, he did nothing of the kind. Instead he made an astonishing winter march around the Vosges which enabled him to take the imperial army unawares and drive it from Alsace. Now it was the turn of the diplomats to achieve some startling results. In the east, they gave effective support to the Hungarians and Transylvanians in their revolt against Leopold I. In the north-east, the wily Bishop of Marseilles, Forbin-Janson, succeeded in keeping the Duke of Lorraine off the throne of Poland and securing the election of John Sobieski who had married a French wife and who pledged himself to aid Hungary and attack Brandenburg. Sweden, in the north, made up her mind on 28 December to send 15,000 men against the Grand Elector. Finally, in the Mediterranean, Messina's timely revolt against the Spaniards was immediately exploited and in September 1674 France dispatched help to the rebels.

1675 was another difficult year. Turenne was killed and

the great Condé, in his last campaign, had to save Alsace from the threat of invasion for the second time. In August some of the king's troops had to be spared to carry murder and pillage to the inhabitants of lower Brittany and Rennes who were in violent rebellion against taxes and nobility alike. The Bretons had, unintentionally, carried the war on to another front which had to be dealt with at all costs. When the bad weather came, thousands of troops were sent to take up winter quarters in the west of the kingdom which, by this time, was in a state of rebellion all the way from the Channel down to Roussillon. Brittany and Guyenne were particular targets and Rennes and Bordeaux singled out for especially severe punishment. But by the end of the winter, the home front was a thing of the past. Having hanged a few thousand of his subjects, the king was able to send back his troops to face the members of the coalition, while the provinces thus terrorized lay low for a long time to come.

The war dragged on for another three years. On the Rhine front, a new generation of commanders fought without distinction. Off the coast of Sicily, the French navy, though still in its infancy, in the course of three battles succeeded in defeating and setting fire to the Dutch fleet and finally killing its illustrious Admiral Ruyter. But the troops which had been landed on the island made no headway under indifferent leaders and were ultimately recalled to France. The offensives which had been launched against the rear of the Empire produced no decisive results. France's Swedish ally was crushed by the Brandenburgers at Fehrbellin in 1765 and by the Danes at sea. The activities of Poles, Hungarians and Turks had harrassed the emperor for a while and then hung fire. But in Flanders, Vauban and Louvois were still systematically laying siege to every major strongpoint and although Valenciennes and Cambrai did not fall until 1677, in the following year it was the turn of Ghent, and William of Orange was faced with the disagreeable knowledge that picked French troops were drawing closer to Anvers and the United Provinces.

The negotiations, which had never stopped, were now coming to a head. The allies were deeply divided, each thinking only of their own interests. The emperor was still obsessed by the Turkish threat. Spain was quite simply exhausted, and the Dutch burghers, in their anxiety to recover the profits of peace and the freedom of the seas, were putting pressure on their unhappy stadtholder. Charles II, besieged by London, Parliament and the merchant interest, all of whom wanted an attack on France, was simultaneously offering his good offices and threatening intervention. The German princes were still open to offer. Louis XIV, having removed all threat of invasion and holding substantial sureties, found himself in an excellent position to negotiate. After the usual jobbery, five main treaties were signed, three of them at Nimeguen, bringing the coalition to an end.

Without losing an inch of their own territory, the United Provinces secured the evacuation of the French forward positions in the Netherlands and the abolition of the French customs tariffs of 1667. A backward glance at Louis' and Colbert's dreams of 1672 shows that this was a triumph for the Dutch. Spain suffered most, giving up Franche-Comté, the remainder of Artois, part of Flanders and Hainault and the region of Cambrai. Louis XIV pushed back the frontiers that were too close to Paris and Vauban immediately set about encircling the newly acquired provinces with virtually impregnable fortresses (August–September 1678). The emperor exchanged Fribourg for Philippsburg and promised to take no further part in the northern war (February 1679). In the same year, Louis XIV brought this to a conclusion in favour of his ally, Sweden, who had actually been beaten. Brandenburg and Denmark were compelled to restore to the Swedes everything they had conquered.

Now, with his own realm enlarged, pacified and inviolate,

Louis was able, in addition to his private gains, to call himself the arbiter of Europe. He lost no opportunity of doing so and neither did his court. Many historians, in fact, regard the year 1679 and after as the 'apogee' of the great reign, in a military and political sense at least. In all other respects, this needs further consideration and will be dealt with in a later chapter.

THE FIRST OPTION: HOME VERSUS ABROAD (1672–9)

First the decision to go to war and then the acceptance of the coalition had brought unavoidable consequences to the internal affairs of the kingdom. In somewhat broad terms, it may be said that Louvois had beaten Colbert or rather that the necessities of war compelled Colbert to renounce some of the best results of twelve years' work.

Financial stability was now out of the question. By 1672 the deficit had passed eight millions. It doubled in the following year and reached 24 millions in 1676. Never again could Colbert pride himself on the splendid surpluses of the first ten years. The good accountant and sworn enemy of the principle of confusion', had to resort to the loathed expedients euphemistically called 'extraordinary measures'. He sold tax exemptions to minor officials and in order to achieve greater success with these measures he saw to it that his intendants taxed the prospective clients at exorbitant rates. In 1673, this traffic mounted to eight millions but he suspended it in 1676 because it was mortgaging the future, although it was resumed again in 1680. On the same principle, he sold off for seven millions half the exemptions on freeholds. The sale of offices reappeared: measurers of grain, sellers of seafood, pigs and fowls, gaugers of liquids and many more besides. In practice this was simply an indirect tax on commodities and trade goods. Half of the royal estates which had been so painfully recovered in the past ten years were sold off again piecemeal. Old taxes were revived, such as the *Édit du Toise* in Paris which had been one of the causes of the Fronde, and the normal ones increased: the *taille* by six millions, the *aides* by five and the *gabelle* by four. Even the clergy were required to increase their '*don gratuit*'. With the threat of the coalition, new taxes were invented: a tax on the mastery of arts and crafts, a pewter stamp, a tobacco monopoly and stamp duty extended to cover all acts of local ecclesiastical administration (even down to parish registers). All these date from between 1673 and 1674 and, as we have seen, led to protests and rebellion not simply against the burden of taxation involved but against the 'innovation' which these new taxes represented and the threat they carried to the thousands of private, local or provincial privileges. In any case, the rebellions were quelled and Colbert turned his attention to making the most of his extraordinary measures.

All the same, he was obliged to fall back on borrowing. In 1672, he agreed, after a certain amount of resistance, to sell to the public 200,000 *livres'* worth of municipal bonds at 6.33 per cent (see p. 317). In 1675 he sold another eight millions and as many again in 1676. After this he was obliged to offer them at the *denier 14* which worked out at more than 7 per cent although he had fixed the legal rate of interest in 1665 at 5 per cent. All this was to pledge the future in order to pay for the present war. At the same time he was borrowing from the tax farmers and from the Genoese bankers at rates as high as 10 per cent by means of a system of anticipating the income of future years in advance. In 1676 this came to an advance of more than 15 millions on the receipts for 1677. This meant putting himself at the mercy of the financiers again just at the very moment when the farmers of the new taxes were demanding a rebate of as much as a sixth. Were the bad times of the cardinals on the way back?

But things were not yet as bad as that. In the same year as the unfortunate affair concerning the four sou pieces, a monetary fraud in which the minister's own nephew was involved, Colbert created the *Caisse des Emprunts* which enabled him to obtain money from the public at only 5 per cent interest. This was a kind of well-run savings bank which was equally useful to the state and to private individuals. The war was barely over before he was trying to abolish some of the new taxes, reduce the *taille* and buy off the majority of the *rentes* he had created, although at the lowest possible rate and on what were often exceedingly harsh conditions for the *rentiers*. 'You work miracles where money is concerned,' the king wrote to him.

All in all, Colbert kept the deficit down and paid for a war of which he had, at least in the beginning, approved. But by 1670 he knew very well, in his more clear-sighted moments, that 'the greatest of all kings who ever ascended the throne', had a temperament naturally inclined 'to war above all other things and that ... the onerous business of financial administration is not the normal and natural function of a king'. 'Your Majesty', he observed at a later date, 'has never consulted the state of your finances before committing yourself to expenses.' How right he was. Louis XIV took not the slightest interest in administrative matters and in his eyes the minister was simply there to provide him with money. But Colbert carried his share of responsibility for the attack on Holland and therefore for the failure of his own schemes.

Moreover his failure did not end here. For ten years an effort of great energy and perseverance had sustained the many *manufactures royales*, *manufactures privilégiées*, trading companies, arsenals, foundries, and private enterprises of every description, as well as commissioners, inspectors and middlemen. For the first time for many years, the king's treasury was supporting, in some cases unaided, a great many undertakings destined to bring wealth and greatness to the kingdom. But in 1673 the king was running short of money and the edifice which Colbert had built up began to fall apart on all sides.

A few examples will serve. Between 1665 and 1673, 175,000 *livres* were spent on the *Manufacture royale de Beauvais* in a wide variety of ways: in loans, subsidies, gifts, bonuses, and orders. From 1674 to 1678 there was nothing.

For ten years the emergent colony of Canada had been kept supplied with soldiers, women, cattle, intendants, priests and occasionally money, but in June 1673 Colbert confessed that 'His Majesty can give no assistance to Canada this year on account of the great and prodigious expense to which he has been put for the maintenance of more than 200,000 men and a hundred ships'. In May 1674 he demonstrated his helplessness at sea: His Majesty 'being pleased to put only forty vessels to sea in the Ocean and thirty, with twenty-four galleys in the Mediterranean, the Dutch will be masters of the seas'. The Canadians must look after themselves.

The great trading companies which had been launched in such a blaze of glory, with impressive monopolies, advances, gifts and loans from the king, were also running into trouble and sometimes disaster. In 1672 the *Compagnie des Indes occidentales* was confined to trading for cattle and slaves in Guinea. In 1673, the company sold its trading rights on the coast of Africa. In 1674, in debt to the tune of over three millions and with no aid forthcoming, it gave up all its privileges and went into liquidation. The greatest of all, the *Compagnie des Indes orientales*, was forced to let its colony in Madagascar die out, to see a number of its outlets in Ceylon and the Indies taken over by the Dutch and to distribute a first 10 per cent dividend to its impatient shareholders raised from capital. It survived, thanks to the courage of a few pioneers and the acumen of a few businessmen, but was obliged before very long to abandon its monopoly (1682). The *Compagnie du Nord*, which was to build its own fleet and supplant the Dutch in the North Sea and the Baltic, was unable to send its vessels to sea after the beginning of the war for lack of military protection. Its Bordeaux office went into liquidation in 1673 and the principal office in La Rochelle in 1677. The last ship belonging to the company was sold in 1684 while its moving spirits went bankrupt, fled or died in prison.

Colbert managed at least to save his most cherished creations: the Gobelins, the Van Robais works, the *canal du Midi* (which was actually financed by the peasants of Languedoc and Catalonia), and the roads, foundries and ships which were, fortunately, needed for the war. Of the remainder, he managed to scrape up only enough to save a few remnants. Immediately after the treaties of Nimeguen he was asking for 100,000 *livres* a year for commerce – one thousandth of the royal budget – but he did not get it.

There is even a possibility that this overall failure of Colbert's may have been accelerated rather than actually caused by the first great war of the reign.

In the first place, nearly everyone who mattered in France was against him. Merchants, shipowners, middlemen, manufacturers and craftsmen were all accustomed to freedom to pursue their own interests and these did not necessarily coincide with the minister's ideas. Controls, regulations and structures imposed from above were all sources of growing discontent. Colbert's investigators and inspectors were received with, at best, a show of politeness. A recent study of the textile industry of Beauvais has shown that the impressive regulations had little effect on habitual practice. In the matter of apprenticeships, for instance, a thousand contracts were examined and revealed very nearly a thousand irregularities. Again, the compulsory setting up of a 'manufacture of London serge' was regarded as a shocking innovation and quickly sank in the face of general apathy. The arbitrary manner in which the intendants selected those wealthy men in their provinces who were to become shareholders in the *Compagnie des Indes* is common knowledge and these great companies were looked on simply as a disguised form of taxation. Moreover it is thought that Frenchmen preferred to invest their money safely in land or *rentes* or keep it locked up in gold or silver plate. For those who wanted swift or substantial profits there were the traditional means of money lending, traffic in grain or dealings with the king, or, for bolder spirits, the maritime ventures which, while strictly private enterprises, were more common than might be expected, trading to Cadiz, the West Indies or to Guinea with sugar, slaves, and cloth for the greater profit of shrewd merchants from Dunkirk to Bayonne, and Nantes and Saint-Malo especially. Colbert's propositions were too massive and complicated, hedged about with rules and regulations and financially dubious. They inspired no confidence. Or else they were confined to a small circle of relatives, friends and hangers-on like Bellinzani and Frémont d'Auneuil, one of whom ended, deservedly, in prison and the other, because he was cleverer, as a counsellor of state.

For another thing, the competition was largely out of reach. Colbert on his own could not do much against Amsterdam with her Bank and Stock Exchange. Even when the war was at its height, the great Dutch companies were sending well-found fleets out to the Indies to bring home ever richer cargoes, and were paying ostentatious dividends. There could be no competing with the Dutch freighters, the cheapest and most reliable in the world, any more than with the English cloth trade or the dozens of specialities produced by the great manufacturing concerns of Leyden, still securely at the peak of their success and showing no signs of a decline.

Colbert may also have made a mistake that was both monumental and excusable. Comparing his own day with the years before the Fronde, the minister was well aware of what is revealed in most current economic studies, namely a certain decline, a degree of deterioration particularly affecting quality products. In the hope of checking and curing this regression, a process of contraction which may have been going on for some time, he produced a whole battery of such time-honoured remedies as regulations, subsidies, protection, prohibitions, monopolies and incentives to quality. These methods were all very well, and they were vigorously applied, but they may have proved ineffectual because they were not suited to French traditions, to the formidable nature of the competition and, above all, to that very situation, that probable 'Phase B conjuncture' – to revert to the terminology of Simiand – of economic decline, and the increasing shortage of money in circulation which went with them. It is becoming clear that at that time there was a general drop in prices and incomes, and probably also in wages and employment. In such a context, how could the ordinary consumers who made up the majority of the buying public be interested in luxury goods? When merchants are finding it difficult to sell their wares and racking their brains to find cheaper articles and fresh outlets – as seems to have been the case – they are in no mood for industrial regulations and laboriously manufactured enterprises which they are convinced will only lead them, sooner or later, to ruin. It was not enough to subsidize a few manufacturers and businessmen unless the customers could be subsidized as well. The minister was conscious of the decline and tried to counteract it but it is doubtful if his choice of remedies was a happy one. Can any minister, however great, do anything in the face of such difficulties and stagnation? Faced with the sovereign conjuncture of indifference at home and too much power abroad, and then, to cap all this, the war, the wonderful thing is that not all Colbert's work was utterly wrecked.

PART THREE

The Time of Scorn:
Great Options and Great Changes
(1679–89)

Louis XIV, forty years old and in the full flush of health and victory, could sit back and take a look at the results of his twelve years' rule. His frontiers were enlarged and fortified, the European coalition overcome, his law made to run both north and south, his influence growing in the eastern Empire, his armies unbeaten, a fleet still in its infancy but full of brilliant promise, more or less rapid developments in Canada and the West Indies and trading posts established in Asia and Africa. At home, all opposition crushed and a land still rich and prosperous enough to bear, somehow, the burden of war, the new building and the court. Flattered on all sides, trusting in God and his own powers, nothing could stop him now.

It was true that he had lost Lionne and Turenne and condemned Colbert and Condé to varying degrees of impotence. It was true, also, that a petty Pyrenean bishop was busy plotting in Rome and some obdurate Huguenots persisted in their heresy but these were minor details which would be overcome in time. The domestic troubles of the English concealed from him the fact that England's power was unbroken just as he failed to see beyond the labours of the Dutch to rebuild their country to the growing wealth and the new spirit of youth pervading William's land. A few subsidies handed out to Charles II and the Dutch merchants would, he thought, be enough to deal with all that. As for the Empire, where the Germans were slowly becoming a nation, surely its princes could be bought and was not its leader fully occupied with the revolts in Hungary and the Turkish threat?

Louis was in a position to dare much and he meant to do a great deal: to extend his frontiers still further, make his name respected everywhere, impose his will on the Roman pontiff and even on the heretics. To the option for war, now more firmly established than ever, were added progressively those of Gallicanism and religious persecution.

But these new aspects of the reign were to become a part of other, far-reaching changes.

The dashing, nomadic monarchy gave way to the majestic monarchy of Versailles and the gallant, loose-living young king to the model husband. Discordant notes began to creep into the courtly chorus of praise. A succession of weak pontiffs were followed by a great fighting pope. Even the hitherto nervous Leopold was to be transformed overnight by one great victory over the infidel into a respected emperor. Without warning the Dutch Stadtholder became the King of England. ... And even the kingdom of France itself, that great unknown quantity of the reign, was slowly changing its face.

The apparent apogee concealed ten years of great changes which Louis, when he understood what was happening, thought to master by the power of his arms, his will and his scorn. Emperor, kings, princes, merchants, Huguenots, prelates, even the Pope himself: Louis' scorn covered them all as, in the last resort with a few reservations, it also took in the humble mass of his subjects.

8

RELIGIOUS DESPOTISM

To attempt to penetrate Louis' religious feelings is difficult, probably presumptuous and perhaps useless. What he did, of course, matters more than what he thought. The majority of historians, at least, believe that sometime between 1679 and 1688 the king's somewhat formal religious observance changed into a deeper piety. Some place the change very early on; Orcibal and some others put it very much later. At whatever date, the part played in it by age and the widow Scarron is still a matter for argument, while that of the king's confessors is often dismissed altogether. The king may simply have believed that his own was the only true religion, that religious unity was essential to the kingdom and religious argument, which he neither would nor could understand, useless and dangerous because it led to the formation of sects and cabals, and that the clergy, like the other orders, were simply there to obey him and owed no duty to the decisions of any Italian even if he were the Pope. From 1679 onwards, in this as in many other spheres, the king would brook not the slightest hindrance to his wishes.

JANSENISM SPARED

Hardly were the Nimeguen treaties signed than a new attack of Jansenism seemed to be in the offing. On 17 May 1679 the Archbishop of Paris expelled forty postulants from Port-Royal with the object of hindering recruitment to the order. In the months that followed such celebrated figures as Le Nain de Tillemont and M. de Sacy were compelled to leave. The great Arnauld, who was thought to have too strong an influence in Paris, went into exile in the Netherlands and, by an unfortunate coincidence open to interpretation as an act of God, the same year saw the last of Madame de Sablé, Madame de Longueville, the Cardinal de Retz and the Bishop of Beauvais, Buzenval. Finally, in November, Louis XIV dismissed Arnauld de Pomponne from his councils.

Ever since 1669, the precarious and insincere 'Peace of the Church' had maintained some semblance of a truce between Port-Royal and its enemies, who had actually believed, with the Nuncio, that Jansenism was 'extinct'. In fact it was more thoroughly alive than ever for the simple reason that the battle it was fighting was no longer a purely theological one. The famous monastery had grown larger and more crowded. Pious laymen flocked there, great ladies endowed new buildings and there was a constant stream of illustrious visitors. The *Messieurs* abandoned polemics to devote themselves to apologetics and teachings: Arnauld, Nicole, the first edition of the *Pensées* (1670), Godefroy Hermant's *Vies de saints*, Robert d'Andilly's *Instructions chrétiennes*, the letters of Saint-Cyran, an *Ordinary of the mass* in French, the first volume of the Port-Royal Bible (1672), *l'Éducation chrétienne* (1688 onwards), *la Grammaire et la logique de Port-Royal* and then (1687) the *Règles de l'éducation des enfants*. All these were works of uncompromising gravity, full of moral strictures and inclined to the doctrine of '*richérisme*' which exalted the dignity of the simple priest and called for a simplification of the liturgy to bring the celebrant closer to his congregation. With their distrust of the fallen nature of man, their mingled richness and severity, it might be thought that they would appeal only to a limited audience. In fact the very opposite occurred. When historians discover and examine the catalogues belonging to libraries of the period they are continually surprised at the amount of space allotted to the devotional and doctrinal works of the Jansenists. Even Saint-Cyran and the *Bible de Port-Royal* might be found among a merchant's books, alongside the *Ordonnance du Commerce* and handbooks on practical accountancy, and this not only in Paris and Rouen but everywhere from Orléans to Nantes, in Languedoc, Grenoble and all over the north of the realm. Seminaries imbued with the spirit of Port-Royal were already sending out their first priests to carry into the depths of the countryside a seriousness, devotion to duty and a proud humility. In many cases, and especially in the diocese of Beauvais, the so-called Catholic 'reforms' meant in reality Jansenist reforms.

Jansenism, from a scholastic argument, had become one of the greatest currents of French thought. It had moved out from its close, Parisian circle to take root in the remotest provinces and even to make contact with the great mass of the faithful. Such a success was acceptable neither to the Jesuits nor the king's Government, and this apparently explains the attack of 1679 which commended itself more readily to the king in that the two bishops who had resisted him so stubbornly over the affair of the *Régale*, Pavillon and Caulet, were both Jansenists.

It was probably the affair of the *Régale*, then coming to a head, and the fact that the king had other, more serious worries which saved the Jansenists and earned them a further fourteen years' reprieve. Louis XIV had other enemies to deal with and chief among them was the Pope.

GALLICANISM

The Gallican quarrel was a secular affair and had numerous facets, many of them highly complex, which came to the fore one after the other. Briefly, the French Church laid claim to certain 'liberties', or customary privileges, in relation to the Holy See, some in favour of the bishops, some in favour of the ordinary priesthood and the remainder dealing with the authority of the king or the *parlements*. There were in fact several different brands of Gallicanism but all were united in rejecting a certain number of papal rights. Lively clashes, as opposed to simple scholastic arguments, broke out from time to time from 1661 onwards, notably in the maintaining of theological theses, when the Jesuits and their pupils advanced propositions in favour of the inferiority of the councils and even of papal infallibility, which instantly provoked fierce opposition.

Louis XIV believed quite simply that the clergy of the realm were his servants and the Church's possessions his to dispose of at will. His only interest in any theological disputes was to assert his own supremacy. He allowed a score of minor conflicts to pass almost unnoticed until the day when the affair of the *régale* assumed an unexpected importance.

The *régale spirituelle* had been established by a decree of February 1673 which also extended the *régale temporelle* to cover the entire kingdom. This was an autocratic measure, certainly, but owing to the state of subjection of the French clergy, not one which led immediately to any serious protests. The *régale spirituelle* concerned the king's right to nominate to certain convents, for which nothing had been laid down in the Concordat of 1516, and also to certain benefices without cure of souls, while a see was vacant. The most delicate point was the extension of the *régale temporelle* – the reversion to the crown of the revenues of vacant sees – to the outermost provinces of the kingdom which had been hitherto exempt. In addition, by an edict of 1675 this move was made to act retrospectively which meant that all existing bishops must ask seizin for their own sees. Préclin, in Bloud and Gay's strongly Catholic '*Histoire de l'Église*' remarks that the bishops 'were too fearful or too servile to dare protest'. Two recidivists, however, did protest. These were the firm and dedicated Jansenists of Languedoc, Pavillon of Alet and Caulet of Pamiers. The first died in 1677 and it seemed for a while as though the affair would become just another episode in the Jansenist quarrel. Caulet's appeal to the Pope and above all the character of the Pope himself gave it a completely new dimension.

Innocent XI (1676–89), pious, sensitive, upright, frail and thrifty with no trace about him of patron of the arts or doc-tor of the faith, was a fighting pope of a kind rarely seen in the seventeenth century. The crusade against the Turk was his great cause and one to which he sacrificed much else. Basically autocratic and with a high opinion of the dignity of his sacred office, he was not a man to support the pretensions of Louis XIV. In 1678, two short, sharp briefs put the king in his place over the affair of the *régale*. At the end of 1679 a third brief threatened Louis with sanctions. Caulet had put the problem very clearly: 'Unless the sovereign pontiffs and prelates take immediate steps, noth-ing will be safe from the invasions of princes.' (June 1679.)

In 1680, the Pope attacked. He rejected Louis' nominee for the post of mother superior to the convent of Charonne, thereby extending the quarrel to the *régale spirituelle*; he also rejected the capitulary vicar whom the king wished to appoint to the see of Pamiers after Caulet's death. Neither side would retract, in spite of secret diplomatic overtures, and every bridge seemed to have been burnt. The affair be-came the talk of court and town alike. The Assembly of the Clergy of 1680 affirmed, in a somewhat roundabout way, its 'close attachment' to the king. The intendant, Foucault, descended on Pamiers with a troop of soldiers, confiscated all Church possessions and appointed a capitu-lary vicar who would be more amenable while the refractory one was executed in effigy.

Louis' method of bringing matters to a head is well known. Out of the blue, in the spring of 1681, he assembled a kind of miniature council consisting of all those bishops present at court. There were fifty-two of them and they should all have been at home in their own dioceses. These formed the basis for an 'Extraordinary Assembly' of the French clergy which did its best to support its king without an open breach with its Pope. The result was to so-called declaration of the 'Four Articles' (March 1682), a somewhat guarded affirmation of the crown's independence in the temporal sphere, of the superiority of the councils and the validity of the 'rules, customs and constitutions accepted in the realm', which it left carefully undefined. This vague pronouncement which probably had little basis in law and was the work of an Assembly without any real spiritual authority, was given a mixed reception. The bishops made certain mental reservations; the *Parlement* went still further. Louis XIV, well satisfied, decreed that the declaration was to be studied yearly in all seminaries and theological colleges and subscribed to in writing by all students of theology. Innocent XI, whom Bossuet and the Assembly had hoped to placate, exploded. His brief *Paternae charitati* of 11 April 'denounced, denied and undid' all the Assembly's work in the matter of the *régale*. The Assembly, which was still in session, protested vigorously: 'The Gallican Church is governed by its own laws and maintains them inviolably', while at the same time asserting its 'entire obedience to the throne of St Peter' and respect for the uses of the papacy which were 'so close to the life of the first centuries of the Church'. But for all these protestations, there was no sign of a withdrawal and Innocent XI was quick to take a firm line by refusing canonical investiture to all Louis' newly appointed prelates with the result that by 1688 thirty-five sees were vacant.

From 1682 onwards, therefore, France was faced with the danger of schism. To all appearances, neither side would give way, but in fact negotiations were going on and from time to time each rendered the other some small services. However unyielding, the Holy Father was acquainted with the demands of courtesy and had no hesitation in granting the young comte du Vexin who was ten years old and the offspring of a doubly adulterous union, all the necessary dispensations to enable him to receive the revenues of several abbeys. The Great King, on his side, was thanking the Pope effusively at the very moment when the Brief of April 1682 burst on him. But, beyond these exchanges, there was no relaxation of the official hostility. Even when Louis XIV believed that he had stamped out heresy, Innocent merely thanked him in an offhand way, waited six months before ordering a 'Te Deum' to be sung and deprecated 'the motive and the means of these onversions by the thousand none of which were voluntary'. In 1687, at the very moment when Louis XIV was having to face the hostility of the Protestant nations and the general coalition, Rome and Paris very nearly came to blows over unimportant temporal matters which will be dealt with further on. Would the Most Christian King yet again send troops into Italy to lay hands on the Papal States? But Louis had other troubles to worry him just then, and Innocent XI conveniently died, to be replaced in April 1689 by a more congenial pope.

THE EXTIRPATION OF PROTESTANTISM

In the midst of this conflict with the head of the Catholic Church, Louis made himself a great many new enemies by deciding to stamp out heresy in his kingdom.

The progress of Louis' policy with regard to 'those of the so-called reformed religion' has been described time and time again. It moved from a limited toleration to first legal and then violent persecution culminating in the revocation. A score of historians, essayists and novelists, each with his own religious, political and philosophical prejudices, have either stressed the king's guilt in this or striven to find excuses for him but nearly all of them have shown the deplorable results of the 'Edict given at Fontainebleau in the month of October 1685'. Now it seems that things were more complicated than was for a long time believed.

The first point that must be stressed is the highly irregular religious situation obtaining in France at that time. Ever since 1598, two religions had existed side by side on a perfectly legal basis. Nothing of the kind was to be found in any other country in Europe and all the political, legal and religious thinking of the age was firmly against any such division of a nation into two Churches. Hardly any Catholics had accepted the Edict of Nantes, that temporary expedient imposed by thirty years of indecisive warfare and authority of Henri IV. The Assemblies of the Clergy regularly culminated against 'the regrettable freedom of conscience' (1650), against the Protestant temples, 'synagogues of Satan' and against the *religionnaires* themselves, whom they stigmatized as 'rebellious slaves' (1660). The *dévots* and the *Compagnie du Saint-Sacrement* devoted all their efforts to bringing about the revocation. To begin with, at least until the grace of Alès (1629), the Protestants themselves regarded the edict as unsatisfactory and the majority of them would have liked to see some form of 'cantonment', an autonomous organization within the kingdom after the pattern of the United Provinces. Richelieu had put an end to these dreams and had forced a million Huguenots into a disadvantageous defensive position. From the beginning of his reign, Louis XIV had suffered from the religious anomalies of his kingdom and thought of various ways – legal, religious and financial – of doing away with them but had rejected 'extreme and violent remedies' (Memoirs for the year 1661, revised 1670–72). He must have had weighty reasons to restrain him up until that date and, no doubt, right up to 1680 or even 1684. What were they?

At that time, like Richelieu and like Mazarin, he regarded as his 'hereditary' enemy the ultra-Catholic house of Habsburg. Like his predecessors, he needed the alliance of a great many Protestant states and princes against it. This was not the moment to make life difficult for the Huguenots. It is for this reason that, for a long time, even after 1680, we find him going back on his anti-Protestant statements, slowing down the prosecutions and occasionally suspending them altogether. Time and again, the diplomatic situation, his prime consideration, forced his to temporize.

It has been maintained, also, that before 1679, Louis could not summon up enough enthusiasm for the outward appearances of his faith to take a firm stand against heresy. There has been talk of a 'conversation' which took place after 1679 under the influence of Bossuet, of Mme de Maintenon and of his Jesuit confessor: Louis repented his adulteries, meditated on mortality and twice went back to the queen. It seems to be a fact that he attended communion more frequently after 1680. Previously he had been content with performing his Easter duty. By degrees we find him saying his rosary and taking part in the worship of the Holy Sacrament. The secret remarriage which may have taken place a few weeks after his widowerhood in 1683, marked a turning point. In 1684 he forbade performances of opera and comedy during Lent and rebuked courtiers who neglected their religious duties. It was then that the court, newly installed at Versailles, became devout, a *dévot* being, as La Bruyère later observed, 'a man who, under an atheist king, would be an atheist'. Yet in 1685, Mme de Maintenon herself was complaining that Louis still gave so little thought to God. So the king's purely religious motives do not emerge clearly. Did they in fact play any part in restraining him at first, or dictating his later actions?

Or it may be, more simply, that his attention was absorbed by other tasks and he thought that the severities of the law,

the influence of good bishops, the spectacle of such illustrious converts as Turenne and the promise of money and
'favours' to the converted would do their work in time, and
that in any case, both before and even more after 1680, the
peaceful projects in which Spinoza, Leibniz, the Emperor
Leopold and the Pope himself were engaged would bring
about a moving reconciliation between the members of the
reformed religion and the Church which, in view of the
Turkish threat, was highly desirable. Also worth mentioning is the palliative influence of Colbert who was by no
means a religious fanatic and who knew better than anyone the economic power of the Huguenots, out of all proportion to their numbers, including as they did numerous
tapestry-makers, clothworkers – Van Robais in particular –
contractors and craftsmen of all kinds, as well as merchants
from Dunkirk to Bayonne and chief among them the re-
nowned Le Gendre family, the famous bankers of Rouen
and Lyons, all of whom belonged to the reformed religion.
The *Compagnie du Nord* alone was run and financed essentially by four men and the members of their families, the
banker, Formont, in Paris and the shipowners, Pagès, Raulé
and Tersmitten of La Rochelle, all fervent Huguenots. How
could the king do without such support? But by 1680, Colbert's influence was waning and in 1683, his voice was
silenced for ever. The venerable leader of the opposing fac-
tion, the aged Le Tellier, was free to devote his last energies
to bringing about the revocation.

According to Louis' last great historian, Jean Orcibal,
the revocation was a last-minute decision taken for political
reasons in a particular diplomatic situation. Ever since
1679, Louis had been solemnly informing the Pope of every
move he made against the Protestants with the idea that this
would earn him some reward, such as his own way in the
matter of the *régale*. Innocent XI never took the bait but
Louis found himself obliged to persevere. In 1683, the em-

peror had saved Christendom from the Turkish threat with
no help from the French. Now Louis, in his turn, felt it
incumbent on him to distinguish himself as a defender of
the faith, since that was the only grandiose gesture within
his power, and the only one which could win over the
Catholic princes, even in Germany, who had rallied to their
victorious emperor. In England, with the accession of James
II in February 1685, the throne was once more in Catholic
hands. Holland was in any case hostile and Sweden and
Denmark were in French pay. An unbroken series of peacetime annexations, a swift and easy victory over Spain and
the conclusion of a twenty-year truce at Ratisbon on 15
August 1684 seemed to indicate the aquiescence of Europe
to his conquests. In this climate of peace and victory, what
fresh deed was there to raise Louis above all other monarchs?
The religious unification of the kingdom would provide
the crowning glory of his reign and, at the end of 1684, the
decision seems to have been taken.

The ministers, in other words Le Tellier and Louvois,
had other reasons. To begin with, there were legal quibbles.
The practice of billeting dragoons was nothing new; soldiers
had long been 'lodged' on delinquent taxpayers or in disturbed provinces, and at the beginning of the century even
Austria had been subjected to Catholic *dragonnades*. This
practice had been revived, after a short intermission, and
worked wonders. The lists of converts flowed in in their
thousands. Louis may have believed it, more likely he pre-
tended to, but at all events the fiction could be maintained
that France was now populated solely by Catholics and there
was no longer any need for the Edict of Nantes. There were
other, more practical considerations. Converts were exempt
from taxes and the burden of these would therefore fall on
the Catholics. All, wrote Louvois to the comptroller-general,
must be reduced to the same condition. Furthermore the
missionaries, as the priests attached to the 'new converts'

were called, were beginning to fall short, both in numbers and quality. It was Mme de Maintenon's belief that it was necessary to plan for the future by providing a strongly Catholic education for the children of converts and even for obdurate heretics, but there was one obstacle in the way of this in the shape of the continued existence of pastors who were accused of encouraging feigned conversions and of organizing, in the words of Louvois, a 'cabal of converts'. It is not impossible, as Lavisse maintained, that the revocation was directed primarily against these, on the principle that once Protestantism was made illegal the pastors must disappear.

The Edict of Fontainebleau, while prohibiting all former members of the reformed religion from leaving the country, was fundamentally ordering their exclusion. Since Protestantism no longer existed in law, all churches were to be demolished, all assemblies forbidden – even in noble households – and all children made to attend mass. The remaining obdurates could continue to enjoy their property on condition that they never met together, even 'under pretence of prayer'. The revocation was reinforced by complementary measures such as the expulsion of Protestants from Paris, the massacre of the Waldensians in Savoy, refusal of burial, fresh *dragonnades*, children carried off, returning pastors hunted down and the penalty of death promised to any 'caught making assemblies' – and actually carried out on six hundred of them who were discovered by the intendant Baville's bullies.

The mass exodus has been described perhaps a hundred times: mule trains crossing the Alpine passes, flotillas sailing down the rivers of Charente to be picked up by Dutch ships off the coast, and then the individual refugees, overcoming countless obstacles with the aid of organized escape chains. Out of a million Huguenots, perhaps 200,000 left: labourers, craftsmen, merchants, intellectuals, soldiers and sailors, though not many peasants, making for asylum in Holland, Switzerland, England, Brandenburg, Germany, Scandinavia and even Russia, to say nothing of those who sought safety in the Cape and other colonies. The French as a whole remained largely indifferent to this loss of population, wealth, talent, power and intellect. The whole of Catholic France followed Bossuet in praising 'the new Constantine', 'the new Theodosius', who was at last restoring its fundamental unity to the kingdom. The revocation was strictly in accordance with the spirit of the times. Those who protested were few and far between, a handful of humble curés like the priest of Saint-Pierre d'Oléron and some liberal prelates like Le Camus who based their arguments on the factitious nature of the conversions. Four years later, the admirable Vauban had the courage to write, 'Kings are indeed master of their subjects' lives and goods, but never of their opinions, for men's inmost feelings are beyond their power and God alone can direct them as he wills.'

Moral considerations are outside the province of the historian but even so it must be said that the revocation was an immense blunder. The past Protestant allies were offended. The Grand Elector actually dared to break with Versailles, in spite of the handsome pension it gave him. The Protestant adversaries were strengthened in their determination to attack France, especially William of Orange who cemented the unity of the Netherlands at a time when it was tottering. The Catholic princes sent polite congratulations which did not affect their attitude to Louis XIV in the slightest. The Pope applauded half-heartedly, deplored the use of violence and made the disgraced Le Camus a cardinal. The émigrés enriched all Europe with their skill and industry, peopled Berlin, brought new blood to Brandenburg, carried the secrets of paper-making from Angoulême and clothworking from Saint-Quentin to Britain, and created a real centre of resistance in Holland with a formidable propaganda team and probably an active spy network which lost no time in infiltrating their country of origin. The revocation was both useless and ineffectual. It disturbed, divided and impoverished the kingdom and strengthened all its enemies. More important still, it paved the way directly for the revolution in England.

However cautiously he had begun, the English Parliament feared that their own too Catholic king might come, in the end, to similar measures. William of Orange cunningly set in motion a rumour that, at the request of his father-in-law, James II, a French force was about to appear and reduce the Anglicans to the same condition as the Huguenots in France. Orcibal has argued with great plausibility that it was fear of French *dragonnades*, as well as the manifold errors of James II himself, which was responsible for the remarkable ease with which the English revolution took place. William donned the British crown and, as the saviour of the Church, became the hero of Protestantism. It is permitted to add that the fears of the Anglicans may not have been entirely unfounded.

Having quarrelled with the Pope and with all the Protestant princes, whose hands he had helped to strengthen, Louis XIV sat back and contemplated a 'wholly Catholic France' which was comparing him to Hercules and to Apollo vanquishing the serpent, Python, and producing marble, medals, odes and even music to celebrate his glory.

How he quarrelled with the rest of Europe remains to be told.

9

THE ARMED PEACE
TO THE GENERAL COALITION

(1679–88)

TEN years of peace, ten years of triumphant supremacy –
but only on the surface. Even after the Treaties of Nimeguen had been signed the armies remained on a wartime
footing and the major changes which took place in the administration of the realm show that the king was not
content.

In spite of his valuable annexations, in spite of his triumphant resistance to the princes united against him, in spite
of all the adulation with which he was surrounded, Louis
did not forget that he had gained nothing from the Dutch
republic which in June 1672 he had believed lay at his mercy,
that he had yielded up his advanced positions in the Netherlands, that his north-eastern frontier remained wide open
from the Meuse to Alsace and that Alsace itself was only
partially subdued and not complete without Strasbourg.
And so, of his own accord, he dismissed Pomponne who was
a nephew of the great Arnauld and as a diplomatist somewhat over-cautious, and replaced him with Colbert de
Croissy, the wily and ambitious lawyer who had already
made his mark as intendant for Haute-Alsace and laid the
foundations for the policy of 'reunions'. This may be seen
as a reinforcement for the Colbert clan, but there could be
an equally strong case for seeing it as the beginning of the
'reign' of Louvois. Certainly the best and most up-to-date
historians of the monarchy in its period of conquest and
administration, and in particular Georges Livet in his work

on Alsace, discern the harsh, ruthless authority of the younger Le Tellier growing and spreading from as early as 1673. Louvois stood for war, aggression and the use of force, and no one before him had ever planned for them more efficiently. But once again, Louvois would have been nothing without his king who shared his views and to some extent used him as a vehicle for the expression of his own deepest nature, the proud and ruthless energy of his own dazzling maturity. Louvois was not the evil counsellor who led Louis astray: he epitomized Louis himself at a certain stage in his life and he died with the period in the king's career which he stood for.

THE REUNIONS

With the object of acquiring both strategic advantages and prestige, the servants of the monarchy resorted to a very old dodge put forward by an intendant of Alsace named Baussan in 1650. This was the systematic exploitation of any clauses in the treaties of Munster and Nimeguen which were at all vague or ill-defined. Legal experts had been set to work well in advance, preparing dossiers and instituting searches into such lands, seigneuries, or fiefs of any kind which were or might be dependent on those regions ceded to the king by the treaties. In many cases the incredible complexity of Alsatian lands and a not entirely accidental confusion in the wording of the treaties facilitated such claims. From 1679 onwards they were followed up systematically. Four special courts were set up to assemble the facts of the cases and pronounce their verdicts, the outcome of which was invariably a rapid 'reunion', in other words annexation of the territory in question. These were peaceful annexations, made on a legal basis, but they were backed up by the ever-present force of arms which was a sufficient menace to discourage any serious show of resistance.

By 1679, the *Parlement* of Besançon had 'reunited' eighty villages of the *comté* of Montbéliard which were attached to the castellanies of Franche-Comté. The remainder followed the next year. A special Chamber formed by the *Parlement* of Metz looked into those places which might have formed part of the temporal estates of the *Trois-Evêchés* and summarily reunited villages and fiefs as far afield as the Saar and Luxembourg. In Alsace, the intendant Jacques de La Grange set to work methodically, with the help of the Chamber at Breisach, to bring together the most widely scattered lands under his control and sever all their connexions with the Empire, both in the prefecture of Haguenau and in the two landgravates of Upper and Lower Alsace. All the nobles of Alsace, even the Duke of Zweibrücken and the Margrave of Baden, now had to swear fealty to the King of France alone for their lands. Finally, at the conferences of Courtrai, Spain was obliged to accept the loss of a number of towns and villages in the Netherlands, including Givet, Revin, Virton, and of part of Luxembourg.

The annexation of Strasbourg in September 1681 was decked in no show of legality. Thirty thousand men were drawn up secretly outside the walls of the city which had no choice but to surrender. A month later, Louis XIV went in person to take possession of the Protestant city and restore the cathedral to the Catholic faith. Politically, the annexation of the bridge-city was justified by its strategic importance and its dubious neutrality (three times in the last war it had welcomed the Imperial troops), but the suddenness of the move shocked Europe. On the same day, the Duke of Mantua, crippled with debts and depravity, finally ceased haggling and sold Louis the fortress of Casale, the opposite number to Pinerolo in eastern Piedmont and the key to the Spanish Milanais. These two annexations occurring simultaneously put Europe thoroughly on its guard.

From the beginning there had been protests from a great

many princes of the Empire, from Spain and even the King of Sweden, who as the new Duke of Zweibrücken was also an injured party. William of Orange was uneasy at the advance into Luxembourg. The annexation of Strasbourg unleashed a fresh flood of anti-French propaganda throughout Germany and served to strengthen the 'nationalist' party there. However, Louis XIV's diplomats played a subtle game with great skill, in spite of the fluctuations of their hand. Spain was weak, Holland divided, England a prey to factions, the emperor kept busy on two fronts, in Bohemia and Hungary, and irked by Louis XIV's alliance with the Hohenzollerns. Even so, there came a moment when William of Orange, the Kings of Sweden, Spain, the emperor, and even part of the Empire formed the beginnings of a coalition against Louis XIV as he moved against Luxembourg (1682). But the Turks were at the gates.

KAHLENBERG

Now that they were no longer at war with the Poles and Muscovites, the Ottomans, under their energetic vizirs, the Köprülüs, were free to turn their attention to assisting the Hungarians in their religious and nationalistic revolt against the emperor. By the end of 1682 their intervention was a certainty and for the second time Leopold appealed in terror to the Empire and to Christendom for aid. Innocent XI, filled with the crusading spirit, offered him prayers, diplomatic assistance and a million florins. Venice, most of the German Catholic princes, and Bavaria and Saxony in particular, sent help. The Diet of the Empire promised 40,000 men and volunteers flocked from all directions, among them a little abbé from Savoy whose services had been rejected by Louis XIV: the future Prince Eugène. The King of Poland, in spite of all that the French diplomats could do, yielded to his chivalrous Christian instincts and to his desire for glory. But the emperor soon took refuge in Vienna where, by the beginning of July, he was besieged by a vast Turkish army numbering over 200,000 men.

At this point the King of France was not obsessed with his ambition to become the first king in Christendom. He had always aided the Hungarian Protestant, traded with the Turks and striven to keep back the emperor in the east. He had already advised the Poles to remain neutral and to the Pope's envoy he replied simply that he could pledge himself to nothing but would show his 'generosity' by observing a kind of truce towards Luxembourg. Nevertheless, in August he marched his troops into Brabant and Flanders where his legal experts had unearthed for him a claim to 'reunite' Alost and the old city of Ghent.

A few days later, on the heights of Kahlenberg, the army led by John Sobieski overthrew and routed the Turks. Leopold returned to Vienna while his generals set about the systematic reconquest of all Hungary after two hundred years. The battle of the Kahlenberg on 12 September 1683 marked a great turning point in the history of Europe. It was the beginning of the end for the Turks and brought about the birth of the first united state of Austria-Hungary. The triumphant and victorious emperor gained increasing respect as the head of German-speaking Christendom. On that great and decisive day, France was notable for her absence.

For the present, Louis went on amassing small gains and making soothing noises to the rest of Christian Europe.

THE TRUCE

The setting for Louis' small gains was the Netherlands. At the very moment when the battle of Kahlenberg was being fought, Louvois' armies were sacking Spanish Flanders and Brabant, Catholic provinces though they were. In October, having learned of the Turkish defeat and hoping for support from either Holland or Vienna, Spain abruptly declared war. Louis, made uneasy by William's donation of 10,000 men to assist Spain, uttered a few well-chosen words of reassurance to the United Provinces. Brandenburg and Denmark to the north were allies, and in the east Leopold was busy reconquering his kingdom of Hungary. Louis was able to walk calmly into Courtrai and Dixmude, ravage the regions of Bruges and Brussels, bombard Audenarde and Luxembourg and capture the latter stronghold in June, advance into Catalonia and bombard Genoa. At the same time he was preparing against any subsequent interventions on the part of the emperor by fortifying his Rhine frontier and mustering an army at Sarre-Louis. Everyone, even the emperor whose generals had wisely directed his attentions to the east, was urging Spain to negotiate. The treaties of Ratisbon were signed in August 1684. Concluded between Vienna, Madrid and Paris, they established a twenty-year truce. Louis was to keep his *réunions* made prior to 1 August 1681, with the addition of Strasbourg and Kehl, as well as Luxembourg and a number of villages and strongholds in the Netherlands, but was to advance no further.

In the same year, he had left it to his ministers to explain to Europe why the Most Christian King failed to support the Holy League which was formed at Linz in March, under the aegis of the Pope, between Austria, Poland and Venice, with the addition, two years later, of Russia. Colbert de Croissy and Louvois maintained that the king was already rendering inestimable service to Christendom by launching occasional forays against the barbary pirates and now and then, in between treaties, bombarding one of their towns. Once the truce was signed, setting a limit to his own conquests, Louis left it to Racine to explain to the Academy how his enemies had been 'forced to accept' his conditions, 'being unable, for all their efforts, to move one step outside the small circle within which he had been pleased to confine them'.

Such words did not augur the good behaviour which might have been hoped from the promise of a twenty-year truce.

FURTHER AGGRESSION

For the next four years, in fact, Louis continued to flout the rest of Europe more self-assuredly than ever.

In 1684, he sent a peace-time demand to the Republic of Genoa to stop building galleys for Spain and send senators to Versailles to apologize. Duquesne's fleet carried the summons and, without waiting for a reply, burned the town in a six day bombardment. In January 1685, the doge, although not officially permitted to leave Genoa, travelled to Versailles to offer the republic's submission. For twenty-five years Louis had adored these splendid audiences of apology: he had no suspicion that this was to be the last he would enjoy.

After bombarding Algiers three times without great risk to itself, his fleet appeared off Cadiz in June 1686. Faced with this threat, the King of Spain revoked the measures he had introduced against French trade in Cadiz which was encroaching on the exploitation of the Spanish Indies and capturing a large part of Spain's American income. The French fleet was a good deal in evidence during this period of truce.

The Great King was also adept at intimidating smaller nations by land. He stepped in to forbid the Duke of Savoy to make a journey to Venice, to prevent the marriage of his daughter and stop him extending a welcome in Turin to Prince Eugène who had been expelled from France and fought with the imperial armies against the Turks. Victor Amadeus put up some show of resistance but in the spring of 1686 he was unable to prevent Catinat massacring his own Protestant subjects, the Waldensians, on the grounds that they might assist the Huguenot refugees from Dauphiné. Catinat wrote after this crusade into foreign territory that he left behind him 'utter desolation, without either men or beasts'.

Yet this caused less uneasiness than the affair of the Palatinate although here Louis showed a degree of moderation which in view of his previous record was not taken seriously. The king was satisfied with an appeal to the Holy Father to arbitrate in the succession of the Palatinate, part of which, according to him, rightfully devolved upon the second Madame as the sister of the deceased elector. Admittedly he put his demands in no uncertain terms and threatened to occupy the country. This was in 1685. In the same year a dangerous ally ascended the throne of England and the Edict of Nantes was revoked.

In a Europe where great changes were occurring or about to occur, this kind of aggressive bravado served to bring the princes together in self-defence against the Most Christian King's future moves. The discussions, agreements and defensive alliances which took place in 1686 have been grouped together under the general, if somewhat inaccurate name of 'the League of Augsburg'. This league was concluded only within the Empire but it included, apart from Bavaria, Franconia, the Palatinate, the duchy of Holstein and a few more, Sweden and Spain, on account of their lands inside the Empire. This was a rallying of the Empire, no longer in a position to be afraid of Louis XIV's designs on the imperial throne which had threatened certain military and financial arrangements, but the League made clear that it had no intention of submitting to any further 'unjust claims and illegitimate demands'. Possibly a greater threat to Louis XIV was the secret alliance between the Elector of Brandenburg and the emperor immediately following the revocation and then the united front slowly formed among the Protestant princes, for Louis could still fear isolation even if he did not think it likely to happen.

Nonetheless, Louis XIV and Louvois preferred to stick to their policy of intimidation rather than humble themselves to negotiate. The affair of the franchises resulted in a real break with the papacy. The business of Cologne set fire to the powder barrel (1687–8).

All foreign ambassadors in Rome had renounced the diplomatic immunities which had made whole areas of the city where the ambassadors lived a refuge for the rogues and prostitutes in which Rome abounded. Louis XIV, for reasons of prestige, refused. In 1687, Innocent XI declared that he would receive no new French ambassador unless Louis bowed to the general rule. The response was magnificent: God, the king declared, had appointed him to set an example to others, and not to be given one. An ambassador was dispatched and promptly excommunicated. In January 1688, Louvois prepared to send troops against Rome and to seize Avignon, which was done in October of the same year. Never had France been so close to schism.

It happened that at the same time, the archiepiscopal and electoral see of Cologne was vacant. Louis XIV had his own candidate in one of his agents, Furstenburg, who was already bishop of Strasbourg. The emperor had his – a young Bavarian prince. Neither of the two was strictly eligible but the Pope decided against Louis XIV by sending the necessary dispensations to the Bavarian in September 1688.

At this precise moment, while it was still possible to negotiate, Louis once again opted for the use of force. He occupied Cologne, occupied the Palatinate, occupied Avignon, marched into Mayence and into the see of Liège. What grounds had he for this rush to declare war?

He certainly had his reasons, although none of his calculations came to anything. The first of these was the hope of a renewal of the Turkish war, in spite of the fall of Buda and Belgrade and the subjection of Hungary and Transylvania to the victorious Habsburg. There was also the hope that William of Orange, totally absorbed by English affairs, would be kept busy there for many years to come. A swift blow by a well-drilled army could well carry the day. As it happened it failed to do so and the race against time was wasted. The second coalition had begun, and a few months later Louis was without a single ally. France was attacked on all sides, north, east and south, at sea and in the colonies. This was the beginning of the great trial and it was to continue, apart from one brief truce, for more than twenty-six years or throughout the remainder of the reign.

But the Europe in which it began had changed. The old allies and the old dependents had gone. The revocation had united the Protestant states which had once been in Louis' pay almost to a man. The emperor was more powerful than ever and had become the acknowledged leader of Germany and of Christendom. Within a few weeks, the two great maritime powers had joined forces under the formidable leadership of William of Orange.

Faced with this grave and protracted threat, what was the attitude of the French king? And what of his subjects?

IO

THE KING AND THE REALM
BEFORE THE GREAT TRIAL
(1688)

VERSAILLES

THE king had only moved into Versailles, which was still a building site, in May 1682. Mansart had just finished the two wings and was working on the Orangery. He began on the demolition of the porcelain Trianon in 1687 in order to replace it with the present building. The Galerie des Glaces was finished but the chapel not yet built. Work was going on continually on the inside and there were alterations to the gardens and fountains. In May 1685, Dangeau counted 36,000 workmen and soldiers on the site of Versailles, and to divert the waters of the Eure, Vauban employed troops on the aqueduct of Maintenon which finally remained unfinished owing first to epidemics and later to the wars.

Many attempts have been made to portray the almost indescribable setting inhabited by the king, his second wife, his complex family and the multitude of gentlemen and servants who made up his household. The rigours of an etiquette of Spanish formality did not prevent serious overcrowding in which, from time to time, the royal family was all but submerged. Access to the monarch was at the same time easy and very difficult, while after a few days the corridors and galleries became so deep in refuse that the king and the court were compelled to seek a change of air at Marly or elsewhere. Louis' personal valet, Bontemps, never succeeded in ridding the château of rogues and loose women. The flower of the nobility was lodged in conditions of unspeakable squalor under the roof. The time was passed alternately in gaming, entertainments and in prayer. But the stables were growing and the ministers' wing was becoming inhabited. All Europe knew that this artificial capital was the scene of all major decisions and already dreamed of imitating it.

Louis was over fifty now and, except at table, the burden of maturity was bringing with it a greater moderation. The widow Scarron, created Marquise de Maintenon by Louis in gratitude for the education of his bastards, was his constant companion, director of his conscience, silent and omni-present counsellor and, of course, his mistress. His religious attendance increased and sometimes even satisfied his wife and his confessor. Although ignorant of theology and prob-ably quite incapable of understanding it, he played the role of caesar-pope and lived to all intents in a state of schism.

Of the old, talented staff bequeathed to him by Mazarin, nearly all were gone: Lionne, Turenne, Colbert, Le Tellier and Condé were all dead. Louvois' influence was waning: Maintenon, who favoured the more pious Colberts, could not abide him, and 1689 was a particularly bad year for him as he was held responsible for the capitulation of Mayence, and Seignelay became a member of the council, relieving him of some of his responsibilities. For two years he dragged on in semi-disgrace and died in 1691, swollen with ill-gotten gains, gluttony and dissipation. The citizens of Paris treated his corpse, as they had Colbert's, with an open dis-play of contempt.

The king, left to his own devices, governed with the aid of the families and dependents of his former colleagues: the brothers of Colbert and Croissy, the son of Seignelay, the son-in-law of Beauvilliers and a few Le Telliers with the exception of Louvois' son, Barbezieux, whose influence was not great, but there were other kindred of the Le Tellier family, and through them of the Colberts, the Phélypeaux de la Vrilliers and the Phélypeaux de Pontchartrain and revenants like Pomponne and an Arnauld who were allied to the Colberts and hence to the Le Telliers. There were no dynasties, only a single family, rife, like all families, with internal squabbles. All were genuinely of the nobility, not necessarily even the recent nobility (apart from the Colberts) and placed by the king above dukes who were obliged to address them as 'Monseigneur' while receiving only a plain 'Monsieur' in return. Louis chose his servants without imagination from among those singled out by Mazarin and their descendants.

Five were members of the *Conseil d'En-Haut* at which from time to time the Dauphin put in a bored appearance. The other councils developed into a matter of routine, attended by the Chancellor, Boucherat, who was not a minister at all, various departmental heads and a number of small fry. Everything of any importance took place in the king's own room or in that of his wife, especially private audiences with the *contrôleur-général*, a secretary of State, a confidential servant such as the army commander, Chamlay, or the king's Jesuit confessor. In practice, major decisions took the form of royal decrees which were simply the expression of the king's will, countersigned by a secretary of State. Minor details were taken care of by 'orders in council', simple decrees (passed in the king's absence) which were roughly comparable to modern administrative orders.

One whole section of Versailles, known by the rather grandiose title of the 'ministerial wing' was given over to clerks and offices. These administrative departments became steadily more specialized, not to say involved, as the monarchy took on an increasingly bureaucratic tone, a process described by Pagès, for reasons which remain somewhat obscure, as a 'deformation' or even a deviation of the *Ancien*

Régime. The old administrative forms were beginning to acquire a highly novel basis of properly constituted records and before very long would give way to a new kind of administrative procedure which, in many respects, remains with us today.

Versailles must have been a curious place: a mixture of work and play, splendour and filth, piety and licence. Certainly, it was a far cry from Versailles as it used to be pictured, and sometimes is still, as a place of literature and learning. Hardly any of the 'great' ministers, 'great' generals or 'great' writers ever lived there. Lionne, Turenne, Pascal and Molière were all dead before the place was properly inhabited. Colbert, Corneille, Le Tellier, Condé, Lully, Lebrun (in 1690) and Louvois (in 1691) died almost immediately afterwards. Boileau and Racine were the only ones – a sadder and wiser Racine, writing entertainments to order (*Esther*, 1689) before producing his last great work, *Athalie*, in 1691. More than anything else, Versailles meant Maintenon and her good works, Le Pelletier and Boucherat, pale shadows of former greatness, the unstable Luxembourg and an undistinguished brood of lesser generals, culminating in Villeroy – these and a maelstrom of horses, lackeys, clerks, priests, courtiers, navvies and ne'er-do-wells.

Yet it was here that one man, alone, with his passion for work and his selected handful of advisers, once again made his choice for war. Now, on the eve of so many years of conflict, what of the rest of France, so remote from the world of Versailles?

THE FAR CORNERS OF THE REALM

For actual social conditions in France at this vital period, we have a certain amount of indirect evidence, none of it particularly new, and an impressive quantity of first hand testimony, most of which has lain undisturbed in the records. The first falls easily into a number of categories: complaints, broadsheets, stylistic exercises and commonplaces. The complaints are letters from local administrators mentioning storms, rains, excessive heat or cold to account for the 'poverty of the people' and obtain tax relief for those under their jurisdiction. The broadsheets are the remarkably brilliant pamphlets smuggled in from Holland, with titles like *'les Soupirs de la France esclave'* and proclaiming how the country 'yearned for liberty' (1689). Under stylistic exercises come the *Caractères ou les Mœurs de ce siècle*, to the fourth edition of which La Bruyère appended the famous 'wild beasts' (1689). For commonplace, there is the note of January 1686, discovered by Clément among Louvois' papers, deploring the scarcity of money, the increasing number of business failures, more and more farms abandoned, craftsmen fleeing abroad, depopulation and other disasters. Documents of this kind, always vague and clearly exaggerated, tell us very little. Colbert was always fulminating against dissatisfied merchants who were busy all the time filling their own purses, and officials and intendants who overstressed the sufferings of their provinces to obtain tax relief and so make themselves more popular, while from the Huguenots, snug in their Dutch refuge, abuse was only to be expected and La Bruyère was above all an exponent of style.

Let there be no exaggeration. This was before Fénelon preached or Boisguillebert thundered or Vauban produced his accounts. France in 1688 was not the France of 1695 or of 1710. If she had been, she could not have withstood twenty-two years of war.

Louis had governed his own country for between twenty-seven and twenty-eight years and in that time the population of France had undergone almost a complete revolution, from generation to generation, from age-group to age-group, and each had grown to maturity in a different climate.

In the early years, adults were still burdened by the memory of the long and terrible years of the Fronde when armies, epidemics and famine had come together or in turn to decimate families, wipe out the aged, scatter the people, reduce the number of children in some cases by half and recall or even outdo the horrors which had fallen on the people in the 1630s. The king's accession was marked by a fresh crop of horrors: the harvest of 1661, coming on top of several bad years, was catastrophic and in some places those of 1662 and 1664 were almost as bad. While the king and his court pursued their revels, the poor folk were dying in numbers twice or three times what was usual and children were not born or died in infancy. As a result, even in time of peace the old familiar troubles reappeared: market riots, robbery, theft and poaching, gangs of beggars, more disease, unemployment, corpses in the streets and the evident inadequacy of such charitable measures as existed. It seemed as though there was no end to the tally of death.

However, there was an end, for a brief while. The year 1663 marked the beginning of ten years of comparative prosperity, apart from a few outbreaks of plague which came from the north between 1665 and 1668. The weather, which is reasonably well documented, was favourable again and produced good harvests. The price of corn and bread fell as low as in the good old days of Henri IV and other prices followed suit. 1668 and 1673 were years when goods were particularly cheap. The armies were on a peacetime footing and such fighting as there was was done outside the kingdom and without too many depredations on the way. Colbert's first steps were providing work for artisans in town and country. Until the ultra-protectionist tariffs of 1667, exports were booming: French trade outdid all rivals in Spain, especially in Cadiz, and was causing them some uneasiness even in the Levant. In Amiens, the only 'industrial' centre for which any production details are known (or becoming known), there was a notable increase in the number of products, although it never reached the pre-1635 figure. The kingdom showed signs of a return to a more ordered state of affairs and although the pressure of taxation from the Church and the secular lords on an unwilling population seems to have increased, the king's taxes did not go up and their collection became more efficient. The few reliable documents available to us reveal no drop in wages. For ten years, in the absence of the traditional plagues, with the price of bread very low and work comparatively easy to come by, the poorer classes must have known a degree of affluence which is reflected in the king's own finances. This does not mean, of course, that there were no local outbreaks of disease, rebellions or tax riots, but all these things were a part of the normal life of the country. Yet even so, the kingdom's overall production does not appear to have reached the same level of prosperity it had known before the Fronde. On the other hand, the large numbers of children born before 1645 had reached maturity and were in their turn producing offspring which had not yet suffered from the worst ravages of famine or disease. It may be that from 1670 to 1675 there were too many children and young adults, work may have become less plentiful and, in consequence, family incomes diminished.

What is certain is that from 1674 onwards there was a definite change. Soldiers, food shortages, epidemics and special taxes reappear. The 'times were out of joint' as the saying went: there were more wet summers, the harvest of 1674 was a bad one in many places and those of 1677, 1678 and 1679 were even worse and, what is more, the effect was cumulative. 1681 was a poor year in parts and 1684 very often catastrophic. The price of staple foods shot up: corn and bread rose between 1677 and 1684 to nearly double what they had been in 1667–72. Wages, on the other hand, had not gone up

at all and in view of the increase in the adult and adolescent
population, the amount of work available had probably decreased. The consequences are easily foreseeable. At some
time or other (but mainly round about 1679 and 1684), the
death roll all over the country began to rise again, while the
number of baptisms fell nearly everywhere to less than the
death rate. Here and there disaster struck with fearful suddenness: there was a widespread outbreak of 'dysentery' in
Eastern Brittany in 1676 and the years of 1679 and 1684 were
marked by classic demographic crises in the regions of Beauvais and Anjou. By 1674 the country was again suffering
from the depredations of the military: winter quarters and
staging posts connected with the first coalition; the savage repression of revolts in the south and south-west (1675); garrisons quartered on recalcitrant taxpayers and obdurate heretics. The burden of taxation, direct or indirect, was greatly
increased after 1673: the slight relaxation which followed the
peace of Nimeguen was not maintained because the army
was kept on a wartime footing and there was no reduction
in the expenses of the court or the building programme.
Subsidies to the arts, manufactures and trade had, on the
other hand, virtually disappeared. In addition, the number
of taxpayers seems to have gone down. For one thing, those
Protestants who were more or less converted were exempt
from the *taille*, while the more obdurate, who were often the
richest, were emigrating in their tens of thousands. For another, the products of the high birth rate before 1648 had
grown older and fewer and those reaching manhood between 1675 and 1685 were the generation born during the
Fronde, many of whom had suffered again the lean years
from 1661 to 1663. The new royal demands fell on a smaller
population, already suffering from the effects of famine and
sickness.

From 1685 to 1689, however, the weather was good again.
The magnificent harvests and remarkably low prices made

1688 in many places a record year for cheap grain in the seventeenth century. Undeniably, this must have afforded the common people considerable relief, a relief which is reflected in the parish registers, but now it was the turn of the *rentiers* to complain.

Before turning to their grievances, let us sum up in a few words what is known, or conjectured about the immense variety of the common people who made up the real stuff of France. On the eve of the second coalition, they were living in a kind of truce, symbolized by the low price of corn which, for most people, was a commodity which had to be bought. It was true that work was not abundant and that wages had not altered for thirty years, but there was no shortage of food. The provinces, except in Protestant areas, basked in a kind of peaceful interlude. A comparative order reigned, with no major rebellions, no pronounced unrest or egregious poverty – apart from the built-in wretchedness that was an inevitable part of the worker's situation whether in town or country. But from 1674 onwards, soldiers, new taxes, food shortages and epidemics reappeared almost everywhere and the people became reacquainted with suffering. Most serious of all – if current research confirms the hypothesis – was perhaps that the adults in the prime of life (that is, between twenty-five and forty) who constituted the most active section of the population in 1689, had been born between 1648 and 1663. Numerically, therefore, this age group was extremely limited and greatly inferior in relation to the fifteen age groups born before 1648 and to the fifteen born between 1663 and 1678. Yet it was on this section of the population, at once the smallest and the most vital, that the burden of payment for the coming war was to fall most heavily. Moreover, it had as yet no suspicion of what else, besides war, lay ahead in the last, terrible decade of the seventeenth century.

MERCHANTS AND RENTIERS:
THE WEALTH OF FRANCE IN 1688

Few voices were raised in protest at the decline in landed income which formed the main source of revenue in France until after 1695 when that of Boisguillebert spoke out most forcefully. But by 1680 or thereabouts, and sometimes earlier, complaints were being made which can be found at length in the reports handed to ministers or their immediate associates, such as Louvois or Desmarets. With the collapse of landed income, there was a rush of complaints about depopulation, the shortage of money, the increasing numbers of business failures and the depreciation of offices. From all this writers and teachers have concluded, perhaps a trifle hastily, that the first thirty years of Louis' personal reign can be summed up in terms of depression, recession and deflation, Simiand's 'phase B'; a depression which is soon seen to be more or less world-wide.

Before accepting these views wholesale, it will be as well to check whether there is any foundation for them.

In the matter of land which was, and long remained, the most important factor, two things may be taken as true: prices and tenant farms had fallen off appreciably in thirty years. Agricultural prices are well known and more could easily be discovered about them. After a good harvest the price of corn fell to a level unequalled for another three-quarters of a century and anyone with a surplus to sell found trouble in getting rid of it. Even timber and livestock which had been subject to enormous increases in price from 1500 to 1650 – and which in Picardy had gone up four times again from 1600 to 1650 – now remained obstinately stable: incredibly, even the butchers were cutting their prices! All, therefore, from the little man with a surplus only in a good year who made occasional sales to the average vendor and, most of all, the big operator, had some reason to shout. And although they were able to recoup their losses in times of scarcity (scarcity, however, being rare at this period), it was naturally the big investors and the wealthiest farmers who shouted the loudest.

All ritual lamentation set aside, they do seem to have had sound reasons for complaint. A nineteenth-century economist, Daniel Zolla, wrote a memorable essay attempting to trace the history of landed income in the seventeenth century. His earnest, though somewhat random studies and painstaking, if naïve methods led him to some remarkably clear-cut conclusions: from 1660 onwards, but especially after 1670, the revenues (and prices) of land in France suffered a literal collapse. A number of regional studies of greater depth and accuracy have been made since Zolla. Here, without false modesty, are my own conclusions for the region of Beauvais.

Beauvais was a very old *pays* comprising a part of Picardy and a part of Bray, grain producing and pastoral regions respectively. After 1660 nearly all farm rents in kind showed a decline both in quantity and in market value, often of considerable proportions. Farm rents payable in cash, by far the greater number, never rose and in nine cases out of ten actually fell. Moreover, a study of the actual payments made by farmers reveals a rapid increase in indebtedness from 1660 to 1690. In many cases the normal period of arrears lengthened from a few months to two, three and even five years. Furthermore, conditions were the same in the towns where housebuilding seems to have come to a standstill and tenants found it almost impossible to keep abreast of their payments. Shortage of money, currency crises, a pinch felt in town and country, all these emerge with consistent clarity from perusal of the documents. The same contracts brought the landowners less corn which was generally worth less, or less money which was invariably late and became more and more so. Recent research on Languedoc has led to similar conclusions.

The landowners naturally fought bitterly to preserve at least their former level of income. We find them cutting down leases, making over farm rents from grain to cash, amalgamating farms in order to attract better farmers, employing land surveyors to assess their acreage exactly and seizing the goods and chattels of defaulting farmers. Where landowners were *seigneurs* as well, they ransacked the records for ancient rights which had fallen into disuse, making their copyholders provide sworn returns, exacting tithes, dues and *corvées* (a number of which had lapsed during the troubles) and even going so far as to impose unauthorized levies (particularly in western Brittany before the uprisings of 1675). These increased demands on the part of their overlords only served to increase the people's discontent without compensating for the long, oppressive and ineluctable depression in landed income. Intensive study has established that at this period the rate of income from land was less than 3 per cent and then only if the farmers themselves paid up. This general debilitation which was responsible for the marked drop in land prices (30 to 50 per cent is the figure sometimes put forward, although there is no easy way of checking it), does, however, provide an explanation for the popularity of annuities and perhaps also for the renewed interest in trade which, although risky, could bring in substantial profits.

There has, as yet, been no serious study of annuities. These were loans at interest transacted between private individuals. All that is known is that there were tens and hundreds of thousands of them and that no real understanding of the economics of the *Ancien Régime* is possible until someone has sorted out this vast and complex subject. Some facts, however, can be stated here and now. In 1689 or thereabouts, a great many private fortunes were based on annuities and the number and extent of these was constantly increasing. This is understandable. In the jurisdiction of the Paris *Parlement* after 1665, the legal rate of interest was 5 per cent and it was probably 5.5 per cent elsewhere, that is, twice the income from land investment. Payment was easy and assured because the creditor could always distrain upon the goods of the debtor for his money. Unfortunately the facts about these annuities are not at all clear and there is even some question whether the capital which went to 'purchase' the income was always actually paid over, but the fact remains that their very popularity is both an indication that all was not well with the land and the countryside and at the same time a proof that France was not yet ruined.

There are still too few serious, detailed studies of merchant society, but those which do exist do not give any strong indications of French decadence. Historians who are fortunate enough to find themselves in possession of the records of a business, or even of an inventory of the estate of a particular merchant are astonished by what they find there: vast stocks of merchandise, manufacturers employed by the retailer, close and continual contact between the major cities of the realm and their foreign agents, abundance of ready money, immense resources of credit and bills of exchange and the recurring names of Spain and the Antilles, Cadiz and San Domingo – and Cadiz meant all of Spanish America, a customer rolling in money – which even then formed the background to French trade. This preoccupation with Spain and America has been neatly, if somewhat briefly, described by Albert Girard and will be dealt with at greater length before very long by Huguette Chaunu. France set out with her textiles and her grain, often with her own ships, in search of the treasures of America.

While the historians of Marseilles are slowly reconstructing the history of their port in a series of fat volumes, Jean Delumeau and his students at Rennes have been digging out the history of Saint-Malo from its magnificent and hitherto unknown archives. Light dawns in 1680 when the unfairly named 'corsair' city was probably the chief port in France and one of the richest in the world, with a turn-round of 2,000 ships a year, traffic amounting to nearly 100,000 tons burden (more than the great Spanish American ports), 120 large ocean-going vessels and probably ten times the number of small ships of a few tons perfectly capable of crossing the Channel. Trade out of Saint-Malo was world-wide, covering all Europe and America and even Pondicherry (1686) and Greenland (1688) but there were particularly strong connexions with Newfoundland (one hundred vessels a year), Cadiz and the Mediterranean. The massive, granite walls of the great business houses already towered above the city walls and the vast fortunes which have made names like Magon and Danycan a legend for posterity ran into millions of *livres*. Legendary, too, were the great fleets out of Saint-Malo which, in 1661, could carry nearly a hundred tons of pure silver in a single convoy.

'The war on French trade' is the name given by the English historian G. N. Clark to the struggle which was about to begin, a struggle otherwise referred to merely as the war of the League of Augsburg. William of Orange, King of England and Stadtholder of the United Provinces, may have attached small importance to the economic considerations but the merchants of his two countries were fully aware of the deeper causes that were at stake. French trading interests were too well established in Asia, in the Mediterranean, on the slave coasts of Africa and, above all, in Cadiz and America. This had to stop.

This trade war does at least prove that in spite of the peasants' wretchedness, the landowners' complaints, rural depression and the misdeeds wrought by armed intolerance, the kingdom of France was far from exhausted. Once again, how could it have endured the quarter century which lay ahead of it without the staggering resources of its merchants, shipowners and financiers, without the endurance of its *rentiers* and without the stubborn, furious and backbreaking toil of its millions of peasants?

And yet, in a kingdom where splendour stood cheek by jowl with discord, a kingdom ruled for a bare six years from Versailles, voices were beginning to be heard which had nothing to do with the 'classic period' of the old textbooks which took so little account of history.

NEW VOICES: THE DAWN OF THE GRAND SIÈCLE

The reader will probably have observed, perhaps with some asperity, that this book takes little account of that minuscule *élite* of writers, painters and engravers which, in its time, has occupied some thousands of worthy souls. Indeed, the success of such a man as Pradon should, in a sense, be infinitely more interesting to the historian than the genius of Racine because it is the expression of a particular time, place and society. An anthology of 'genius' is often highly subjective and the aesthetic joys or cultural outlets to which it gives rise have a greater bearing on the history of recent taste than on that of social life in the past.

However that may be, it was in the penultimate decade of the century that Paul Hazard discerned the beginnings of his *'Crise de conscience européenne'*.* Leibniz who lived through it, had a simpler definition: *Finis saeculi novam rerum faciem aperuit.*

In France, as elsewhere, criticism of accepted beliefs and official doctrines was not at that time a new thing. After all the humanists, basically Montaigne had said nearly all there was to say. And then, apart from one or two outbursts, the

---

*La Crise de la conscience européenne, by Paul Hazard (1935) available in translation by J. Lewis May, *The European Mind 1680–1715*, Pelican, 1964.

criticism was muffled or confined to small groups of mech-
anists or free-thinkers, while the mathematicians and
scholars went on as before. But the coming of Descartes saw
the appearance of his method 'for the good conduct of
thought' and of this system of doubt which was the essential
liberating instrument.

In the intellectual field, at the time with which we are
dealing, that is, at the period when the Protestant William
of Orange took over England and roused Europe against
French aggression, three things are certain. Descartes had
triumphed, the so-called 'classical' generation was dead, and
the kingdom and Europe as a whole had been subjected to a
spate of dynamic and irreverent critical works. A few examples will serve.

In the field of scholarship, Richard Simon, a member of
the Oratorian Order, created biblical exegesis in his vigorous
Histoire critique de l'Ancien Testament (1678). Expelled
from the Oratory and his book pulped by order of the king
and afterwards placed on the Index, Simon persevered with
the preparation of his attack on the generally accepted text
of the New Testament. A great scholar and a great Christian, he placed weapons in the hands of the atheists and free-
thinkers. His colleague in the Oratorian Order, Père Malebranche, less revolutionary but equally stubborn and still
more influential, devoted his life to the reconciling of Carte-
sian philosophy with Christianity. With the same decency,
certain of their Jesuit opponents, by letters and accounts of
their travels and later by the famous *querelle des rites*, carried on the work of the free-thinker La Mothe Le Vayer
who, fifty years earlier, had written a treatise on 'virtuous
pagans', using the Chinese as examples. It was becoming
apparent once again that the teachings of the Church, maintained by the Sorbonne and by the king, were utterly at
variance with the facts of geography, history and ethics.

Others, taking advantage of current problems, went still

further. By attacking sorcerers, oracles and celestial portents (such as comets), they denounced superstition, demonstrated that the teaching of the Church was riddled with it, that the Church had fallen into an idolatry worse than atheism and that all things considered, atheism was more moral than this corrupt form of religion and could, moreover, claim a greater number of martyrs. Tribute has been paid to the irony of Fontenelle and to the intellectual dynamite of Pierre Bayle whose famous *Dictionnaire*, containing all the seeds of Voltaire, was soon to appear. It was no accident that the major works of these two pioneers were written between 1682 and 1689.

Another significant point was the appearance in England, very nearly at the same time, of Newton's *Principia* and the first works of Locke, heralding a scientific and political revolution which the refugee journals, the effective loudspeakers which Louis XIV had helped to establish in London and Amsterdam, were swift to propagate. At the very moment when the *Caractères* was turning society upside down, another great and subtle opponent entered the royal circle. This was Fénelon who, in company with his friend the Duc de Beauvilliers, was tutor to the Duc de Bourgogne. The same year also saw the eruption of the quarrel between the Ancients and the Moderns, a relatively unimportant dispute among men of letters which, although it appeared to sing the praises of the '*siècle de Louis*', nonetheless helped to undermine the sacrosanct tradition.

Bossuet was almost the only one to hear these first, ominous rumblings and almost alone in taking up the hopeless struggle. He had spoken out against Richard Simon in 1678 but in 1682 he was still busily engaged in reconciling Descartes and St Thomas (*Traité de la connaissance de Dieu et de soi-même*). Then his eyes were opened by the bold propositions of Malebranche and in 1687 he sounded a warning of the 'impending great attack on religion'. The following year

he published his *Histoire des variations des églises protes-
tantes*, an earnest and already overdue plea in favour of the
concept of authority. While maintaining the controversy
with the main voices from abroad, he trounced the biblical
exegetists and over-critical scholars, as well as preparing a
'*Défence de la Tradition et des Saints Pères*', both of which
stood in some need of defending.

But philosophers, scholars, theologians, jurists and
satirists presented no immediate threat to Louis' kingdom.
Moreover, it is not always easy to know how great their influence really was, or how extensive their audience. There
can be no doubt that the appetite for scandal on the part of
both court and city assisted in promoting the success of the
Caractères and also the books and pamphlets imported from
Holland. Almost certainly, the immediate impact of Leibniz
and Spinoza was practically nil and it took Voltaire to explain the English thinkers to the fashionable world. All the
same, historians coming across the catalogues of great provincial libraries, or even quite small ones, for a number of
years, are surprised at the changes which occurred in the
ten years from 1680 to 1690. Before this period, the serious
bookshelves of magistrates, canons and educated bourgeois
were adorned with tales of chivalry, Latin works and massive treatises of law and theology in varying proportions.
Afterwards, a new wind blew, sweeping away tradition.
Travels, controversies and explosive pamphlets stood side by
side with romances and operatic librettos although the solid
phalanx of Jansenist literature retained its place almost
everywhere. On the evidence of certain still unpublished
work carried out at Amiens and elsewhere, it appears that
the crucial date was around 1690. It was not until after this
date, while the 'great reign' creaked sadly to its close, that
Michelet's *grand siècle*, by which he meant the eighteenth,
the century dedicated to the ideal of liberty, really began.

PART FOUR

The Time of Trial
(1689-1714)

THE SECOND COALITION
(1689–97)

WAR

HAVING angered the Pope by his display of 'caesaro-papism' and his arrogance, bitterly offended Protestant Europe by the Revocation of the Edict of Nantes and by his brutal persecutions and tried the patience of Spain and the Empire by his 'reunions' and aggressions, Louis XIV now thought to avert a general war by striking one or two swift blows on his own account. He therefore began moving his armies into Avignon, the Palatinate, the Electorate of Cologne, to Ireland and even from Canada to New York (late 1688 to early 1689).

The admirable result of this was that within a few months the whole of Europe, with the exception of some insignificant neutrals (Denmark, Switzerland, Portugal), was united against him under the leadership of the Stadtholder of the United Provinces whom Louis had permitted to become King of England. He was obliged to sustain a war in the north, the east, the south-west and the south, as well as in Ireland, North America, the Antilles, the Indies, and more or less everywhere at sea. The Most Christian King's sole and quite unintentional ally was the infidel Ottoman, still keeping the emperor and his best troops fully occupied on the borders of Hungary.

The coalition, though quickly formed, took rather longer to get under way. The sack of the Palatinate, the burning of Heidelberg and the destruction, stone by stone, of Mannheim, Spire, Worms and Bingen had been enough to unite the German princes. The assistance of French officers and ships at James II's landing in Ireland early in 1689 decided the English Parliament. The invasion of Savoy by Catinat's army which triumphed without risk to itself or even so much as a declaration of war at Staffarde in 1690, was enough for Victor Amadeus who took his stand on the Treaty of Vienna which, for a year or more, had been gradually turning into the charter of the allies. Holland and Spain (where the French queen had died at the beginning of 1689 and was swiftly replaced by an Austrian one) had naturally joined forces months before, added to which Louis himself had actually bothered to declare war on them, on various pretexts.

It was to this gathering of divergent interests, some of which happened temporarily to coincide, that William of Orange, now William III of England, endeavoured to give an organization and a soul. He brought them together at conferences in Holland but his task was not an easy one since each member was pursuing his own private ends. All the same, the coalition was in possession of good armies, a strong seapower, and above all, sound financial resources. The allied armies numbered more than 200,000 men and Louis XIV could count on at least as many, all of which amounted to a force quite unprecedented in European warfare.

The commanders were not bad although Condé, Gustavus-Adolphus and Montecuccoli had left behind them no worthy disciples. France was fortunate in Luxembourg who had flashes of genius, but he died in 1695. The allies lost the Duc de Lorraine even earlier and left Prince Eugène to shine against the Ottoman. They were left with William who was full of military enthusiam, and a few conscientious German princes. But by the end, the French were in an even worse mess. The coalition armies were made up of troops from the Empire, Germany and Holland: Spain had run out of *tercios* for lack of money and the English were cautious about leaving their island. The French forces remained a curious mixture, a quarter or a third of them foreigners, although there was some attempt at conscription for the militia, of which more will be said later on.

Given the absence of any exact agreement among historians, sea power must have been fairly well balanced. The Spanish fleet was negligible, the Dutch to begin with outdid the English in numbers, effectiveness and in daring but later on the positions were reversed and the British were even emboldened to launch systematic raids on the least well-defended French ports. The French Atlantic fleet and the new, swift and well-armed Mediterranean galleys enjoyed the advantage of illustrious admirals – Tourville and Châteaurenard – who were later reinforced by such daring freebooters as Duguay-Trouin and Barth.

The defence of Louis' kingdom was supported by French wealth, the effectiveness of her fiscal administration and the aid of a number of financiers. This time, thanks to the London merchants and the bankers of Amsterdam, her enemies, too, were able to count on sound financial backing. However, the men who paid tired sooner than the men who fought. Of the latter, there was no shortage: they could always be replaced by fresh recruitment and could live off the land. The French, especially, acquired a lasting reputation at this time.

The absence of any continuous front, the always seasonal nature of the fighting, the widely scattered battlefields, and for the period, the massive numbers engaged, the generally undistinguished leadership and the clearly well-matched forces are all things which help to explain the turn taken by the war. For nine years the conflict ranged over a wide area with each side in turn gaining the upper hand but without ever achieving a decisive lead. A great deal of blood was shed, ten or twenty thousand killed in a single day at times, as firearms became more formidable and their targets more closely packed. By the fourth or fifth year of the war both sides were tired and, what was more important, running out of money, so talks were begun. The discussions went on for five years or so, with marches and countermarches, trickery, jobbery and haggling. An end was reached in the summer of 1697, at a château of William's near Ryswick.

In the beginning, Louis XIV had endeavoured to strike a great blow at the very heart of England while simply defending his own frontiers. He therefore lent assistance to James II, a Catholic and, he claimed, the lawful heir to the throne, to land in Ireland where supporters, enthusiastic but unarmed, were waiting for him. James occupied papist Ireland without much trouble, then advanced into Ulster, already Orangist, with the object of joining forces with his faithful Scots who were already up in arms, and laid siege to Londonderry. Louis XIV dispatched reinforcements and these were landed by Châteaurenard's fleet after eluding the English ships which then appeared in Bantry Bay, underwent a fearful bombardment and retired in confusion. But James, ineffectual, ill-equipped and poor, dallied in Ulster, giving William III time to bring up a substantial army and inflict a crushing defeat on him at Drogheda on the Boyne. Poor James needed all his French protection as he fled precipitately and took refuge at the château of Saint-Germain-en-Laye which Louis, in a splendid gesture, placed at his disposal. But on the same day, Tourville inflicted a severe defeat on the Dutch fleet (which was covering the timid English navy) near Beachy Head and went on to ravage the British coastline and make London shake in its shoes, although without destroying many enemy vessels. This day, 10 July 1690, was typical of the whole war, with one defeat and one victory. ... Two years later Louis, having promoted himself somewhat irresponsibly to the post of commander-in-chief, was planning a great invasion of England. He had gathered a large army on the Cotentin peninsula and was awaiting the fleets from Brest and Toulon to transport it. With forty-four vessels against eighty-nine, Tourville met the Anglo-Dutch fleet near Barfleur. The French claimed a victory but in the days that followed the enemy burned fifteen of their ships at Saint-Vaast and Cherbourg and the English crowed in triumph. Subsequent events seemed to prove them justified for there was no invasion, nor, indeed, were there any further great naval battles.

On the remaining fronts, the honours were divided or allowed to fade quietly away.

In the Netherlands (which although Spanish were defended chiefly by the Germans and the Dutch) things had begun badly. In 1689, marshal d'Humières permitted the pillaging of frontier towns and villages. The following year an intelligent offensive on the part of the allies, planned by William III with an eye to Champagne, was checked adroitly by Luxembourg at Fleurus, an ideal battleground. In 1691, Louis took command in person, captured Mons with the help of Vauban and was treated to a species of triumph by his courtiers. It is true that all he did next was to set fire to Anvers. Then, early in 1692, Luxembourg took Namur and he and William met again at Steenkirk in the same year, resulting in a hard-won victory for the French. The next year it was the turn of the French to conduct a small offensive. Luxembourg wanted to take Brussels, and Louis XIV Liège. There was a certain amount of dithering, then William stepped in and resolved the difficulty, and Louis conducted a majestic retreat. It was his last personal campaign; thenceforward he fought from his desk. Luxembourg was left with the increasingly arduous task of halting William yet again. This he did at Neerwinden in July 1693, bringing back so many prisoners, canon and standards that he became known as the *tapissier* of Notre Dame, but he left many of his best men on the battlefield and 'Nervinde', as it was called at Versailles, was in reality an indecisive butchery.

Year by year, the same scenes repeated themselves, with one side taking the initiative, capturing a town or two, only to be checked by the other which in turn lacked the strength either for pursuit or for a decisive victory. Then, with the onset of bad weather, there was a polite cessation of hostilities. This could, and did, go on for a long time. The only important event was the death of Luxembourg in 1695. He was replaced by Villeroy who promptly lost Namur, avenged himself by bombarding Brussels and then sat back and waited for peace.

Military activity on the other fronts was much the same: a series of advances and withdrawals that never came to anything. This was so in the Empire where Louvois had established sound positions in 1688 under circumstances already described. Marshal de Duras lost a good many of these in 1689 but took his revenge by setting fire to the unlucky Palatinate once again. Then, in the following year, the Dauphin, an indifferent commander, and Marshal de Lorge who was a much better one, fought a spasmodic campaign and at least managed to keep possession of the Rhineland as a buffer to Alsace. In 1692, French troops marched into Bavaria and then marched out again. In 1693 they distinguished themselves by extensive ravages and by burning down Heidelberg for the second time, but an offensive directed towards central Germany came to nothing. Then they went on advancing, retreating and pillaging beyond their own frontiers while they waited for peace.

In the south-east, the honours were evenly divided. In 1690 Catinat was encamped in Piedmont, the year after, in Savoy and the *comté* of Nice. In 1692 the armies of Savoy came down the Durance and occupied Embrun and Gap, but in 1693 Catinat had his revenge, invaded Piedmont and won a victory at Marseilles, although without destroying the opposing army. He made his way back across the Alps. . . . There seemed no reason why this toing and froing should not go on for a long time when, as we shall see, the diplomats took a hand.

A French army had marched into Catalonia very early in the war but it was not until 1693 that it reached Osas and 1697 that it captured Barcelona, thanks to a fleet from Toulon. Considering the weakness of Spain, this campaign could not be described as a miracle of speed but even so, the fall of Barcelona had an effect on the last stage of the negotiations.

In the colonies, where the French were to some extent abandoned to their own somewhat limited devices and to their courage which was very great, the honours were divided also. English and French colonists took it in turns to threaten Quebec and New York. In the end, however, Le Moyne d'Iberville gained possession of the Hudson's Bay trading posts (Port Nelson in particular) and nearly all of Newfoundland. In 1697, Boston and New York were quaking at tidings of another Franco-Indian raid and this drove the English to peace. The planters of the small but wealthy West Indian island of Saint-Christophe (St Kitts) retaliated by seizing the French half of the island. In Africa, the French lost Goré and St Louis in Senegal. In Asia, the Dutch captured Pondicherry (1693). For the first time, the fighting in the colonies steadily mirrored the progress of the war on the Continent and this phenomenon spread rapidly, giving a new and highly important turn to the conflicts of the eighteenth century.

After the Barfleur incident, the war at sea was economic rather than strategic, involving no more great naval battles in which whole fleets were deployed. The admirals themselves set the fashion when Tourville and d'Estrées attacked a strongly guarded convoy of Anglo-Dutch merchant ships destined for the near east off Lagos, in Portugal.

Eighty ships out of two hundred were lost and the allies
admitted to a loss of forty million *livres*. After this, captains
and shipowners, especially from Dunkirk and St Malo,
equipped with privateer's papers, sallied forth heavily
armed to ravage the enemy trading fleets. They are said to
have sunk four thousand English merchant ships but this
seems an excessive figure even if it includes small coastal
vessels and calls to mind the other side of the picture: the
French vessels lost, French trade harassed equally by
enemy ships, the English raid on Camaret in 1694, the bombardment of French ports and the burning of Dieppe.

By 1693, both sides had realized the impossibility of final
victory and were ready to negotiate. Louis XIV behaved
with great moderation (which was more than he would
have done before) and made quite serious offers. But almost
at once the haggling began and Louis refused point blank to
recognize the new King of England. Talks were resumed
in 1694 and again in 1695 since there was, after all, no possibility of invading France or England, no possibility of destroying either fleets or empires, little chance of the French
penetrating into the heart of the Empire, Piedmont or
Catalonia and still less of their remaining there. Keeping
four or five hundred thousand men under arms was proving
ruinous even to the Dutch exchequer, while the youthful
Bank of England was experiencing severe difficulties. As for
the state of French finances, that will be seen . . .

The Duke of Savoy, the last to join the coalition, was
the first to leave it and this decision gave the final push
towards peace.

THE COST OF PEACE

Victor Amadeus had only one thought, which was to free
his country from the oppressive presence of the French and,
if possible, at the same time from the awkward proximity

of Spain in the Milanais. After endless circumlocutions, he came to a preliminary agreement with the King of France in 1695. The fortress of Mantua, which was in French hands and under siege by a combined Austrian, Spanish and Piedmontese army, would succumb, after a show of resistance and be disarmed and restored to its owner. This piece of play-acting was carried out very prettily. In the following year it was followed by another of even greater subtlety. The duke, pretending to be hard-pressed by Catinat and deserted by his friends, made public the secret Treaty of Turin, joined forces with Catinat's fifty thousand men and ravaged the Milanais. The emperor and the King of Spain, with plenty of other things to worry about, pledged themselves (by the Treaty of Vigevano, October 1696) to undertake no further fighting in Italy. The trick had worked. In order to pay for this defection Louis XIV had been obliged to give up Casale and Pinerolo, his old strongholds in Italy, as well as all his recent conquests including Nice, Susa and Montmélian and consent to the marriage of the Duc de Bourgogne to little Marie-Adelaide of Savoy. The break-up of the coalition had cost him dear.

But it speeded up the process of peacemaking. With England on the verge of bankruptcy, New York and Boston threatened, the territories of Hudson's Bay and Newfoundland already lost, William III was prepared to consider peace at last. The French diplomats held out a well-timed lure, promising that Louis would finally abandon the Stuarts and recognize William. From then on, once the capture of Barcelona and the sack of Cartagena (America) had decided Spain, it only remained to convince the emperor. He, however, was triumphantly driving the Turks beyond the borders of Hungary, recapturing Transylvania at last and feeling securely in command of his army, although in point of fact he was probably less so than any of the German princes who had, nonetheless, recognized his son as 'King of the

Romans', in other words as heir to the Empire. For a full month, Leopold the Victorious remained alone in a state of war with France, having been deserted by all his allies in September 1697. Then he gave in and added his signature to all those which had been appended to the various treaties of Ryswick (or Rijswijk, as it is in Dutch).

After nine years of indecisive slaughter, none of the belligerents, with the exception of the Duke of Savoy, had realized all their objectives in the war. The aim of the coalition had been to restrict France to within her frontiers of 1648 and 1659 but in general they had been obliged to settle for those of 1679 with the addition of Strasbourg which the emperor let go most unwillingly. But each did obtain appreciable advantages on their own account. Even the king of Spain, for the first time in fifty years, lost nothing, although admittedly Europe was only waiting for his death to strip the carcase.

As for Louis XIV, who is our prime concern, he could undoubtedly preen himself on a highly effective defensive strategy, some splendid actions and the fact that he had kept hold of Strasbourg. But in the long run he had to pay dearly for the Peace of Ryswick.

Louis had gone to war in order to put the Catholic Stuart back on the English throne, to install his own candidate in the Electorate of Cologne, to claim a share in the succession to the Palatinate and to confirm his possession of the territories he had 'reunited' with France. At the same time he set himself to oppose the Pope in Rome, Avignon and France. What, after nine years, had become of these accumulated claims?

At a very early stage, Louis had restored Avignon to the Pope (1689) and given way completely in the matter of the franchise (1690). In 1693 he came to a satisfactory agreement with Innocent XII over the affair of the *régale* but was obliged to go back on the declaration of 1682: the Gallican

bishops had to go before the Nuncio and sign an unequivocal form of disavowal. This was the end of royal Gallicanism and caesaro-papism. The ultramontane, protestant
and 'politic' were free to mock at this 'extraordinary recanta-
tion', this 'abjuration' on the part of the French clergy,
this 'submission' on the part of the Great King. In order to
gain at least a benevolent neutral, to try and thrust a spoke
into the coalition, and not to add to the number of his enemies, Louis renounced religious despotism and would
remain, until the end of his days, an obedient ally of Rome
and of the Company of Jesus, as the Jansenists were very
soon to find out.

In the two German quarrels which had helped to bring
about the war, Louis XIV obtained no satisfaction. The
Electorate of Cologne eluded his protégé and the Palatine
inheritance escaped the second Madame. Both obtained at
least some compensation but it was the Pope, as the accepted
arbiter, who settled the indemnity due to the Princess Palatine.

Of all the 'reunions' put into effect before 1689 and all the
conquests made during the war, none, with the exception of
Strasbourg, was left. Spain recovered the whole of Catalonia
and all the Netherlands positions which had been annexed
after 1679: Courtrai, Mons, Ath, Charleroi, even Luxembourg and its flat countryside. The whole of Lorraine which
had been occupied for so long and which Louis declared was
indispensable to his kingdom, was restored to its young
duke, with the exception of Longwy and Saar-Louis. Instead of the sovereign rights over the four great roads which
she had once possessed, France was reduced to a mere right
of way. The 'gaping wound' on her eastern border remained, and gaped wider than ever. To the emperor or the
German princes, he was obliged to restore the region of
Trèves, the towns and villages of the Palatinate, the duchy
of Zweibrücken and the advanced positions on the right

bank of the Rhine: Kehl, Fribourg, Alt-Brisach and Philippsburg. The last French strongholds in Italy were, as we have already seen, ceded to the Duke of Savoy in 1696. The United Provinces gave back Pondicherry but received two more than compensating advantages: the right to maintain troops in certain strongholds of the Spanish Netherlands close to the French border, referred to, significantly, as 'the Barrier', and also considerable commercial privileges (exemption from French entry dues such as the 50 *sous* per ton, concessions in the provision of salt and fish, the abolition of the 1667 tariff which had been reintroduced during the war, and so forth).

The other maritime power, actually ruled by the same man, the arch-enemy, enjoyed still more advantageous conditions. France and England both handed back their colonial conquests and this meant that while the former recovered a bit of the West Indies and two slave-trading posts she had to give up Newfoundland and its fisheries together with the Hudson's Bay territories and their furs, and to lift the threat hanging over Boston and New York. Last and most important of all, Louis made the supreme concession of recognizing William and promising to give no further support, even in secret, to the Stuart king living in exile in France and his Jacobites.

No one could have foreseen, nine years before, when Louvois' armies were advancing on all fronts, that there would come a time for such a host of concessions, so wounding to the royal pride. For a country which had not been defeated and which had been waging a war outside its own territorial limits, the punishment seems even somewhat excessive. Louis was now almost in his sixtieth year. Had he learned moderation?

There is no avoiding this question, which is raised, likewise, by Louis' next war. And yet in 1697, necessity and hope for the future both urged the king to prudence. The necessity was the appalling state of his finances and the very real sufferings of his country. The hope, which was also present at every other court in Europe, was the imminent death of the childless King of Spain. Louis had always intended to assert his claim to the coming succession. Wisely, he realized that he could not achieve it alone and his far-reaching concessions might well earn him some friends in Spain, the support of the Duke of Savoy and possibly make an ally even of his inveterate enemy, William.

But if, in 1697, the concern of princes was chiefly with the King of Spain's health, the people were thinking above all of licking their wounds, the people of France as much as the rest.

THE BURDEN OF WAR

To feed, arm and equip 200,000 men and two fleets for nine years on four main fronts and as many distant theatres of war, against almost the whole of Europe, the Bank of Amsterdam and, before long (in 1694) the Bank of England as well, was a gigantic task, the cost of which, in terms of money, was literally beyond measure. Moreover it could not be reckoned in terms of money alone because, in addition to the actual cost of the war, there was the burden it placed on the economy and, in very unequal proportions, on the different classes of the country's population.

Colbert, at the end of his career, had for the most part abandoned his old dreams and done his best to bolster up the country's finances which were shaken rather than stretched unbearably by the first coalition. His successor, Le Peletier, probably began by making a mistake in abolishing the *Caisse des Emprunts* which might still have had its uses. Le Peletier was a cautious and conservative man, thoroughly honest and unassuming (which is more than can be said of Colbert) and for five years he carried out the task bequeathed to him adequately enough. He lowered the *tailles* slighly, maintaining the level of income from tax farms, repayed part of the national debt and almost entirely did away with the bad habit of 'anticipating' or spending future income in advance, resorted to by Colbert. In 1686 and 1687 the budgetary deficit (by now a matter of course) was even reduced to a few millions. By the end of 1688 the country was at war again and in 1689, the normal revenues of a hundred millions proving quite inadequate to finance one, the *contrôleur général* was already being obliged to look for money wherever he could find it. Le Peletier, who disliked 'extraordinary measures' and felt himself quite unequal to handling them, resigned with dignity. He was succeeded by Phélypeaux de Pontchartrain.

He is one of those ministers who commonly fall victim to historians infatuated with Colbert, but this 'foil' had charm enough, a little later, to attract the young and critical duc de Saint-Simon who praises his 'enlightened simplicity and cheerful good sense' while at the same time stressing his exceptional intelligence, wit and competence and his admirable knowledge of men. One only has to read a few lines of Pontchartrain to understand and appreciate his subtlety, especially after such heavyweights as Colbert and Louvois. As intelligence carried to a very high degree can sometimes make up for everything else, Pontchartrain addressed himself, with cynical efficiency, to the strict task imposed on him by his king: that of continuing to support the war by any means.

Not a great deal more could be expected from the 'ordinary' sources of income, whether direct or indirect, farmed out or otherwise. These had clearly been stretched to their utmost. The *tailles* rose by about a tenth from 1688 to 1694 then fell to their original level and then below it. Something had occurred in 1694 of which more will be said later. The *fermes unies (gabelles, aides* and customs, *the cinq grosses fermes* and *domaine*) were pushed up from 66 to 70 millions (in 1690), then dropped to 61, to fall again when the war was over. A number of privileged classes were encouraged to increase their *dons gratuits*, a more or less unofficial form of taxation: the *pays d'État* achieved wonders, the cities paid once, jibbed at a second demand and evaded a third: the clergy of France provided several millions for which the monarchy recompensed them by delivering the lower-clergy to the bishops, a move of fundamental importance of which more will be said. All this did not go very far and it fell off abruptly following the disasters of 1693–4. But the war demanded twice the amount of the normal revenues, or not far short of it. Pontchartrain had two ways out: the 'extraordinary measures' or the imposition of a new tax which should be effective and really general.

The first method, the traditional one, had its advantages and Le Peletier had already resorted to it, without enthusiasm. Pontchartrain manipulated it with a virtuosity recalling the colleagues of Richelieu or Mazarin (basically, in fact, he was reapplying the old recipes of former wars). He created and sold new offices, as varied as they were unexpected: tax assessors and financial reckoners (attached to the courts), receivers of communal dues (attached to municipal magistracies), official funeral criers, official refuse collectors, inspectors of accounts of arts and crafts (attached to the so-called 'corporative' institutions), oyster-sellers, wigmakers and qualified doctors, registrars of births, marriages and deaths, officers of *ban* and *arrière-ban* (from whom the nobility purchased exemption from military service) and a hundred others equally ingenious. Payment of some of these was a charge upon the state, which pledged only the future: payment of others was a matter for the public or for the various 'corps' which, in the event, concerned only the tax payers. In 1692, Pontchartrain had the idea of selling mayoral offices (except in Paris and Lyons) to the highest bidder, together with half the other municipal offices, and this brought about the final disappearance of communal 'liberties'. Existing officers had their commitments doubled, were obliged to purchase new offices and in many cases had to submit to a so-called rise in increment which was really a clever compulsory loan: for the sake of a thousand *livres* a year more in some uncertain future, the officers had to pay up the corresponding capital of anything from sixteen to twenty thousand *livres* on the spot. Speculation on the love of offices and bourgeois vanity produced 170 millions in six years. The honest Le Peletier, in a comparable period, had made no more than twenty millions out of such sales.

Like his predecessors in office, Pontchartrain also created annuities. Up until 1694 these amounted to less than a hundred millions at what was to begin with a reasonable rate of interest (5 or 5½ per cent). Thereafter, the number increased rapidly, sometimes with scant regard for legality, while the interest augmented. At the end of the war, the State was obliged to approve the interest rate of 7·14 per cent and for a while even 8·3 per cent, which proves that credit was very low, but this improved after the peace. Colbert had done much the same in the days of the first coalition. Like him, Pontchartrain sold, at the rate of 8·33 per cent interest, tax exemptions payable in cash, even – and the echoes of this scandal have never died away since no historian has yet dared to publish the names of the beneficiaries – sold titles of nobility to wealthy commoners, and actually went so far as to send blank certificates of ennoblement to his intendants, leaving it to them to dispose of the goods as advantageously as possible. In a great many towns we even find wealthy merchants purchasing the office of lieutenant, captain, major or colonel in the civil militia which gave them, together with certain fiscal privileges, the right to parade in armour at the head of antiquated companies of archers, crossbowmen and popinjay hunters.

When the exploitation of vanity and self-interest proved insufficient, it was necessary to resort to time-honoured methods of monetary jiggery-pokery. Colbert had ventured to do this twice, in 1666 (an attempt at revaluation) and 1674 (the nasty business of the 4 *sou* pieces) and had failed both times. In this respect the virtuosity of Pontchartrain and his department compels a certain admiration : in less than ten years he made more than eighty millions out of currency manipulations. The technique was comparatively simple. The principal coins, the gold and silver *louis*, carried no face value and circulated, in theory, at the value fixed for them by royal decree. Consequently, it was only necessary for these decrees to be issued at the right moment and in the right direction for the state to benefit from a rise (or, as we should call it, a devaluation) or fall (an augmentation) in the value of the *louis*. In 1689 and 1693, operations were conducted on a grander scale which meant in practice that Frenchmen were obliged to sell back their old coins to the Mint and receive in exchange others which were supposed to be worth much more but were as like the former as two peas in a pod. The difference went to pay for the war. There was also some subtle play with the bi-metallic standard (on which the worthy Le Peletier had already exercised his talents) by making slight variations in the value of gold without affecting that of silver, or vice versa.

By 1694, however, the taxpayers were more than 20 millions in arrears and the tax farmers were quite unable to collect their dues. There were no more buyers for offices, annuities and all the other financial inventions and even the latest currency manipulation began rather badly. The kingdom was in the grips of a general exhaustion which served to aggravate the famine and was in turn aggravated by it. What it amounted to was that the country could not pay any more while the rich were no longer prepared to : their confidence had collapsed. Whether he liked it or not, Pontchartrain was forced to listen to the reformers, and Vauban* in particular.

Vauban had put forward a proposal for a new tax payable by all Frenchmen, whatever their privileges, on the basis of a duly certified declaration of their incomes. The idea of a fair assessment and equality in collection involved two formidable innovations which did not appeal to Pontchartrain in the least but making the rich pay for once did hold out some hope of putting a little money into the exchequer. After a good deal of machination, the proposal was announced by the estates of Languedoc, with the encouragement of the intendant of that region. Somewhat softened by the exchequer, it became the first capitation tax (1695), applicable to all Frenchmen, even princes of the blood, but not to the clergy who were of another essence. The subjects were divided into twenty-two 'classes' according to their occupations and titles. This involved a good many absurdities since income was not related to *estats* and *mestiers* but in the end this irregular innovation brought in some 22 millions a year of which a good third came from the pockets of the privileged. After three years and three months, a little later than the promised date, the capitation tax was removed.

It had at least helped a little to finish the war, the cost of which, oddly enough, decreased in its last years owing to the military and financial exhaustion of all parties. Then, having done his duty, Pontchartrain received the ultimate reward: in 1699 he was made chancellor and this eminent position he filled with great dignity until 1714.

That the country was clearly exhausted was already apparent from the drop in the amount raised by the machinery of taxation and from the lack of interest in fresh offers of offices and annuities. The explanation is simple: never,

---

*For Vauban, that great and generous personality, see Rebelliau's short, posthumous work (Fayard, 1962).

since Richelieu, had such heavy demands been made on such a small body of taxpayers and one which was being reduced continually by new exemptions and fresh outbreaks of famine. In addition to the taxes, old and new, there were also the maintenance of armies whether in transit or in camp, (staging posts, implements), levies resulting from the newly created offices, monetary fiddles, economic depression and the burden of a kind of despotic brutality which is so often one of the hidden side-effects of war. To demonstrate the cumulative effects of all these demands would take a lengthy examination of material still in process of compilation. A few examples will suffice.

Study of the archives of Saint-Malo gives a clear picture of the decline of the great port. Before the war, a hundred Newfoundland fishing boats set out every year. There were forty-seven in 1689 and six in 1690. In 1687, the traffic out of Saint-Malo bound for the West Indies exceeded 3,000 tons. In 1690 and 1691 it did not reach 2,000 and then it collapsed, remained negligible for four years until, in 1694, it ceased to exist. Seen from Nantes, the same traffic fell by more than half, from seventy-three ships in 1687 to twenty-three in 1694 and fourteen in 1696. Calculated in tonnage, the world trade out of Saint-Malo dropped by a third, from 90,000 to 60,000 tons. Admittedly some of this loss was made good by piracy but this had its own, enormous risks and the freebooters sailed mostly from Dunkirk.

In the great textile cities of the north, such as Amiens and Beauvais, complaints of a drop in trade due to the financial ruin of customers took on a new urgency, and it is a fact that half the looms in these two towns fell idle, unemployment was rife and charitable institutions were besieged by the needy.

However necessary to the war, the monetary manipulations were regarded as nothing more than swindles, especially by state creditors, *rentiers* and officers. The most able and far-sighted businessmen managed to make money out of them by the knowledgeable use of hoarded *louis*, or by sending money out of the country and playing the market. The general result of this was a drop in the price of French currency abroad and a progressive lowering of the exchange value while inside France there was a danger of increased hoarding, which did in fact occur, at a time when the amount of currency in circulation was notoriously inadequate. Louis XIV might send his silver plate to the Mint – an ostentatious gesture which paved the way for others less admirable – but the majority of well-off Frenchmen were more inclined to play the market or to melt down their money into plate or candlesticks whose value at least seemed safe from royal manipulation. However, in this order of things, the last years of the reign were to produce still more startling effects.

Meanwhile, the great companies which had outlived Colbert were experiencing their death throes. The tapestry-workers, hungry and out of work, were leaving the Gobelins and going back to their native Flanders, although there were some who found a refuge with their charitable compatriot Behagle, the liberal director of the Beauvais factory. The Highways Department which had received over 1½ million *livres* in 1687 was allowed less than 100,000 from 1690 to 1692, and this at a time when the Stuart and his followers were eating up 600,000 *livres* a year at Saint-Germain. Absurdity was piled on impossibility.

The aggravation of old burdens and the imposition of new ones had the curious effect of giving the royal administration a more settled, effective and authoritative place in the kingdom. Military organization, supplies, troop movements, coastal defences, new taxes, letters patent of nobility or offices for sale, all these were added to the work of the intendants, under the direction of Pontchartrain. Brittany, the last province to retain any semblance of independence, had received its intendant in 1689, although he was prudently given only the provisional title of *commissaire départi*, and one reason for his presence was the need to ensure the defence of the coast. From now on, each intendant had his own offices which were becoming increasingly organized, and a fair number of assistants whose usefulness no one dreamed any longer of disputing, as Colbert had once done. An administration with increasing powers and influence was developing within the kingdom. A time was coming when it could be said with some truth that the king was 'present in every province' in the person of thirty or so intendants who were at last really powerful and effective.

At the same time, these provinces were feeling the weight of another and possibly more dictatorial authority. After his reconciliation with Rome in 1693, Louis XIV was not long in granting the bishops a free hand within their own dioceses. In return for the four millions agreed to by the Assembly of the Clergy in 1695, the edict of 21 April 1695, followed by the declaration of 15 December 1698, delivered up the diocesan priests to the tender mercies of their bishops who were now in possession of absolute power to give (or withhold) authorization to particular preachers for Advent or Lent, and to give (or withhold) authorization to priests other than parish priests (the vast majority) to hear confession in a given place at a given time under given circumstances. More important still, every prelate was thenceforth entitled, on his own initiative, to relegate to a seminary for three months any members of the second order who displeased him, without prejudice to subsequent proceedings. In theory, these arbitrary decisions were to do away with a kind of parochial Gallicanism, known as '*richérisme*' which had developed at the beginning of the century and which placed bishops and parish priests on the same spiritual level as pastors of souls. The movement, fed by the writings of one of Boileau's brothers (*De antiquo jure presbyterorum in regimine ecclesiastico*, 1676), and later of Eustache Le Noble and the fanatical priest of Beauvais, Guy Drappier, became associated with the later form of Jansenism when it found a place in the *Réflexions morales* of Père Quesnel who was to rouse the ire of the, by that time, episcopal, jesuitical and ultramontane monarchy. The subjection of the country priesthood, in return for money, was to impart a distinctive colouring to eighteenth-century Jansenism and exercise a distant but clearly discernible influence on the anti-episcopal attitude of the humbler French clergy during the events of 1789. The Great King's political, religious and financial actions during the time of the second coalition carried within them far-reaching consequences.

Still others were emerging. In 1688, Louvois decided to strengthen the army by the addition of provincial militia. This was not so much an innovation as the revival of an old institution which had never really died out, like all the institutions of the *Ancien Régime*. Civil militia had once existed to provide protection for the old walled towns, and they existed still, although in a decaying form. Some frontier provinces still maintained special troops, raised from among the local population, to assist in the defence of their territories. The *boulonoises*, the *petites milices* of Dauphiné, the Béarnaise forces and, most of all, the *miquelets* of Rousillon had distinguished themselves particularly during the late war and no less a person than marshal de Noailles had paid tribute to them in 1691. When an emergency arose, as in the year of Corbie, the militiamen were called out willy nilly, primarily for local defence, and returned home once the danger was past, or simply whenever they got tired of the army.

Louvois decided that in future all the parishes in France were to raise thirty regiments, comprising twenty-five thousand militiamen, for the duration of the war. Initially, the men were elected but before long they were chosen by lot and whereas at first only unmarried men had been taken, as the supply of bachelors dwindled, young married men were also called up. The militia's arms and equipment, and even the cost of its sojourn in winter quarters, was paid for by the parish. Militiamen fought honourably in Catalonia, and in the Alps, for they were not kept purely for defence as had at first been promised. In spite of this, the militia in France began its career by being immensely unpopular. Inevitably, large towns and privileged persons were exempt and practically none of the promises given to the militiamen were honoured. The cost of maintaining the men, and even their sergeants and officers, fell entirely on the already overburdened rural parishes. The young men fled and their parents, or even their parishes, paid for replacements, who were the dregs of society. The French peasant's rooted dislike of any form of military service, which was to be a characteristic feature of French history for over a hundred and fifty years (and incidentally explains the popularity of guerrilla activities), had its beginnings, therefore, in the war of the League of Augsburg and reached a new intensity during the war which followed. By uprooting and degrading the countryman, turning him into a brigand and a deserter, the militia acquired a hideous reputation from the first. Even so, it was only one tribulation among many more serious and universal ones.

1693–4: THE GREAT FAMINE

A minor official of the bishopric of Beauvais noted in his memoirs that in May 1693, 'the price of corn and other cereals which was already high, rose considerably. ... Other commodities became proportionately expensive. This, combined with the desolation brought about by the war and the slump in trade meant that the people suffered terribly from poverty and disease.' The following spring, April 1694, the same man observed that all about him he saw:

An infinite number of poor souls, weak from hunger and wretchedness and dying from want and lack of bread in the streets and squares, in the towns and countryside because, having no work or occupation, they lack the money to buy bread.... Seeking to prolong their lives a little and somewhat to appease their hunger, these poor folk for the most part, lacking bread, eat such unclean things as cats and flesh of horses flayed and cast on to dung heaps, the blood which flows when cows and oxen are slaughtered and the offal and lights and such which cooks throw into the streets.... Other poor wretches eat roots and herbs which they boil in water, nettles and weeds of that kind.... Yet others will grub up the beans and seed corn which were sown in the spring ... and all this breeds corruption in the bodies of men and divers mortal and infectious maladies, such as malignant fevers ... which assail even wealthy and well-provided persons.

There are many documents in a similar strain which have been, or may one day be published. They cover most of the realm, with the possible exception of Brittany and the Mediterranean south. Few achieve the minuteness and exactitude of the foregoing, from which the more revolting details have been omitted, or its naïve description of the climatic conditions of 1692, with its cold, wet summer, and 1693, when, in spite of all the novenas and processions, the corn was 'blighted' by foggy and belatedly warm weather.

It is blindingly clear to us today that from the summer of 1693 to that of 1694 the great majority of people in France – and a good many in other countries – were threatened with, suffered or actually died from starvation. In a great many places, the annual death toll rose to two, three, or four times its normal level, and sometimes more. Many families were broken up. Less than half the usual number of children were born and of those that were brought into the world, at least

half perished in infancy. The marriage bells were all but
silent. There were fears of a return of the plague: in the
rich land of Burgundy where the people had only 'bracken
bread' to eat, the old folk were wont to say that 'the plague
always began with eating bracken'. The priest of Saint-Just-
en-Chevalet recorded that in Vivarais people were found
lying dead 'in the fields with their mouths filled with grass'.
Even a cursory glance at the parish registers reveals, all too
clearly, the magnitude of the disaster: France buried at
least a tenth of her population in the space of a few months.

The worthy official of Beauvais pinpoints the reasons for it
with a naïve accuracy which even the great economists of
the time, Boisguillebert and Vauban, could not have
equalled. The seasons were not merely 'out of joint', they
were so for several years on end. The harvest of 1691 was
poor, the harvest of 1692 worse and that of 1693 disastrous;
disastrous, but not non-existent; estimates vary from a third,
a half, and two thirds of the normal. The basic causes of the
famine were cumulative and accelerating. As usual, a succession of bad harvests set prices rocketing: between the
summer 1688 and spring 1694 they rose to five or six times
their original level, or even more. At Provins, for example,
the cost of rye was multiplied nearly nine times. Increases on
this scale surpassed even those of 1649 or 1662. Bulk buying
for the army, buying up at rock bottom prices before the
harvest, barefaced speculation (in which magistrates and
churchmen did not scruple to set the example), the lure of
high profits to be made from exporting by sea which led to
the denuding of the more fortunate provinces (Brittany),
and the fear of scarcity which, amounting to a panic, led to
more market rioting, and raids on convoys of grain, were all
additional factors contributing to the abnormal rise in prices.

For the basic trouble was still cost. Want and famine are
deceptive words. What they really meant was high prices.
There was flour and bread for all but not all could afford to

buy it. Famine is a strictly social calamity. It is only the epidemics which follow that often leap the barriers of class, and even then the rich are able to flee the main centres of infection and take refuge in the country. There can be no understanding of a tragedy of this kind until it is realized that the vast majority of people in France, even in country districts, *had* to buy their bread, that there were provinces where three-quarters of the peasant population were unable to produce enough to feed their families and were forced to earn their bread as journeymen or by home industries. Now it is a fact that hard times led to less work in the fields, in barns and at the loom. With everyone retrenching, so the outlets were throttled. Moreover, it was even customary to cut the labourer's wages 'because times were hard', although, in fact, this sliding scale in reverse, a particularly charming touch, was less important than increasing unemployment and prohibitive prices. It is not hard to see that if an artisan spent half his income on food for his family, he was in an impossible position when the price of food quadrupled and his income ceased altogether. He was left with no recourse but charity – inadequate in the towns and non-existent in the country – or his own savings. Unfortunately (and this is the reason why this famine was so much worse than usual), the people had been in no position to save anything for a number of years.

The small family hoards had been swallowed up by the war. The raising of the old taxes and the imposition of new ones (including the militia), the demands of the new officers and the brutal exactions of excisemen and tax farmers, subsidies, both lawful and unlawful, to the troops who pillaged wherever they passed through or camped, monetary uncertainty, the general drop in exports, and hence in manufacturing and industrial labour, and from 1691 the threat of rising grain prices: all these were heaped on the backs of the limited adult population born between 1648 and 1663 and now overburdened with children, old people and by five years of wartime economy.

If it were possible to produce some scales in which to weigh the poverty and mourning which the common people of France endured at this period, it would be clear that at no time since the Fronde had there been more protracted, cruel and universal suffering.

The Great King's expressions of sorrow for 'his people' may well have been perfectly genuine, although in his fifty-fifth year such displays of sentiment were a little inappropriate, being both tardy and premature. His administrators made copious arrangements for the policing of markets, and for dealing with sharks, beggars and, sometimes, with prices (vague attempts were made in a number of places to prevent them rising), but none of these decrees seems to have been worth much more than the paper they were written on. Corn was brought from the Baltic to feed Paris, where rioting had broken out. It was intercepted by the Dutch, recaptured by Jean Bart and some of it, very little spoiled, arrived almost in time. In this state of affairs, there was nothing that private or official remedies could do.

But unfortunately the trouble spread to the State. From 1693 onwards, the receipts from all forms of taxation fell off sharply. No taxpayer on earth could get money out of the dead and dying. As we have seen, *tailles* and farmed taxes had to be brought down, the latest currency manipulations speeded up, capitation tax swiftly introduced and even, a most remarkable step, expenditure on the war cut down in the very midst of hostilities while at the same time serious negotiations got under way.

On a different plane, the great famine hastened the growth and establishment of an opposition, not the opposition maintained by the refugees in Holland and elsewhere, whose hostility was a matter of fact and whose arguments were now strengthened, but of a real opposition party at home. Already in 1694, Vauban spoke out and began work on his *Dixme Royalle*; in 1695, Boisguillebert published his *Détail de la France* which concentrated much more on the country's slow economic decline than on the recent famine but which none the less drew attention to the important problem of grain supplies and the absurdity of a system of taxation which exacerbated the sufferings of the countryside. The eloquent and often-quoted letter to the king, which probably dates from 1695, may well be attributable to Fénelon:

Your people, Sire, whom you should love as your children, and who up to this time have been so devoted to you, are dying of hunger. The land is left almost untended, towns and countryside are deserted, trade of all kinds falls off and can no longer support the workers: all commerce is at a standstill. ... For the sake of getting and keeping vain conquests abroad, you have destroyed half the real strength of your own state. Rather than take money from your poor people, you ought to feed and cherish them. . . . All France is now no more than one great hospital, desolate and unprovided. The magistrates are weary and degraded. The nobility, whose whole wealth is in decrees (that is, in the event of seizure) live only by letters patent. You are importuned by the murmurs of the crowd. And it is you, Sire, who have brought these troubles on yourself. ... The very people ... no longer rejoice in your conquests and victories, they are full of bitterness and despair. Little by little the fire of sedition catches everywhere. The people believe you have no pity for their sufferings, that you care only for your own power and glory. They say that if the king had a father's heart for his people, he would surely think his glory lay rather in giving them bread and a little respite after such tribulations than in keeping hold of a few frontier posts which are a cause of war ...

Much more than simply a portrait of the realm, this long, literary epistle bears witness to the birth of the opposition which was to crystallize with such insidious strength around the young Duc de Bourgogne and his advisers. All of Fénelon's objectives are there: an end to conquest, peace at any price, priority given to domestic rehabilitation, protection for the downtrodden old nobility and for the much-diminished *noblesse de robe*. This is du Marillac rehashed and given a more aristocratic turn – the pious, Spanish reformist movement which Richelieu had stamped out in 1630 for the next sixty-five years. Fénelon's friends were already gathering material, initiating the great inquiry of 1697–8 into the activities of the provincial intendants which was to capitalize France's exhaustion for political ends.

Over and above these by no means disinterested expressions of discontent, the great famine had an adverse effect on both the immediate and the more long-term future. In the immediate future, the dwindling numbers and capabilities of the taxpayers (at Beauvais, the number of householders paying the local equivalent of the *taille* dropped by more than a quarter from 3,310 in 1691 to 2,428 in 1695) compelled the state to practise severe restraint and, for a time at least, adapt its policies to its resources. In the long run, the famine resulted in further greatly reduced generations which were to upset the balance of age for a long time and pave the way for fresh difficulties in years to come.

The narrow margin by which the coalition had been opposed, the enormous cost of this long war, the drain on taxpayers, the delicate monetary position, the slump in trade, the poverty of the countryside, the sudden drop in population (two or three million, at least) the rise of an aristocratic and pacifist opposition (which was, as we shall see, Jansenist besides), the evident failure of the Revocation and of royal Gallicanism, the dearth of great generals, the losses to the army from deaths and desertion, the unpopularity of the militia, were all aggravated by the terrible famine still fresh in people's minds. The kingdom was in dire need of a long breathing space, a truce in every respect, to give it time to recuperate.

It was the king's and the country's ill-luck that the respite lasted less than five years.

12

THE RESPITE
(1697–1701)

HAVING negotiated so persistently and shown such good sense in his dealings, was Louis, now in his sixtieth year, at last about to silence the voice of glory and magnificence within him and listen instead to the promptings of that cautious instinct which was also a part of his inmost nature? Would he give his people and his exchequer their much-needed rest?

Besides the court, his buildings and religious control, all of which were still dear to him, his chosen field to which he clung from end to end of his reign and in which his own decisions were always paramount, remained that of foreign affairs, diplomacy and war, the sources of Greatness, Glory and Honour. The old king did not even wait for the final Treaty of Ryswick (with the emperor in October 1697) before turning his attention to the impending Spanish succession which was preoccupying every court in Europe. With the help of his diplomats, now under the direction of Colbert Torcy who had succeeded his father, Croissy, he plunged into subtle and cautious schemes which, he believed, while saving the honour of the fleur-de-lys and strengthening his frontiers, would avert the danger of another coalition which he knew the country was unable to support. Caution and subtlety gave the kingdom forty-two months of peace, plus a year of localized fighting. Would this respite be enough?

SIGNS OF RECOVERY

The conflict was over at last and the nation breathed a sigh of relief.

Three of the heaviest burdens which oppressed the countryside were lifted, one by one: the hated militia, the capitation tax and the army subsidies. In the *pays d'élections*, the *taille* which had risen again to 35 millions in 1695 fell to 32 and then to less than 31 in 1699. In the *pays d'États*, the *dons gratuits* fell by a tenth. The receipts from farmed taxes rose slightly, an indication that collection was improving as the country's sufferings lessened. After 1693, the face value of the gold and silver louis stayed fixed at 14 *livres* and 72 *sous*, and from 1697 to 1699 there was room for hope that there would be an end to currency manipulations. The excellent harvests of 1694 and 1695 put an end to high prices and famine and the price of grain soon dropped to the low pre-war levels. All over France it was a brilliant spring, gay with weddings that were quickly followed by christenings. Many families, freed from the burden of too many idle mouths – the aged who had succumbed in 1694 and children too young to work – rejoiced in a renewed prosperity, with bread at 6 *deniers* a pound, plenty of work and wages often somewhat higher since weavers and even labourers were in short supply. In the textile towns and districts, the looms clattered cheerfully once more as low prices, the drop in financial pressure and the reopening of the seas brought huge increases in demand. A sudden shortage due to the poor harvest of 1698 – although in some places the price of corn doubled or even tripled once again – fell far short of an economic or demographic disaster. The realm was even spared the epidemics of disease which struck so savagely in other parts of Europe. The credit for this apparent miracle, which was nonetheless not without exceptions, must go to the relief from taxes, the resistance of the surviving population and still more to the plentiful work available which stemmed from the peace and the resumption of commerce.

For these last years of the century saw an unexpectedly vigorous rebirth of trade, which had only been lying dormant, and of private seafaring ventures, to which piracy had been merely an alternative. In 1698 alone, twelve ships sailed from Saint-Malo bound for the West Indies, as many or more, that is, than in the six previous years. Forty-two put out from Nantes, three times as many as the year before. Put in terms of tonnage, sailings of Newfoundland fishing vessels reached, in 1699, the record figure of nearly 16,000 tons. With the return of peace, the traffic of this great port rose again to its pre-war level of over 80,000 tons, and before long had reached a new peak of prosperity. Last and most important was the triumphant introduction of a new traffic of unparalleled wealth and daring. The merchants of Saint-Malo, La Rochelle and one or two other places set their sights directly on Spanish America, Peru, Chile, the Pacific and China, by-passing the old intermediary of Cadiz. For the first time, to quote Charles Carrière, the merchants of Marseilles made for it *en masse*.

Daghlgren has described, in fine detail, the modest, even unhappy beginnings of this great enterprise with the unsuccessful expedition of Jean-Baptiste de Gennes in 1695 and the more encouraging one of Beauchesne who, setting out in 1698 and returning in 1701, was the first to sail through the Straits of Magellan and trade on the coast of Peru. The people of South America were immensely rich and eager for the luxury goods of France: it was a matter of carrying the merchandise and coming home laden with silver bars and *piastres*. The risks attendant on the voyage, from enemy pirates and the laws of Spain, were considerable, but the profits might run into hundreds of thousands of *livres*, or millions in pure silver. The inhabitants of Saint-Malo, La

Rochelle, Paris, Le Havre and elsewhere invested large sums in these ambitious ventures, with strong support from the Government. The few years from 1698 to 1701 saw the formation of no less than six new companies, for trade either with the South Seas or with China. By 1698, the greatest capitalists of the time were active in the first two companies. Jourdan of Paris and the redoubtable Danycan of Saint-Malo, the moving spirits, were soon joined by the Magons, Crozats, Begons and La Houssayes. To the old indirect markets reached via Cadiz and the direct and growing ones of the West Indies were now added the irresistible attractions of Peru and China. The Danycans and Magons were not the only ones to take advantage of them. At the turn of the century it was as though a wind from the ocean blew through the old kingdom, reviving its manufactures, reawakening and rejuvenating industry and the spirit of enterprise. In cities which had never looked beyond their own continent, names like the Indies, the South Seas and China rang with an almost magical promise. From Dunkirk to Saint-Malo, from Port-Louis to Bayonne and even in Marseilles, the way was being opened for the maritime splendours which were the keynote of the eighteenth century.

Even the king, who gave little thought to it at the time, was to draw such comfort from the 'returns' from America when he found himself once again at war, that tempting theories have sometimes been advanced to the effect that his decision in the grave matter of the acceptance of Charles II's will may have been dictated by commercial or maritime, in short, by economic motives. If Louis XIV was above such base considerations, some of his advisers, and in particular the secretary of state for the navy and the *contrôleur général* of finance, were certainly not.

EFFORTS TOWARDS RECOVERY

Now that peace had been made, the Government, while busily at work on the Spanish question, was reckoning on having several years to play with and even on avoiding a large-scale war altogether. But whether it had in mind the same kind of rehabilitation of the kingdom as Colbert a third of a century earlier, is difficult to say.

At all events, a number of measures directed towards financial, administrative and even religious reorganization were introduced during the last three years of the century.

The most pressing task was that of stabilizing the enormous national debt which amounted to over three millions. The peace and the leap forward taken by trade and manufacturing had re-established a degree of confidence which made it easier for the king to find money. By the end of 1697 bonds – *rentes* – were being offered, and taken up at 5·5 per cent and in 1698 and 1699 it was possible to bring the rate down to 5 per cent. The second were used to repay the first, just as the first had been used to repay bonds previously offered at 7·14 and 8·33 per cent which had been necessitated by the rigours of the war. In short, by a systematic series of conversions which to the *rentiers* could have looked like swindles – the burden of the debt was brought down considerably.

Meanwhile the most recent monetary scheme in 1693 produced another million and a half and succeeded in laying the groundwork for future currency manipulations. This strategy involved an arbitrary modification of the value of circulating currency without a corresponding change in their metallic backing. For example, in the course of 1700, the Government lowered the value of the *louis d'argent* from 72 to 71, then to 70 *sols*. The following year, in a cunning reversal of policy, it brusquely re-evaluated the *louis* at 76 *sols*. This last operation was what we would call a devaluation. Subtle manoeuvres such as these resulted in a relative return to order.

To achieve a real cure would have needed both more time and more courage. The 'extraordinary measures' continued, though in a more moderate form, as did the practice of anticipating revenues. In 1699, his last year as finance minister, Pontchartrain got through 25 millions of the revenues to come in 1700 and 1701. A fresh campaign against abuses was initiated as a sop to public opinion and some twenty millions, or about a fifth of 'rebates' granted by the king during the late war, were recovered from the least shrewd of the tax farmers. But as another war hove in sight, the rigours of the law abated and the tax farmers were able to recoup themselves.

Some of the quantities of offices for sale were not without their uses. Between 1693 and 1703, the gradual institution of controls on legal contracts and of a one per cent levy on all transfers, exchanges, gifts and certain inheritances, while certainly fiscal in origin, constituted the basic charter for the grasping paw of the Registry Office. This was all very annoying to begin with, but its utility was beyond question. During the same period, although there were a number of absurd innovations, the Parisian appointment of a lieutenant of police was extended to the majority of cities (from the end of 1698 to 1699). Seigneurs, local magistrates and members of certain established officer companies squabbled over this important post which carried with it the control of supplies, markets, trades, wages and prices and a large section of the economic life of the community, as well as of its moral attitudes. An Order in Council of 1700 laid down the principal of a new and really universal contribution to pay for the upkeep of a schoolmaster and a schoolmistress for every parish. This, if not purely fiscal, was a laudable step and the more enlightened provinces, such as the Île-de-France, began to put it into practice, but with the coming of war it was quickly forgotten.

A more studied and lasting move, more characteristic of a certain kind of economic revival, was the reintroduction of the Trade Council which had been set up by Colbert and then allowed to drop. It held its first session in the very month of the acceptance of Charles II's will and the date is extremely significant. More so still, is the composition of the council. It comprised, apart from the two initiators, Chamillart and Pontchartrain the younger and a few major colleagues such as Daguesseau and, shortly afterwards, Amelot, twelve great merchants representing the chief commercial cities of the realm which were gradually acquiring chambers of commerce. The seven great Atlantic ports and Marseilles sent powerful merchants – such men as Piécourt of Dunkirk, Mesnager of Rouen and Des Casaux of Nantes – who talked of economic freedom and of treaties with the maritime powers. Through them, Spanish and American maritime interests penetrated to the heart of the government, together with the demand for a freedom of the seas which was the offspring of renewed or anticipated commercial prosperity. Besides their own interests, the 'trade deputies' also served those of the king who employed them on a number of occasions as secret negotiators and later as accredited envoys. This too was an early pointer to the Atlantic trade of the eighteenth century. Ultimately, however, the Trade Council was a purely advisory body.

These scattered moves, which were not always entirely disinterested or truly indispensable, can scarcely be described as forming part of a conscious and deliberate reform. Had the Duc de Beauvillier anything else in mind beyond the education of the Duc de Bourgogne when, with the approval of the Council, he embarked on his great inquiry into the conduct of the intendants, in 1697–8, which was to provide food for so many publications, recriminations and plans for reform, and to afford so much ready-made material for the historian? In all probability, Beauvillier, Fénelon and the rest of the young duke's entourage, all of whom were aristocrats and *dévots*, were seriously in pursuit of information with a view to real action. But the reforming party was unable to do anything definite.

What the great inquiry did do, however, was to throw fresh light on the Protestant problem revealing the Revocation as both iniquitous and ineffectual and setting in motion a kind of general discussion directed both at the intendants and the bishops, which lasted throughout 1698. Many, especially in the Midi where the rumblings of Huguenot rebellion had been heard more than once during the war, were in favour of continued severity: *dragonnades*, compulsory attendance at mass, the abduction of children and Huguenot dead dragged away on hurdles and left to rot with the carcases of animals. The advocates of gentler measures, Bossuet, Noailles, Daguesseau, Pontchartrain and a great many intendants, called for purely spiritual action, without any obligation for stubborn Huguenots to attend mass. A royal declaration at the end of that year, which was followed by an explanatory letter at the beginning of 1699, recommended strict principles while forbidding the use of force in their application. At the same time, this interesting document begins with an exhortation to the clergy and the faithful to set the example and accepts the possibility of the continued existence of the 'so-called reformed religion' in a wholly Catholic France. Without actually saying so the royal declaration implied an admission of partial failure and seemed to hold out hope of a more liberal regime: 'His Majesty wishes no constraint to be employed.' It remained to put this into practice. The Camisard revolt was soon to illustrate the difficulties of this.

For all its vague leanings towards balance, pacification, appeasement, financial recovery and general improvement, the Government was unable to dissociate itself from the difficulties and mental attitudes of its time. Conservative, devout and middle-aged, like its king, it became hopelessly involved in religious disputes, struggled unsuccessfully to free itself from its wartime debts and waited eagerly for the corpse that would allow it to annex a part of Spain. This last was the great political concern.

THE AFFAIR OF THE SPANISH SUCCESSION

While the court, city and country were once more passionately involved in all those current affairs which we have invented 'isms' to define – quietism, Molinism, the new Jansenism and various complicated forms of Gallicanism – matters on which the priest-king also had his say, the only really important affair, the only one worthy of the Master, was that of the Spanish succession.

Charles II, King of Spain, the deplorable heir to a degenerate line, incapable of getting children, doomed from infancy, appeared in September 1697 to be on the point of death. He dragged on for another three years, giving the diplomats time to display their ingenuity. There were ten kings or princes with a claim to the Spanish throne. Only two were serious claimants: Louis XIV, as the husband and son of elder infantas and the Emperor Leopold, as the husband and son of younger infantas. The former claimed release from the renunciation clause of the Treaty of the Pyrenees on the grounds that the queen's dowry, on which it was conditional, had never been paid and his candidate for the throne was naturally his son, the Dauphin. Leopold claimed it for one of his grandsons, the Prince-Elector of Bavaria but his claim was for the whole Spanish inheritance, including the Netherlands, Italy and the Indies. Louis, much more moderate for once, claimed only a slice of the cake, close to his own frontiers if possible or else one that

would be easy to exchange: a sizable chunk of the Netherlands was tempting or, failing that, by a complicated piece
of bartering, Lorraine, Savoy and Nice.

Since the emperor's opposition was a foregone conclusion
Louis set his diplomats to work to win over the Grand Pensioner of Holland, Heinsius, and even his inveterate enemy,
William III, while at the same time maintaining troops
under arms on all his frontiers. Neither could bear to see a
German Habsburg in Madrid, Cadiz, Anvers, Naples or,
above all, in the Indies. A year was enough to produce the
first, premature, plan for a partition. The dauphin would
be satisfied with Naples, Sicily and part of the Spanish
Netherlands, all good exchange currency; the remaining
Spanish possessions in Italy would go to a son of the Emperor Leopold by a second marriage, Charles, and all the
rest to the young prince-elector. When the latter then died,
a second plan had to be formed which was adopted by the
three robbers in March 1700. The Dauphin would be satisfied with the Milanais, a splendid bargaining point, and the
Archduke Charles would keep the rest. This admirable
piece of moderation, in which England and Holland did
their best to believe, broke up the grand alliance of 1689–97
and left the emperor no chance in a conflict of arms. Quite
understandably the French, from 1697 to 1700, were able to
indulge in hopes of peace and go back to work regarding the
future with a certain amount of optimism while they turned
their minds to reforms at home.

But this was reckoning without the Spaniards themselves
who were the persons chiefly concerned in the premature
dismemberment. At the court of Madrid, a Spanish
nationalist party was formed which opposed any form of
partition, preached the integrity of the empire and, out of
pure dislike of the arrogant Austrian queen, turned instead
to the French who were well-represented at the court of
Charles II. The future was to show that this court coterie

met with strong support in deepest Castille. The party besieged the dying king and succeeded in wringing from him,
in October 1700, an unequivocal testament which remained
secret until the king's death on 1 November. Known in
Paris eight days later, its effect was that of a thunderclap.
The King of Spain insisted that the integral unity of his
domains, possessions and empire was to be preserved and to
this end rejected all idea of partition. Secondly, he named as
his heir Louis XIV's second grandson, the Duc d'Anjou, on
condition that he formally renounced all claim to the throne
of France. Should he refuse to do so, his younger brother,
the Duc de Berry, became heir on the same conditions. Failing these two, the Archduke Charles was to succeed.

Louis XIV and his council – the Dauphin, Pontchartrain,
the chancellor, the *contrôleur-général* and secretary of state
for war, Chamillart, Torcy and Beauvillier – held long
deliberations at Fontainebleau on 9 and 10 November. Their
problem was whether to reject the will and stick to the partition treaty of 1700 or whether to accept the will and, by so
doing, violate the treaty. In either case, war with the emperor was inevitable. In the first this was likely to be with
the support of England and Holland, in the second, the two
maritime powers would be hostile. But in the event of the
first, the war would be against the Spanish provinces, legally
occupied by the imperial forces, whereas in the event of the
second, the Spanish territories, occupied by the French,
would be useful bases and the support of the Spaniards and
their arms might be far from negligible. Last but by no
means least, the ultimate argument to a vainglorious sexa-
generian and a king brought up on the anti-Habsburg traditions of the house of Bourbon, it was unthinkable that there
should be a Habsburg ruling to the north, east and south of
the kingdom, and in the Indies, with the constant threat of
a revival of the Empire of Charles V. It was grand and
honourable that a son of France should seat himself on that

throne which, so often in the course of two centuries, had given the monarchy of the Lilies cause to tremble. After earnest consultation with his council, Louis XIV decided to accept the will.

This epoch-making decision has let loose a flood of more or less historical writings. Some, following Michelet, blame the old king, others roundly praise his sense of honour, patriotism and political genius, the rest argue endlessly. From the economic angle, it was certainly the best decision: what could be better than a French ruler for Cadiz and the whole of the Spanish Indies! The members of the newly reconstructed Trade Council, great administrators and great merchants, were well aware of this, and the Dutch and the English even more so, but Louis, as we have seen, had never cared much for administrative details. From a military point of view, his decision might perhaps have been worse and diplomatically all may not have been lost, as subsequent events seemed to show since Amsterdam and London appeared initially to accept the situation. As far as the strengthening of his frontiers and the glory of his house, in other words of France, were concerned, the king's choice was not merely the best but the only one he could have made, given his fundamental character. The only trouble was that the weary nation and its strained finances had not yet had time to recover. The respite had been too short.

However, war was not yet inevitable, or at least not a large-scale war. True, fighting broke out in the Milanais in spring 1701 between Franco-Spanish troops, assisted (with circumspection) by those of Savoy, and the imperial forces under the able leadership of Prince Eugène. The European coalition did not go into action against the combined forces of France and Spain until 15 May 1702. This was because, in England as in the United Provinces, powerful forces were at work for peace which acted as an effective brake to William's rancour and to the hostility of the Grand Pensioner, Heinsius. In Spain, the young monarch made a spectacular entry, being received with enthusiasm not only by the court and the notables but also by the common people. Louis XIV's first two attempts at intimidation did not even meet with any immediately hostile response.

By February 1701, in flat contradiction to his previous pledges and of the will of Charles II, he was maintaining all Philip V's rights to the French throne and having this high-handed gesture solemnly ratified by Parliament. Admittedly, the grand Dauphin and the Duc de Bourgogne still stood between Philip V and the throne and no one could foresee that both would die prematurely. Even so, this first act of bravado antagonized Europe. A second, and possibly graver one, followed almost at once. Anticipating the arrival of Spanish garrisons, French troops marched into the Netherlands and took prisoner the Dutch soldiers of the barrier forts in clear violation of the Treaty of Ryswick. The States-General protested strongly but, while insisting that this was a purely temporary measure, the old king refused to give the Dutch the least satisfaction.

The result was that Heinsius strengthened his ties with Denmark (to the tune of 12,000 men in return for 300,000 *écus* in January 1701) and embarked on energetic negotiations in Europe. Louis XIV, for his part, in addition to his Sardinian alliance, could count on the support of the Elector of Bavaria, Max-Emmanuel, governor of Cologne and Prince-Bishop of Liège. In June, in return for certain subsidies and the promise of further territories in Brazil, he obtained the neutrality, geographically so important, of the king of Portugal. The emperor was also issuing a call to arms to the German princes: the Elector of Hanover, the Elector of Brandenburg, whom he made King of Prussia at the end of 1700, and a host of vassals. Both sides were making preparations.

Even then, early in 1701, in the face of opposition from financial and commercial circles and from their various assemblies, King William and the Grand Pensionary recognized Philip V. This constituted an act of provisional neutrality in the Franco-Imperial conflict. Would it have been possible, by the exercise of great wisdom and diplomacy, to strengthen this neutrality? It is all too doubtful. William was manoeuvring constantly to push his Parliament, his merchants and his people into war. Once again, Louis XIV came most effectively to his aid.

He did so first by refusing to make any major concessions over the Spanish Netherlands which the French army was now proceeding to fortify as though for an indefinite stay. These tactics added British indignation to the resentment of the Dutch and both mounted in concert throughout the summer of 1701.

In the second place, Louis was all too obviously ruling Spain through the puppet King Philip V: Spanish armies were commanded from Versailles, the French fleet cruising off the coast of Spain, the Spanish king and queen were surrounded by French advisers and, above all, there were signs of an incipient commercial merger between the two countries.

Quite apart from the persistent enmity of William and Heinsius, there seems little doubt that what decided the bankers, shipowners, merchants and seafarers upon whom the war ultimately depended was the economic factor. The French merchants were making the most of the gift of Spanish and American markets, of Mexican and Peruvian silver, which had been handed to them. French fleets cruised in American waters and merchantmen from the Atlantic ports, Dunkirk, Le Havre, Rouen, Saint-Malo, Nantes, La Rochelle and Bordeaux, embarked on a peaceful invasion of the harbours of the Iberian peninsula and the Indies. The hearts of merchants and manufacturers in Picardy, Normandy and Laval beat high with expectation as they congratulated themselves on the vast markets which were opening, ever wider and more accessible, to their linen and woollen cloth and other goods. Then, in September 1701, came the ultimate triumph and the ultimate peril, when the King of Spain granted the *asiento* to a French company, one in which both he and Louis XIV had an interest.

The *asiento* was, of course, a monopoly in the supply of Negro slaves to the Spanish colonies, and this much-disputed and highly profitable monopoly had previously belonged to the Dutch. The English, too, had a considerable interest in it. George Scelle in a monumental and too often neglected work (it was published in 1906) has analysed in detail the way in which the French cleverly penetrated the business of a Portuguese shipping company, the Cacheu Company (1696–1701) which also held the *asiento* for a time, and the careful preparations which were made from the moment Philip V was proclaimed, and possibly even before, by the Duc d'Harcourt and Pontchartrain the younger (as skilful in this as in all else he undertook). The long and the short of it was that for ten years the monopoly of providing the vital black labourers for the Indies passed to the French Guinea Company in which, as well as the two monarchs, the greatest capitalists of the time, chief among them Crozat, Legendre and Bernard, were involved.

This triumph was more than the English and Dutch merchants (the latter of whose part in the business has been greatly under-estimated in historical tradition) could stand. The signature of the *asiento* was followed only a few days later by the Grand Alliance of the Hague.

At the Hague, the emperor and the maritime powers came together strongly and gave Louis XIV two months to come to terms. If not, it would be war, the aims of which would be the undoing of the Spanish succession, to close the Netherlands to the French, to gain control of Italy and the Mediterranean and to give the allies an entry into the Spanish colonies and at the same time to keep French trade out (7 September 1701). Nine days later, the death of the exiled King of England, James II, gave Louis XIV the chance to send back a characteristic answer. Disregarding the advice of his council, he yielded to the persuasions of his second wife and of the *dévots* at his court and took the audacious step of recognizing the dead man's son as James III, King of England.

To be sure, he was careful to distinguish between William, the 'actual' and James, the 'rightful' king. The time for petty irritations was past. The English people, profoundly anti-Catholic and weary of the Stuarts, howled with fury. Parliament, which had just finished settling the order of succession to the crown among the Protestant princes and whom William now twisted round his little finger, took instant offence and voted all the subsidies required for the war. Louis XIV had succeeded in raising a veritable storm of national feeling in England. Strengthening and uniting his adversaries was undoubtedly one of his greatest talents.

Now war was inevitable on both fronts, French and Spanish. Even the death of William III, in March 1702, did nothing to delay it. The three allies of The Hague declared war on one day, 15 May 1702.

The third coalition had begun.

13

THE LAST COALITION

(1702–14)

W H I L E the epic story of the young King of Sweden, Charles XII, who at one moment (in 1706) emerged as a formidable arbiter of Europe only to plunge, the following year, into the vastness of Russia, was unfolding to the north and east, a third coalition was moving against Louis XIV now, for the first time, allied to the King of Spain, his own grandson.

For Louis, as for his enemies, the stakes were very high. Every question was coming to a head at once.

There was the question of monarchical prestige. To whom would fall the honour of seating a child in Madrid, at the heart of that empire 'where the sun never sets', to Habsburg or to Bourbon? Who would gain control of Italy: Leopold, Louis or Victor Amadeus? The emperor had overcome the Turks, but could he overcome the jealous or refractory vassals within his empire? Could the Most Christian King and his Stuart protégé shake the Protestant, parliamentary realm of William and afterwards of Anne?

There were the never-ending frontier questions. Would Louis succeed in pushing his borders into the Netherlands, despite the English and the Dutch, and into Lorraine and the Rhineland, despite the emperor and the Empire, or into the Alps?

There were the comparatively recent questions of mastery of the seas. Would the still flourishing Dutch navy and the young and victorious English one be content to let the French, already so strongly entrenched in Dunkirk, go on to gain control of the North Sea, through Ostend and Anvers? Would they leave them a free hand from Gibraltar to Naples and in the islands of the western Mediterranean which, until recently part Spanish and part Genoese and still partly in the hands of Barbary pirates, would one day be British? Would they let them sail their galleons across the ocean bringing back the fabulous metal of the Americas, and thrust with impunity into the ports of China and Peru?

Far beyond all question of honour, dynasties, frontiers, and flags, the immense market of Spanish America was, for the English, but for only a handful of Frenchmen, the ultimate stake. The provision of fabrics and slaves to the Castilian Indies weighed as heavily on these twelve years of war as any considerations of prestige.

But for the old Bourbon king it was, first and foremost, a matter of defending his own house, and to this end he spared neither himself nor his people. The struggle was to be a hard one.

DEFENCE MEASURES

Confronted with Prince Eugène in the Milanais in 1701, the forces of France, Spain and Sardinia had not acquitted themselves spectacularly well. The future, however, was to bring more than mere local skirmishes. Now what was involved was the defence of the entire country, from Gibraltar to the Scheldt and from Lisbon to Naples, as well as two overseas empires and America in particular. But the old king had mustered his forces coolly and neither the extended fronts by land and sea, nor the military and financial strength of the allies could discourage him.

Diplomatically speaking, he had four valuable allies. In between Holland and the Empire, covering the Netherlands, the twofold bishoprics of Cologne and Liège offered him military bases and points of departure. In the heart of the Empire and cornering the Habsburg states, Bavaria could engage the imperial armies and protect Alsace and the Rhine. The alliance with Savoy guaranteed the easy crossing of the Alps and helped to keep one enemy army occupied in Italy while at the same time lending some, admittedly rather lukewarm, assistance in the defence of the Spanish Milanais. Portugal, another ally, had promised to close her harbours to the coalition and open them to the French and Spanish, thus forestalling any invasion of the Iberian peninsula from the west. For a while, these four allies were to save both kingdoms from invasion.

As far as generals were concerned, in spite of the rise of a generation of commanders who were mediocre or worse, selected by the king himself, there still remained of the old guard the marquis de Chamlay, the king's chief adviser and the real commander-in-chief, and the indefatigable Vauban, whose usefulness was greater than ever until his untimely death after falling shamefully into disfavour on account of his excessive bluntness and intelligence. Catinat fell off a good deal and soon left the scene. Villar's real gifts were marred by his unpleasant character and outrageous vanity. Vendôme, when not wallowing in idleness and debaucheries, had flashes of genius, and Berwick, the bastard son of James II, shone only by comparison with Tallard, Marcin and Villeroy. Unfortunately, for all these, it so happened that the other side possessed two great captains in Eugène of Savoy and John Churchill, soon to be Duke of Marlborough, both of whom shared an equal aptitude for politics and diplomacy. In the former this may have been inherited (he was a descendant of the Mazarini), in the latter it was due to his own innate genius joined to that of his wife, the domineering friend of that most English Queen Anne. The third member of this triumvirate, the indefatigable and unbending Heinsius, worked tirelessly at coordinating their various moves and interests. There was no one in

France to match these men. For once, the genius was all on the other side.

In the matter of armies, Louis had taken rigorous action at a very early stage. Even by 1698 entire regiments had been reformed, rearmed, given fresh training and encamped on his borders. Vauban was continually on the move from one stronghold to the next, visiting Flanders and Savoy, Brest and Toulon. Up-to-date weapons were introduced: muskets became general by 1701 and fixed bayonets by 1703, while the artillery was given a new look by Surirey de Saint-Rémy along lines laid down by the Duc de Luxembourg. Most important of all was the immense recruiting campaign which was undertaken and continued in order to cover the vast fronts involved. According to earlier, accurate studies by Georges Girard of material recently re-examined by A. Corvisier, recruitment, whether voluntary or by conscription, impressing and the militia accounted for 220,000 men in the king's service in January 1702, and perhaps 300,000 in the following year. No such host had ever been raised in any European kingdom before. At one time, indeed, the king contemplated some kind of mixture of old soldiers with young recruits but later abandoned it, leaving to the Revolution the honour and the benefits of such a move. There can be no doubt that these multitudes of troops must have been recruited under the worst possible conditions, by press-gangs and the enrolment of beggars, vagabonds and convicts, by the abduction of young men and the selection by lot of militiamen, initially from among the unmarried alone (hence a disturbing spate of marriages) and later from among all those below the age of thirty. They were prone to disband at the slightest provocation and to desert still more readily. From this time on the forces of law were kept constantly busy hunting down renegades. Ill-clad, ill-fed and irregularly paid, the troops regarded plunder as one of their natural prerogatives. Even so, their numbers, their superior arms and the influence of a few hundred veteran officers and two or three fine generals gave them, at times, a certain formidable quality, the more so in that the opposing forces, while better led and better supplied, were largely made up of mercenary regiments of a dozen different nationalities which rendered effective coordination very difficult since those of each nation naturally tended towards their own interests.

The navy was, to all appearances, in an even worse state. The two succeeding ministers, Pontchartrain father and son, were, however, men of initiative and industry. Moreover, they had under them some fine admirals, such as Chateaurenault and Ducasse. What they chiefly lacked was ships. In 1702, the king's navy consisted of barely a hundred ships of the line, including galleys, and their task was an enormous one, given the length of coastline they had to defend. Even with the antiquated Spanish galleons, the Bourbon navy cannot, in terms of tonnage, have amounted to half that of the enemy. But there remained the pirates, a great many of them formidable fighters and famous since the last war. Conscientiously stripped of the romantic finery in which schoolboys' adventures and popular imagery have decked them, the French pirates emerge as merchant privateers from the great ports who armed their own vessels, with the king's consent, in order to protect their trade with Spain, the West Indies, India and the South Seas. It so happened that the interests of these commercial knights errant coincided with those of the king who was consequently prepared to wink at their acts of piracy, contraband and even at their trading with the enemy. The privateers' help was very useful to the king's navy in a great many ways, and saved the king himself from disaster on more than one occasion.

Some kind of economic mobilization of the country was necessary to meet what was obviously going to be a long, hard war. No one in those days had any real idea of what a wartime economy should mean: the national convention was the first really to work out the rules, conditions and disciplines involved. All they knew was that it was an expensive business and that the *contrôleur-général*'s job was simply to find the money by whatever means. Pontchartrain's successor, Chamillart, has acquired a pitiable reputation and one which he owes in part to Saint-Simon. For once that indefatigable scandalmonger was not mistaken in the object of his spite. He was said to have owed his position to his mediocrity and a talent for billiards, since the king could no longer tolerate any but flatterers or weaklings whom he could more readily dominate. The honesty, modesty and strict piety (which endeared him to Maintenon) of the new Maître Jacques (Chamillart was handed the combined offices of war and finance) are beside the point: these qualities were not enough when what was wanted in the face of a coalition without precedent was a man who would be both Louvois and Colbert to the exhausted realm. Would any others have done better? It is hard to say. What can be s id is that he gave himself unsparingly and resignedly to his task, while his successor carried it out with unblushing cynicism. Still, he did scrape up the resources for the war, and if he drained the country dry in doing so, no one ever asked him to spare it. Louis XIV, like so many others, had never regarded the happiness of the people as one of the objects of government.

By 1701, expenditure on the army had leaped from 56 to 97 millions, while the king did not abate himself of a single *écu* spent on maintaining his mistresses, his building works (on Marly in particular), his pleasures and his 'petty cash'. Chamillart resorted to the good old ways of filling the coffers. The *taille* rose by 15 per cent in two years. A decree of 12 March 1701 reintroduced the capitation tax, ostensibly for no longer than the duration of the war and six months after.

It even stated that this would avert the necessity for 'extra-ordinary measures', although this was more than anyone could really believe. The level of the capitation tax very soon went up by a third. A certain imaginativeness early manifested itself in matters of taxation. In 1700, the time-honoured idea of a 'royal lottery' was revived but brought in no more than five millions owing to the state's decision to distribute the prizes mainly in bonds which the public had some reason to distrust. In 1701, a tax was put on, among other things, card playing. The hated militia, revived again after four years, was as much a levy of money as of men. A 'pursuit of tax farmers' was got up, purely as a political stunt to occupy the public attention: the tax farmers who during the last war had made 107 millions, by perfectly legal means (and no doubt a few more on the side), were made temporarily to disgorge a twentieth of it, although they recovered it all again in the following year. At the end of 1702, there was a straightforward rise in the price of salt, from three to five *livres* per *minot*. Naturally, sales dropped at once and the black market flourished as never before. In 1703, duties payable on legal contracts, such as the one per cent, and a score of others were introduced or extended.

But even this was not enough. As early as 1701, the usual bonds, new offices, and tax exemptions were being created, sold, abolished, recreated and sold afresh. A little later it actually occurred to someone to revoke recent letters of nobility and make the new nobles pay for their titles all over again. There was a spate of new currency manipulations. A fresh 'augmentation' (read: devaluation) of two *louis* was carried out in 1701, preceded as usual by progressive 'reduc-tions' (read: upward revaluation). The so-called 'new mint-ing' of coins by which it was accompanied is said to have yielded some 30 millions for the benefit of the state. In the same year, there was a slight drop in the bi-metallic ratio (from 15.6 to 15.4) which led to a rush of gold from the country. Two quite sensible innovations made at the same time as the great overhaul of the coinage were the introduction of paper money and the *Caisse des Emprunts*.

In its original form, the first could do nothing but good. As in 1693, the notes were simply receipts corresponding in value to the gold coins returned to the Mint for melting down and which were then redeemable in coins of the new minting. In October 1701, it was laid down that notes which had not yet been redeemed should carry interest at the rate of 4 per cent. In 1703, the rate of interest was raised to 8 per cent, by which time notes to the value of more than 6 millions were circulating at par, chiefly in Paris. The experiment in paper money was working quite well and Chamillart pledged that all bills would be repaid in coin by 1704. If the war had ended in that year, there would have been no doubt in anyone's mind about the advantages of paper money. Unfortunately the war did not end.

The *Caisse des Emprunts* was a revival of an idea of Colbert's. Its resuscitation dates from 11 March 1702, in other words from before the coalition declared war. Private deposits carried 8 per cent interest – which was high, perhaps even too high – and were now repayable not at will but after a fixed term, in coin. The system functioned perfectly well until August 1704 but as the war dragged on with increasing lack of success, so this too suffered.

At the same time, currency manipulations also took a dangerous turn. There had already been one further devaluation, in May, when the two *louis* went to 15·4 *livres* which was really no more than an extension of existing practice. But in 1703, Louis authorized Chamillart to coin what can only be described as counterfeit money: so-called ten *sou* pieces which contained only six *sous* and three *deniers'* worth of metal. The bad money drove out the good and prophesied the worst.

These wartime measures, in the right proportions, were reasonably well adapted to the failing resources of the kingdom, the strength of the allies and the greatness of the stakes, and would have been enough if the fighting had gone on for no more than two or at most three years. Only on this condition could the king, the State and the mass of the population have borne the burden of the war without giving way.

But it was clear, in the last days of 1703, that the war was likely to be a very long and painful one.

MILITARY SETBACKS (1702–8)

Nonetheless, the struggle had begun well enough. The dilatoriness and internal divisions of the coalition, the speed and preparedness of the French armies and the geographical and strategical support of her four allies may explain these early successes.

It was true that on the northern front, the French and Spanish forces had been compelled to abandon the Electorate of Cologne, Guelderland and Limburg which were awkwardly placed in the midst of enemy territories, but they had entrenched themselves solidly in Brabant while their adversaries argued amongst themselves over tactics and the conquered towns. The French, having made minor sacrifices, were established in good defensive positions. In the east, Catinat lost Landau but Tallard recovered it without difficulty when his adversary of Baden departed for Bavaria, where in this allied duchy Max-Emmanuel was putting up a spirited defence aided by Villars who won two brilliant victories at Friedlingen (October 1702) and Hochstadt (September 1703). But Villars, having quarrelled with everyone, even Chamillart, demanded to be recalled and was sent instead to kill Frenchmen in the Cevennes where the revolt of the Camisards was keeping too many regiments immobilized for too long.* In Italy, Vendôme and Eugène were locked in a fight to the death. They were well-matched. In 1703, while Eugène was occupied elsewhere, Vendôme advanced as far as Trent but was soon forced to retire on account of the defection of Victor Amadeus.

The Anglo-Dutch forces made two unsuccessful attempts to invade Spain and the Indies, one at Cadiz, the other at Cartagena. The French admiral Ducasse successfully defended the first and the Spaniards themselves the second (August–September 1702). In revenge, the coalition fell upon the Spanish galleons and the French fleet convoying them and drove them to seek a poor refuge in Vigo. A number of vessels were sunk or captured and four millions in gold and silver lost, but over thirty millions were saved. All in all, France and Spain put up an effective resistance and no one could imagine that either of the two kingdoms might one day be threatened with invasion.

The defection of the two Latin allies abruptly shattered this comforting illusion. Victor Amadeus, even though he was father-in-law to two sons of France and gorged with subsidies, had never ceased negotiating with the emperor who was, for the time being, his enemy but who promised a great deal more than Louis XIV. Victor Amadeus changed sides in November 1703 with the result that the French army in Italy was now obliged not only to try and defend the Milanais but also to win back Piedmont, if only to guarantee its own line of retreat. Vendôme lost time and in January 1704 the imperial and Piedmontese forces effected an ominous junction. Vendôme redeemed his mistake by holding out for two years on a double front in the plain of the Po and actually took most of the towns of Piedmont

---

*A lively and perceptive account of the peasant religious revolt of the Camisards (1702–10) can be found in Le Roy-Ladurie's recent, admirable *Histoire du Languedoc* (coll. *Que Sais-je?* 1962) pp. 81–7 and also in the same author's *Paysans de Languedoc* (1966) pp. 605–29.

with the exception of Turin. But in August 1705 he was recalled to serve elsewhere and the French army was left at the mercy of incompetent commanders. Disaster was imminent.

The French were betrayed by their Portuguese ally at the same time as by Piedmont. In 1703, two treaties gave the coalition's shipping, trade and troops the entry into Portugal. In return for naval protection, the promise of some annexations in Spain and America and massive imports of port wine for the thirsty English, the king, Don Pedro, pledged his army, his ports and his goodwill. From this time on, Portugal became an economic satellite of England but the immediate effect was to endanger the young Philip V, especially since all the members of the coalition recognized the archduke Charles as king of Spain. All that remained was for Charles to conquer his kingdom. To guard against this danger, Louis XIV sent Berwick with 12,000 men to Spain, to invade Portugal, and at the same time the Toulon fleet patrolled the Spanish coast. Until August 1704, these precautions were enough, but after this matters deteriorated rapidly. In this sector, also, disaster threatened.

The first real defeat occurred elsewhere. At Blenheim, not far from Hochstadt, in August 1704, the French and Bavarians under Marcin and Tallard were routed by the greatly superior armies, both numerically and in generalship, of Marlborough and Prince Eugène. Thirty thousand men were slaughtered, captured or scattered hopelessly. Old-established regiments tore up and buried their standards before surrendering. Versailles was horror-struck and no one dared to tell the old king the news. Bavaria was lost and the remnants of the army fell back towards Alsace, with the victors in pursuit. The enemy crossed the Rhine at the beginning of September but wasted time recapturing Landau, against the advice of Marlborough who was anxious to press on into Lorraine. One foreign theatre of war had been abandoned and a threat of invasion from the east appeared so pressing that Louis dispatched Villars hastily from the Cevennes to the Moselle. The coalition failed to take advantage of the opportunity and marked time throughout 1705. But by then they had won further victories on other fronts.

In the very month of Blenheim, an English fleet captured Gibraltar, practically unopposed. The French fleet out of Toulon sailed out to blockade the fortress which had been heavily garrisoned by its conquerors, but despite some gallant feats of arms, it failed. Some ships were captured and the rest sunk. By the beginning of 1705, the mastery of the Mediterranean had passed into the hands of the British who proceeded coolly to convey the Archduke Charles to the Catalan coast. All Catalonia declared for him for the simple reason that Castille was against him. By the end of the year, Charles III was acknowledged also as King of Valencia and Murcia and had taken from Philip V all the richer, Mediterranean part of Spain. Taking advantage of dissension among the members of the coalition, Louis XIV bravely embarked on negotiations for a peace but Marlborough, in a general tour of Europe, succeeded in reconciling everyone and even in finding money for the emperor.

This was not the end of Louis' troubles. 1706 was a very bad year for him. Villeroy lost the Netherlands, having by his own stupidity allowed Marlborough, who was quick to take advantage of any slip, to defeat him at Ramillies. With the French and the Spaniards out of the way, the states of Flanders recognized Charles III as king. Vauban hastily set about organizing the defence of Dunkirk. The English general, however, aimed further east, took Courtrai and Menin and had crossed the border with the intention of laying siege to Lille when he found his way suddenly barred by Vendôme. The northern ramparts of the kingdom had fallen and a second invasion route lay wide open to the coalition.

In the south, things were going badly. Marcin and La Feuillade were defeated outside Turin by Prince Eugène and Victor Amadeus in September 1706. North Italy was lost. In return for ceding a few positions which he still held in the Milanais (March 1707), Louis XIV was permitted by the emperor to make an honourable withdrawal. A few months later he decided to abandon Naples and Sicily as indefensible. Little by little, Charles III was gaining possession of his kingdom, while the frontiers of the Alps and Provence were now menaced in their turn.

Even in Spain, the situation seemed to hang on the edge of disaster. Philip V and a squadron of French ships failed miserably at the siege of Barcelona. An enemy army under the command of a French Protestant refugee from England, Ruvigny – later Lord Galway – advanced from Portugal, brushed aside Berwick and entered Madrid in June 1706. Philip V did not give up. Forty days later he re-entered Madrid with an army of militiamen, volunteers, guerrillas and unofficial desperadoes who specialized in assassinating foreign mercenaries in the very heart of the city. Berwick succeeded in recapturing Cartagena but the English entrenched themselves firmly in the Balearics. At the end of 1706, Louis was searching everywhere for an opening for negotiations, appealing now for mediation by the Pope, now to Charles XII, carrying on four separate intrigues in Holland and doing his utmost to win back the Duke of Savoy. But all these attempts were premature and came to nothing, rejected by the coalition, made greedy now by victory.

The year 1707 was not unduly catastrophic. Villars made a spectacular drive into the Empire but was recalled to save Provence from invasion by an Austro-Piedmontese army and from bombardment by the English fleet. Drought, disease, desertion and the local militia all helped to defeat this first invasion which did not last beyond the autumn. Vendôme kept Marlborough in enforced idleness on the northern front. In Spain, the king and queen, with the French ambassador and Berwick, recovered the situation and by the end of 1707 only a few Catalan strongholds, including Barcelona and the Balearics, remained in Anglo-Portuguese hands. Louis XIV had grounds for hoping that his grandson might yet reign. Because of this, there was that year less urgency about his negotiations with the Dutch.

But 1708 spoiled it all. An abortive attempt at a landing in Scotland in support of a possible rising in favour of the Jacobite pretender set out too late, began well and ended in hopeless failure. They were not even able to land. No Scots appeared in the Firth of Forth but the English fleet was there in force. The French ships returned to Dunkirk. In Spain, the Duc d'Orléans, who had replaced Berwick, did practically nothing. The English occupied Sardinia. But it was on the northern front that the real catastrophe occurred.

The northern army of 80,000 men was under the joint command of Vendôme and the young Duc de Bourgogne. The two men could not have been more different. Fénelon's pupil was reserved, punctilious, scrupulous, often vague and in the last resort loathed both the war and the army. Vendôme was his complete opposite in everything. While they argued about a plan of campaign, Marlborough and Eugène, whom they should have fought individually, calmly joined forces, making an army of over 100,000 men. Next the French set off at something of a tangent to take Ghent and Bruges without a blow being struck. However, the enemy were driving southwards and Vendôme wanted to halt them at the Scheldt. There was an engagement at Oudenarde on 10 July 1708. The Duc de Bourgogne refused to take any part in the action and Vendôme, in a fury, gave the order to withdraw. Totally disorganized, the retreat became a rout. Small bodies of troops fled in disorder, pursued by the enemy who accounted for some 20,000 in this way. The remainder, instead of blocking the road to Lille, fell back on Ghent and Bruges, leaving the way open for the opposing army to infest the great city. Still Bourgogne dithered. Lille surrendered on 22 October while the duke was calmly playing shuttlecock. Boufflers held out for a further six weeks in the citadel. The invasion had begun with a bang. Every other frontier was threatened. The army, the finances and even the people themselves seemed on the verge of collapse. Only King Philip with his little army was still doing creditably in Spain. Were the king and his kingdom about to sink into the abyss?

THE KINGDOM ON THE EDGE OF THE ABYSS
(1709–10)

The king had just celebrated his seventieth birthday, an unusual age for the period and an age at which, even in the twentieth century, all but such men as believe themselves possessed of a mission are thinking seriously of retirement. Everything about him was dwindling, save his appetite. His legitimate descendants, bloated, befuddled or debauched – all three in the case of the grand dauphin – irritated and disappointed him. Some of his male bastards, the Duc du Maine in particular, did not altogether displease him. With the Duchesse de Bourgogne, a winsome and flirtatious minx, he was grandfatherly and indulgent. He was surrounded by a court, which though often coarse, licentious and atheistical, was well able to assume the mask of pious gravity when occasion demanded. The courtiers conspired in small groups with an eye to the imminent succession and, above all, to the protection of the successor.

The aged monarch received the news of the disasters

which followed thick and fast after the year of Blenheim
with surprising calmness and lack of dismay. He does not
seem to have uttered a word of reproach, either to his children or to his guilty generals. Was this simply the contempt
of the aged for the inevitable failings of a younger generation? Or a refusal to admit that he, who was solely responsible for the choice of his servants, could have been mistaken? Was it weariness and disappointment, a return to his
old lack of confidence, or a kingly determination to suffer in
silence? With such a man, so accustomed to dissimulation
that secrecy, which was simply contempt in another form,
had become as it were second nature to him, it is impossible
to say for sure. What is certain, however, is that the smallest
success, and that of his grandson in Spain especially, filled
him with inner transports of delight and acted as a sharp
brake on his secret negotiations. For at the first defeat this
bold, arrogant and instinctive aggressor would be on the
look out for some unofficial road to negotiation. These attitudes might be called incompatible, even contradictory, if
they were not so much a part of the habit of the times and
if they were less cleverly calculated to drive a wedge into a
coalition which he regarded as purely circumstantial. As sole
master of war and peace, Louis decided after the fall of Lille
to go a long way in making concessions, further than any
king of France had gone before him, even to the verge of
shame.

His reason was that his whole kingdom was crying out for
mercy and calling for peace at any price.

By 1707, the state of the finances, without which no war
was possible, had reduced Chamillart to despair. All historians, each copying it from an earlier source, quote the
desperate letter which the wretched finance minister wrote
to the king at this time, describing his complete physical,
mental and moral exhaustion. But Louis held out obstina-

tely for another year before he finally gave way and took on Desmarets, a nephew of Colbert and a man of a brilliant and wholly unscrupulous mind calculated to inspire nothing but distrust.

For an honest man like Chamillart there were substantial grounds for despair. Direct taxation had been raised to the utmost limit and even somewhat beyond. The *tailles*, which had increased by nearly a third in seven years, were becoming practically impossible to collect and were lagging further and further in arrears. Tax farming, which had brought in 66 millions before the war, now yielded no more than 58, and there was the additional necessity of granting occasional rebates to the farmers. Before long it was not possible to find farmers to collect the king's taxes at all. In October 1709 it became necessary to make an attempt at raising them directly which functioned for five years and it is estimated that the system brought in 35 millions a year, or half the pre-war figure.

The extraordinary measures were pushed beyond all reasonable bounds: new offices, fresh exemptions, further increases in *gages* (compulsory loans from officers), more bonds for sale, new appeals for credit, all of which brought in less and less and pledged the future further and further ahead. Future revenues were still being swallowed up years in advance. The monetary augmentation of May 1704 (bringing the gold *louis* up to 15 *livres*) was followed by a resumption of the by now ritual practice of slowly decreasing the face value of coinage until the moment came for a swift 'augmentation' – in other words another devaluation – which occurred in 1709. The *louis* shot up to 20 *livres* which meant that anyone who had lent four *louis* at 15 *livres* in 1704 was repaid with three *louis* worth 20 *livres* in 1709, or an effective loss of a quarter.

At this rate the state's credit fell very quickly, especially after the first major defeats. Already, immediately after

Blenheim, the *caisse des Emprunts*, which until then had
worked comparatively satisfactorily, suddenly postponed its
dates for repayment. With the next setback, in April 1705,
a further delay was introduced and after that repayments
were made partly in coin and partly in notes. But the paper
money, a useful financial device which had worked perfectly
well for four years, was beginning to show signs of strain
by the end of 1705 and collapsed altogether in 1706. In
January of that year a note for 100 *livres* was fetching only
94 *livres* in cash, in July it was 72 *livres* and in October,
less than 50. At the beginning of 1707, it was down to 37.
In December 1706, the astute and influential Samuel Bernard persuaded the king to authorize his reimbursement
from the Treasury on an estimated loss of 78·5 per cent on
paper money, an operation which indicates both his personal
power and the chaos of the country's finances.

In practice, the state was dependent on imports of silver
from the Spanish Indies. Thus, the arrival of Chabert's fleet
at La Rochelle on Easter Day 1709 with a cargo of thirty
millions in *piastres* was the means of staving off immediate
bankruptcy. It was dependent to an even greater extent on
the great businessmen, shipowners, merchants, investors
and bankers, among whom were to be found a good proportion of Huguenots. They alone were in a position to place
their credit at the service of the state, on a promise of repayment at some future date from the resources of the realm.
Their names crop up everywhere; Bernard, Crozat,
Legendre, Fizeaux, Nicolas, the Genevese Hogguer,
Huguetan, Mallet and Lullin, and have been made the subject of a recent study by Herbert Luthy. Many, including
the great Samuel Bernard himself, did not emerge unscathed
from their complicated dealings. All had some connexion
with the great companies engaged in the Indies trade and
holding the *asiento*, the Guinea, China and South Sea companies which also numbered many of the inhabitants of

Saint-Malo, La Rochelle and Nantes among their share-holders. But by the beginning of 1709, many of these great magnates were running into difficulties, with the possible exception of Legendre on whom Desmarets leaned heavily for the conclusion of the war.

This widespread distress has been stressed so often that this may be the time to look at it more closely.

In many provinces, at least in the north and west, the century had begun with a terrible epidemic of what has been variously described as measles, swine fever or dysentery. A look at the old parish registers finds it occurring nearly everywhere: even in eastern Brittany, recent studies have shown that the death rate for the year 1701 was a record for the years from 1640 to 1750. In the course of that summer and early autumn, hundreds of children and young people perished in parishes where the usual mortality was no more than a few dozen. This was probably no more than one of the ordinary vicissitudes of life, but people were alarmed by it.

After the crisis of 1698–9, the bottom had dropped out of agricultural prices which remained at an exceptionally low level until 1708. Such a phenomenon, rare at any time, was at this date doubly significant. On the one hand, all those with grain to sell – wealthy peasants, big farmers, landowners, seigneurs and owners of tithes – lost money and started to complain once more. The major works of Bois-guillebert and Vauban were written and published against precisely this background of a strong recession. Their protests about the drop in agricultural incomes had, therefore, more foundation than ever and the farmers and workers on the land who, whatever may have been said about the fiscal injustice of the times, constituted the bulk of the taxpaying public and the potential purchasers of small *rentes* and offices, experienced severe hardship which only added to the general monetary instability.

On the other hand, in certain provinces at least, the common folk in towns and villages suffered a great deal less than is generally believed. This was partly because the cost of living was very low, as low as in 1672 or 1687 and sometimes less, and so long as work was available life seemed comparatively easy. Now in those regions which supplied goods to the great Atlantic ports for the markets of Spain and America, there was no shortage of work. The cloth and textile producing districts, town and country, sent their wares to Dunkirk, Rouen, Saint-Malo, Nantes, La Rochelle, Bordeaux and Bayonne. Every merchant and manufacturer was delighted to see the English and Dutch fabrics ousted from the Spanish and American markets and promptly set to to copy foreign textiles. Right up to 1709, and even after, we find an amazing level of prosperity even in tiny villages. This was especially true of Picardy to which weavers flocked from all parts. People married there in great numbers and produced children, while in the 'great winter' of 1709 and the famine of 1710, the hand of death seemed to pass them by, a proof that there was work and food to be had. The same phenomenon seems to have occurred in Brittany and Maine which were likewise textile regions.

In stark and arresting contrast to these privileged manufacturing and seafaring corners of the realm, which may have been very limited, was the bottomless misery of the continental mass.

It is not necessary to describe in detail the exceptional winter of 1709 which froze all the seeds (except in Brittany) and an incredible number of fruit trees, including all the walnuts of Burgundy, to say nothing of birds, beasts and vagabonds. It has been done many times before. If, as was claimed, the wine froze on the king's table, that only proves the inadequacy of the heating at Versailles. The immediate victims of the cold belong, by their numbers, to the realms of news. The real disaster came at the end of the year and, even more, in 1710. Except in those regions where it was possible to sow some spring corn, especially barley, there was literally no harvest. The price of grain, even old, spoiled or imported grain reached astronomical heights: in Beauce and in Brie it was ten, twelve and thirteen times the price of the preceding year. Just as in 1694, the common people, their savings exhausted by the various taxes, had nothing to live on but charity or rotten refuse. There was a constant stream of burials, people died in the streets, there were no more weddings and of those few children that were born, most died in infancy. Before giving up the ghost, the people made some attempt at rebellion. In Paris, the rich, the great and the royal family all came under fire. Songs and lampoons of a violently abusive nature were directed at the old king himself, although he was now somewhat less free with his invitations to Marly and was even finding some difficulty in paying his bills. Defeat, ruin, winter, famine and murmurs of revolt on all sides: as his troubles mounted, Louis resigned himself with great dignity to suing for peace, even on the most ignominious terms.

In May 1709, at the Hague, the minister, Torcy, in person, did his best to satisfy the triumphant members of the coalition. He agreed to abandon Philip V and recognize Charles III as King of Spain and of all Spanish possessions. He agreed to the expulsion from France of the Pretender, James III, the demolition of Dunkirk and to relinquish Newfoundland and even Strasbourg. In return for these concessions, he obtained a two month truce on condition that Louis XIV pledged himself to take up arms against his grandson and help the allies drive him out of Spain. This was the ultimate humiliation. The peace party, led by Beauvillier and Bourgogne, might have accepted it. The old king rejected it out of hand, refusing 'to make war on his children'. He even went so far as to issue a dignified letter to his people (his advisers, and even Vendôme in 1706, had suggested a meeting of the States-General . . .) explaining his reasons for continuing the war.

The talks were resumed, however, the next year, at Gertruydenberg and came up against what was basically the same obstacle. Urged on by his ministers, his children and even by Villars, Louis offered subsidies to help his enemies drive his grandson out of Madrid. The Dutch, who were the chief negotiators, wanted armed intervention, and Marlborough and the emperor were still more determined. Worn out and deeply uneasy but conscious of the limits of possibility, and of the straightforward honour of his kingdom, the old king broke off abruptly, with the agreement of his ministers. The war would go on. After Malplaquet, a blood-bath and a partial defeat in September 1709, it was little more than a series of reverses, in which the wretched French armies, hungry, decimated and disorganized, were fighting almost on their own soil.

PARTIAL RECOVERY (1711–14)

Between the conditions rejected by Louis in 1709–10 and the treaty which he finally agreed in 1713–14 there are certain clear gains. In a word, Strasbourg and the King of Spain were saved. This evidence of recovery requires some explanation.

The army was decimated and exhausted but lack of work, money and food drove the poor peasant youths and to an even greater extent the apprentices and 'idle' city workers who normally made up the bulk of the troops to enlist in ever greater numbers. As a result, Louis was able to strengthen his forces on the various frontiers and even to send some aid to his grandson in Spain whom he had temporarily neglected.

This military development was made possible by the invariably clever and occasionally daring financial measures of the Colbertite, Desmarets, the comparative success of which took Europe by surprise. A new tax, the *dixième*, which horrified the privileged classes because it was based on the fundamentally egalitarian principles laid down by Vauban, brought in some 25 millions a year, in spite of numerous objections and attempts at sabotage. Considering the difficulties against which it was having to work, the tax office, which had been set up to replace the vanishing tax farmers, was not giving disappointing results. The finance minister was shrewdly making gradual reductions in the value of the *louis* and this apparent revaluation would have led to a substantial increase in the revenues from taxation if it had not been for the quantities of devalued notes which still existed, though much reduced by successive bankruptcies. From time to time the shipowners of Saint-Malo and the other great ports trading with the Indies would bring back millions of silver *piastres*, most of which were taken over by the king. The *Caisse des Receveurs généraux*, otherwise the *Caisse Legendre*, collected all notes issued by officers and tax collectors, discounted them and bolstered up the failing credit of the monarchy with the strong name of the internationally famous Huguenot family of Rouen, Legendre. In addition to all this, the harvests of 1710 and 1711 were excellent throughout the kingdom, preventing an increase in the burden of suffering.

A generally younger and better equipped army was in a position to take advantage of the talents of its last great commanders, Vendôme, who was to die in 1712, and the ageing Villars. The latter contained the advance of the coalition in the north of the realm, between the Canche and the Scarpe, practically single handed from 1710 to 1712, giving way only slowly and ceding a few unimportant positions here and there. The former, after falling temporarily into disfavour, rendered energetic assistance to Philip V, who was again in danger of losing his capital and his kingdom, in recovering both after the decisive victory of Villaviciosa in December 1710. As these events showed, the young Bourbon was firmly entrenched in Spain and had the active support of his people. The degenerate French navy achieved a last blaze of glory when Duguay-Trouin with eleven ships bombarded Rio de Janeiro in September 1711, put to flight a Portuguese army and picked up 20 millions in prize money, divided between the king and a few capitalists, as well as giving Portugal's ally, England, some cause for alarm.

It is customary to celebrate the victory of Denain in epic terms. The old king addressed a few stirring words to his marshal and Villars departed in considerable anxiety for the northern front where the terrible Prince Eugène had raised his head again, and had taken all the last forts which still barred the road to Paris with the exception of Landrecies. A councillor of Lille, Lefebvre d'Orval, proposed a plan which the Maréchal de Montesquiou decided, not without some reluctance, to adopt. Prince Eugène was deceived by a feigned move on Landrecies, in July 1712 Denain was taken and the enemy's supply lines severed. This virtually bloodless surprise move was, more than anything, a psychological and diplomatic triumph. By showing what the French army could still do, it encouraged the negotiators to resume the talks at Utrecht which had been broken off three months earlier. An analysis of the facts reveals, moreover, that the chief architects of the victory at Denain were the English who had withdrawn their considerable forces – and their sterling – from the coalition.

But for England and a few lucky accidents, would the endurance, courage and resourcefulness or sheer cunning of her people, her administrators and her marshals have been enough to save France? In April 1710, Queen Anne was more inclined to listen to her waiting woman than to the imperious Lady Marlborough. A year later, the Emperor

Joseph I died unexpectedly, leaving his lands and before long the Empire to Charles III who was already claimant to the Spanish throne. Between April 1711 and March 1712, the measles and the ineptitude of his doctors deprived the French king of his son, of his grandson and his wife, and finally of the eldest of his great-grandsons. Unimportant as it might seem, the first of these led in England to the ascendancy of the Tory party which was the peace party, being made up of landowners who were finding that the cost of the war far outweighed its profits. A new parliament brought a swift change of government. Early in 1711, the English were already putting out feelers towards negotiation with Versailles. In October a secret treaty, emanating from London, was signed and contained the basic conditions of the future peace of Utrecht. The second event, the death of the emperor, had hastened its conclusion since no Englishman (or Frenchman either) could tolerate the thought of a single Habsburg ruling simultaneously in Vienna, the Empire, the Netherlands, Madrid, Italy and the Indies. Finally, the series of deaths at the French court raised a much more pressing question than that of the Spanish succession, which was that of the succession of France. Philip V and the delicate Duc d'Anjou whose extreme youth and the devoted care of his women had saved him from the doctors, became the only heirs in the direct line. Realizing that he had to make some firm pledges, Louis XIV agreed, and made his grandson agree, to Philip's solemn renunciation of the French crown – and to the renunciation of the crown of Spain, by all the Bourbons of France. At about the same time, as Queen Anne's health declined, he made a solemn recognition of the Protestant succession in England and sent the Stuart Pretender to live in Lorraine.

In the end, internal developments in England, untimely deaths and the need to regulate the dynastic succession with Louis XIV's own good sense, slowly overcame the reservations of the Dutch and the even stronger ones of the emperor. From 1713 to 1715, a whole series of treaties, for which only the names of Utrecht and Rastadt have remained in general use, sorted out the avalanche of conflicts which had been going on for fifteen years. These treaties gave a new shape to Europe and to the world and established firmly what has been described, with some exaggeration, as the 'dominance of England'.

As for Louis XIV and his kingdom, our only concern at present, the important thing is that Louis achieved at least one of his objects in the war. Philip V remained king of all Spain and the Indies, but was obliged to cede his Belgian and Italian possessions to the emperor. Thanks to the English, to Desmarets, to Villars, to gallant armies and to the common people's stubborn determination to survive through these terrible years, the frontiers of the kingdom remained almost intact. In the direction of the Alps, the king was unable to annex Nice or Savoy, as he had so often cherished hopes of doing, but he did reach an agreement with the Duke (now King) of Savoy, the ubiquitous Victor Amadeus, in the matter of some useful border rectifications, following the line of the watershed. The emperor accepted with a bad grace the confirmation of the limits of Ryswick (Joseph and Charles had had ideas of recovering Alsace and even the *Trois-Evêchés*), which meant Strasbourg and Landau. In the north, it was necessary to give way. The Netherlands, which had now become Austrian, acquired a part of French Flanders and Dutch garrisons were installed at the kingdom's doors (at Furnes, Ypres, Menin and Tournai in particular) as a result of the painful conclusion of the third 'Barrier' treaty in November 1715. Lastly, England had to be given the supreme satisfaction of the demolition of the fortifications, sluices and even the port of Dunkirk itself. But who, in 1709 or 1710, would ever have dared to hope for such conditions?

Apart from these relative successes, which were so only in comparison with the disasters which could have come about a few years earlier, the time for a settlement of accounts was drawing near, highlighting the cost of this peace, which was higher than ever, and the burden of the war, which was heavier.

This was the beginning of the end for the French American empire which the enterprise and daring of individuals had stretched from the St Lawrence to the Arctic Ocean and the Mississippi. Newfoundland, Nova Scotia and Hudson Bay were ceded or restored to the English, who very nearly acquired Cape Breton as well. At the same time, the English annexed the small, wealthy West Indian island of Saint-Christophe (St Kitts), and the Dutch part of Guiana. There were no particular changes in the East Indies, where a kind of tacit neutrality had reigned among the belligerents of Europe but here Louis XV later took it on himself to complete his great-grandfather's work.

The attempt at strengthening the kingdom's northern and eastern borders seemed to have failed completely. Lorraine was still independent and Louis had been further obliged to promise the States-General of the United Provinces that no town or fortress in the Netherlands would ever revert or be ceded to the French crown or to any prince or princess of the French royal house. More than that, he acknowledged the right of Holland and the Empire to keep in future an armed watch on Vauban's 'iron belt'.

The satisfaction of the dynastic aims – Philip V in Madrid – was less real than apparent. The French Bourbon became a Spaniard while at the same time continuing, in spite of treaties and renunciations, to hope for the French succession and fully intending to indulge himself with plotting in Austrian Italy. The time was not far off when, having barred French vessels from the Indies and the South Seas, he would actually have the effrontery to seize a great many of them in the Peruvian port of Arica (September 1717), an action which made the real meaning of the treaties of 1713 and 1714 all too clear. They spelled economic disaster.

A return to the commercial legislation of 1664. This was the first condition imposed by the English and the Dutch. (The latter should not be overlooked: the suggestion that they were in decline has been utterly and convincingly refuted in the recent work of Christensen and Glamann). What this meant in particular was that the French market was wide open to English goods of all kinds whereas the English market was quite the reverse. In practice, however, Louis XIV's ministers did obtain some slight alleviation of this commercial *diktat*. It also meant, much more seriously, that France no longer had any trading privileges in the Spanish Empire than those which she had enjoyed in the days when there had been a Habsburg in Madrid. This, as far as British trade was concerned, was most important of all.

The dreams of a few great Atlantic merchants and of a few great statesmen such as Pontchartrain, Daguesseau and Amelot, faded into nothing. Portugal and Brazil were lost already, as a result of the treaties of 1703, now Spain and Spanish America looked like going the same way as the French lost all the privileges they had gained there since 1700. To be sure, there were still a score of ways round the treaties and later events prove that good use was made of them, but for the most part these did not add up to much more than shrewd private dealing which carried great risks and often came to grief. For the next thirty years the *asiento*, with its vast profits, passed out of the hands of French merchants into those of the British. In addition, Philip V made them a grant of land on the Rio de la Plata for the 'keeping and refreshment' of their Negro slaves besides allowing them to import from Europe on their own vessels all the goods and provisions they wanted to support them, thus opening the way to every kind of trading, and, better still, permitting one English vessel of five hundred tons to trade annually in the Indies. This single non-Spanish ship, the 'leave ship', no sooner unloaded than it was loaded again, became the basis of a curious contraband system and one of the pillars of English commercial wealth in the eighteenth century.

This, in basic terms, was the price of peace and Louis XIV was forced to accept it, in spite of his military recovery and the obliging, but scarcely disinterested, behaviour of England. The things that mattered most, the existence of the kingdom and the honour of the dynasty, were saved, but all else was lost.

We have already seen how, year by year, the cost of the war, of financing the war and of the wartime economy had affected the people of the kingdom : taxes and the depradations of tax collectors and soldiery alike, the militia and the continual hunt for deserters; scarcity and famine, made worse by the war, poverty and profiteers; monetary difficulties, the dread of counterfeit coin and 'notes' of all descriptions, all devalued by 80 or 90 per cent; the growing burden of debt placed on the peasantry and the impossibility of finding farmers to collect the king's taxes or private revenues; demographic crises of a mild or catastrophic nature; swine fever, typhoid, scarlet fever, dysentery and measles affecting everyone from the court to the remotest countryside; bands of beggars, brigands and deserters lurking in every forest in the land and emerging to ravage everything in sight; sudden panic uprisings in rural communities precipitated by a new tax, whether real or imagined, a new government agent, a load of grain, troop movements or the rumour that brigands were massing in the region, the army, as it had in the previous century, putting down disturbances in the Cevennes, in Central France, Guyenne or anywhere else.

It is a grim picture of a kind of primitive, anarchic wretchedness which emerges, at least in the backward interior of the kingdom, as early as 1703 and remains constant even in years of comparative recovery. In 1712, the harvest was again a poor one, in 1713 it was bad, in 1714 a shortage of fodder and a mysterious epizootic disease killed thousands of head of cattle. To some extent, this fresh accumulation of disasters may help to mix the colours for the last sombre scene in the picture: the old Monarch's legacy to his great-grandson, a little boy of five.

PART FIVE

1715:

The Time of Reckoning

14

THE LAST YEAR

THE KING

In September 1714, Louis entered the seventy-seventh and last year of his life. His splendid health was in ruins, wrecked less by age than by his doctors. Purges, bleedings, emetics, antimonies, there was nothing in the whole nightmare pharmacopoeia that he had been spared. Then the surgeons had taken a hand, breaking his jaw while ostensibly extracting one or two bad teeth. No one thought of putting him on a diet for his terrifying and voracious appetite. Instead they let him stuff himself with gargantuan helpings of spices, game, sweetmeats and sorbets. He suffered, very early in life, from digestive and bowel disorders and these were followed, inevitably, by gout and then by 'vapours' and dizzy spells, and finally by wasting and in August 1715 by the dark blotches of gangrene on his lower limbs. By this time, people in England had long been laying bets upon his life. There is no doubt that he himself knew death was approaching and that he was preparing himself to meet it with the kingly dignity which rarely failed him.

Around him, the superficially controlled chaos of the court continued its accustomed antics, its rounds of journeys, reviews, audiences, gaming, concerts and church-going. In fact, the court was making ready for the accession of the Duc d'Orléans and a complete upheaval in the government and administration, or rather gave itself up without further pretence to debauchery, atheism and intrigue or, at best, to witty conversation in agreeable and fashionably appointed salons. Slowly, bowed down by the weight of years and bereavement, the king had withdrawn himself from the hubbub until it scarcely touched him. He took refuge in what family he had left – Maintenon and two of his bastards – spending his evenings listening to chamber music and trivial anecdotes and drinking orangeade. Priests, old men and memories made up the rest of his surroundings. Grammont and Villeroy, his last remaining contemporaries, talked to him of the past and performances of Molière's plays reminded him of the Enchanted Isle.

Yet even then he remained the impenitent bureaucrat, still forcing himself to work at the affairs of state. He had two tormenting obsessions: his country's religion and the succession of France. There was a third also: the need to maintain peace.

He had expressed this longing for a lasting peace more than once in the last years of the war, in the opening lines of his will (2 August 1714) and again in what may have been the last words he spoke to his great-grandson: 'I have loved war too much. . . .' His last instructions to his ambassadors, especially to his ambassador in Venice (1715), show that he had thoughts of a permanent understanding with the emperor as a way to ensuring peace in Europe (the colonies were another matter). The idea seemed a new and sensible one, but it remained an idea.

The Dauphin's poor health and the contemptuous dislike (assiduously cultivated by the *dévots* by whom he was surrounded) which he felt for his nephew Orléans whom custom and usage designated as regent, prompted Louis to make two very unwise moves. The first of these was a most unusual measure which called down the fury of Saint-Simon. Louis' bastard sons, Maine and Toulouse, already legitimized in 1694 and given precedence over dukes and peers, were declared, by a decree of July 1714, able to succeed in the absence of legitimate princes. However, this tremendous innovation seems to have met with no opposition. The *Parlement* ratified it without batting an eyelid (it had other, more pressing, religious problems on its mind). A few days later (23 August 1715), Louis added a codicil to his will by which he hoped, as his father had done before him, to lay down conditions for the regency. A council of fourteen persons, designated by name, were empowered to override the regent's decisions by a majority vote. The 'safety, keeping and education of the king during his minority' was entrusted to the Duc du Maine while Villeroy was to be his governor, Fleury his tutor, and Le Tellier his confessor. All these splendid arrangements, aimed at prolonging the dying man's rule through that of his favourite bastard, survived him by less than twenty-four hours.

Like any other old man of the period, Louis was preparing somewhat apprehensively to render up his accounts to God. Encouraged by those around him, he devoted himself with renewed persistence to God's service, as though in compensation for past errors.

A fresh wave of official persecution descended on the members of the reformed church who, since 1698, had been protected by a kind of tacit, partial tolerance in Paris and in a number of other provinces. In 1711, in the principality of Orange, the king broke his promise 'never to trouble any person concerning religion'. There followed a series of laws recalling the severest (and least respected) measures immediately before and after the Revocation and in particular one forbidding doctors 'to visit the sick a third day unless they have been given a certificate, signed by the confessor of the said sick person that they have confessed'. A royal declaration of 1715 aimed chiefly at backsliders defined these quite

incredibly: the mere fact that a Protestant by birth had resided in the kingdom since 1686 was held to constitute proof
of Catholicism, which was contrary even to the provisions of
the Edict of Fontainebleau. These were no more than the
senile outbreaks of pious rage in a monarch whose ultra-
Catholic despotism was at odds with the charity and good
sense of most of his administrators and his bishops. The
number of times this persecution was resorted to was
enough in itself to show that the laws were seldom effective.
As the king actually lay on his death bed, the first reformed
synod of the century was meeting near Nîmes, in the heart
of the fervently Christian province of Languedoc. Louis had
written in his will: 'We have done all we could to bring
back to the Church those who were cut off from it.'

He also wrote there: 'Our chief care ... has always been
to maintain the purity of the Roman Catholic religion in our
kingdom, and to keep it from all kinds of novelties.' Reference to the many and specialized works on the subject will
tell the complicated story of the devious intrigues and covert
opposition, the disputes among persons, cliques and influ-
ences which all too often lay at the root of the differences of
French Catholics at the end of the reign. The king, whose
mind was no more inclined towards theology than his soul
towards mysticism, wanted an end to these disputes and a
catechismal faith, and had an instinctive distrust of any
group with a tendency to individualism, or even of any
person attempting to think for himself. Any 'novelty'
which in his view was bound to be heretical, or any organized group, which was bound to be plotting, made him
angry and perhaps (a memory of the Fronde?) also afraid.
In order to safeguard the 'purity' of his religion, he intervened, sometimes brutally, at others misguidedly.

Brutal was the imprisonment of some of the unworldly
mystics who collected about a somewhat hysterical visionary,

Mme Guyon (1697) and her 'Quietists'. Still more brutal was the action taken against the last remaining nuns of Port-Royal-des-Champs: the dispersal, *manu militari*, of the twenty-two survivors (1709), the destruction of the buildings and the ploughing up of the land where they had stood (1710), the violation of the tombs and the conveyance of the bones to the common sewer by the cartload and finally the demolition of the guilty church itself (1712). These were unworthy victories which did not prevent a resurgence of the Jansenist quarrel in 1702 which once again shook the clergy and the nobility, court and country, even into the depths of the provinces.

This useless brutality alternated with moves of elephantine subtlety. Louis appealed to the Pope for a solemn condemnation of Quietism and of Fénelon in particular. The attempt was a failure. The Pope took his time and at last dispatched a small brief in which he did not condemn anything very much but declared that he was acting *motu proprio* (1699). Obstinately, Louis clung to the same tactics in dealing with the resurgence of Jansenism, now tinged with Gallicanism and *richérisme*, and asked the Pope to decide or in other words to uphold him. Once again, the Pope took his time before responding rather unfortunately with the Bull *Unigenitus* of 1713, which came too late and only raised further storms. The archbishop of Paris, fifteen prelates and hundreds of parish priests and members of religious institutions as well as the Sorbonne and the Gallican *Parlement* virtually went over to the Jansenist cause, much to the amusement of Protestants and atheists alike. Some refused to publish the Bull, others shifted their appeal from the ill-informed Pope to a better informed source, that is, to a council general. The Archbishop of Paris was in a state of semi-rebellion, as also was the illustrious *parlementaire* Henri Daguesseau while the ministers Pontchartrain and Voysin did their best to support them. Louis wailed and ranted, stormed and threatened to 'kick' or to 'trample on the bellies' of his adversaries, then wept again. His last and most singular plan was to assemble a council of France at which he would dictate to his clergy and excommunicate recalcitrants for all the world like a little Gallican Pope. He died before he could put this incredible daydream into practice.

The last months of the man who had once been the Great King were thus much occupied and bitterly troubled by religious matters, and these played a large part in the confusion, ineffectualness and hostility, if not in the ultimate contempt by which they were marked. Louis was made deeply unhappy and sought to justify himself. He is said to have cast all the blame for his failures on to the bishops who had advised him: he had merely followed their advice and if he had done wrong then they would have to answer for it before God. ... No more, perhaps, than the passing pettiness of a dying man.

Thereupon, he fell into a kind of coma from which he roused himself on the evening of 31 August to say an *Ave* and a *Credo* and died a few hours later on the morning of 1 September. Everything suggests that, setting aside the customary civil and religious displays, France, from the greatest to the least of her subjects, experienced a profound sense of relief.

THE GOVERNMENT

The void was closing in on the old monarch. Beauvillier and Chevreuse, long his trusted counsellors, were recently dead. Fénelon, now rising into favour once again, was soon to follow them. Pontchartrain had retired, an old man, in 1714. Only three of his council remained: Voysin, Torcy and Desmarets, all of them Colbert's relatives and the last two his nephews. The services of the administration had multiplied and grown up around them and now included quite specialized offices and departments, intendants in charge of commerce and even the beginnings of the modern Highways Department.

In the provinces, the machinery of royal administration, though slow to get under way, had been smoothed and filled out into the beginnings of a bureaucracy, better informed and better able to enforce obedience. The intendants had little in the way of centralized help, but they had numerous assistants, called *subdélégués*. Inspectors of manufactures were placed on the spot, less to see that the rules were carried out than to pass on information. The old administration with its venal officers persisted, though less rich and respected, but those responsible for the collection and handling of finances were becoming increasingly separate from it and played what was clearly an important role in administration. At the same time, the shrewd and excellent semi-private administration of *fermes*, whether public or private, showed notable efficiency. The *maréchaussée*, or police force, was still totally inadequate and the army was called in in case of need, but some of the habitual trouble-makers were beginning to settle down, the beggars in the ever more numerous public hospitals and those soldiers who were retained on active service in brand new barracks, of which there were as yet still too few. This was the start of the administrative monarchy. The ordered France of Louis XV was emerging.

But before this could come about and the kingdom provide the admirable spectacle of organization brought about by what was on the whole a competent and efficient administration, it still had to undergo the considerable reaction caused by the imminent regency. Moreover, people's minds had already turned to this, plots were being hatched and weapons got ready to bring down the men who had ruled under the dying despot. Memoirs, intrigues and pamphlets show that a real, if secret, opposition was already in existence as early as 1695. Between 1705 and 1710, there was a genuine political conspiracy, activated by Fénelon and Beauvillier with the tacit consent of the second dauphin, aimed at setting up an aristocratic and pacifist monarchy in which the old nobility and the intermediate bodies should occupy or reoccupy pride of place and all the *'vile bourgeoisie'* and the common nobodies from whom Louis XIV had drawn his ministers, secretaries and intendants would be sent back to their scribbling or their farming. Untimely deaths, the king's resistance and French military recovery had destroyed all these hopes and with them the cabal with its mixture of the most reactionary (in the literal sense of the word) ideas with the most daring projects for reform. But it was no more than a delay. When the king entered his last illness the dukes and *parlementaires* depending on Orléans at last knew where they stood and made ready to turn the State of Louis XIV upside down.

All that vast, rambling ministerial family which, for half a century or a century even, had as it were held in trust all the great offices of state, the Phélypeaux, Le Telliers, Colberts and Voysins, all so closely interrelated, who had been so busily placing their nephews as intendants, prelates and abbots, all those genuine, but recent nobles (two generations at the most), were to return to the 'void' to which they were condemned by Saint-Simon, duke and peer, friend of the regent and great man of the coming day, and all his aristocratic party. With them, back into ignominious bastardy, would go those offspring of a double adultery, Maine and Toulouse, the living proofs of the dying monarch's unregenerate soul.

Louis' body was still lying in state when the anticipated revolution took place. It placed all power in the hands of the dukes, under the complaisant eye of Philippe d'Orléans. Down with the bastards, the vile bourgeois and nearly all the administrative structure built up so painfully since Richelieu. To describe the fate of this short-lived aristocratic revolution is not our province here but some indication of its speed, violence and scope is a help in order to grasp the strength and nature of the resentments which had accumulated in the course of an overlong reign.

Such an upheaval would not have been possible without the connivance of the Paris *Parlement* and this had been ensured in advance. The *Parlement* had already clashed with the old king over the matter of the Bull. Daguesseau had not been afraid to resist and had bravely faced the prospect of the Bastille. Tamed and despised for too long, the Paris *Parlement* had begun to jib and had chosen a propitious ground on which to take its stand: Gallicanism brought it many powerful supporters. The same impatience was showing itself in the provinces. The *Parlement* and States of Brittany had not waited for 1 September 1715 to resume their nationalist and financial opposition. A great revival of forces long underrated was in the wind and now and then, in that fine summer of 1715, a hint of a new Fronde blew in the air. As it had set aside Louis XIII's will, so, with the utmost legality, the Paris *Parlement* set aside that of Louis XIV. Only the *Parlement* was entitled to do so. Orléans and his friends must have had to pay for this longed-for decree. But every *parlement* in the realm was to spend the eighteenth century getting its revenge for fifty years of captivity.

To any well-informed person, the violent reaction of the regency must appear inevitable. For no less than a quarter of a century, the real direction of French thought had eluded the royal patronage. Intellectual life had deserted Versailles for Paris, the court for the salons. The principles of law, contract and constitution, new or refurbished, had spread in enlightened circles. The example of England was quoted openly and if the memory of Charles I's end on the scaffold was temporarily (and yet not altogether) forgotten, people recalled the theories and the facts which had led to the expulsion of James II. This was the period when, like Bayle, the young Arouet was cherishing English ideas. The popularity of such literary symbols as the Chinese or Egyptian sage and the good Indian demonstrated, pending the arrival of Rica and Usbeck,* the vanity of a score of accepted ideas. The fashion was for anti-despotism, irreverence, irreligion and laboratories. Ever since 1700, commercial deputies had openly defended the idea of economic freedom. A hundred 'advisers' followed the admired lead of Boisguillebert and Vauban in expounding ways to restore the shattered finances, enrich the kingdom and guarantee universal peace. Prominent among these picturesque figures who propagated a thousand fantasies and one or two ideas of genius, was one John Law.

In the midst of this whirl of wit and ideas, gaiety and folly, old Colbert's system, old Bossuet's obstinacy, old Maintenon with her bonnets and her Jesuits and the old monarch himself, shrivelled and motionless, all seemed very out-of-date and ridiculous, like something left over from another age. There must have been many who thought with a comfortable sigh, on that morning of 1 September 1715, that at last the reign of the old was ended.

Once the first moment of euphoria was past, it was not long before the new men who seized hold of power with such joy came face to face with the real problem. Ever since the peace, the brilliant and clear-sighted Desmarets had been presenting it constantly to the old man he served and offering a variety of solutions, all of which were set aside or put off until tomorrow, in other words for the successor to deal with.

In 1715, Desmarets estimated the net revenues of the state

* The writers of Montesquieu's imaginary *Lettres Persanes* (1721). (Trs.)

at 74 millions, against an expenditure of 119 millions: a deficit for the year of 45 millions. The theoretical gross national debt would have been of the order of 2,000 millions, a fantastic but possibly accurate figure. The amount due for immediate repayment would have been over 400 millions. The Treasury was virtually empty and even the anticipated revenues for the years 1716, 1717 and 1718 already spent. Officers' salaries were rarely paid and the State prisoners (especially in Paris) no longer saw anything of their 'quarters', that is of their three-monthly dividends. The State's creditors held 'notes' from the war treasurers, 'promises' from the *Caisse des Emprunts* and 'assignations' against future receipts, all of which papers were highly vulnerable and circulated with considerable losses. When they were presented too insistently, Desmarets dribbled out a *rente* of 4 per cent on future receipts. From September 1713, the currency manipulations had begun again. Every two or three months saw a 'diminution' of the two *louis* aimed at increasing, if possible, the cash yield of the taxes. In December 1715, the reverse procedure was set in motion, as usual, and a sudden 'augmentation' brought the coinage thus devalued to the lowest level of the great reign, in May 1709. The vicissitudes of the *livre* and the *louis* (which were by no means at an end) caused much public anxiety, interfered with business, upset the exchange, and led to ruinous losses and some undeserved profits among the general public. But it is questionable whether metal coinage at its official valuation any longer played a major role when merchants gave it different valuation in their own dealings and with so much paper money in circulation.

This situation, which was worse than that left by Richelieu and Mazarin, was almost entirely brought about by twenty years of war. Desmarets had the nerve to propose drastic remedies. A saving of 25 millions on military expenditure, the retention of all the new taxes (initially promised to last only for the duration of the war), a general increase in taxation, old or new, whether direct or farmed, and for the national debt, both permanent and repayable, bankruptcy pure and simple, at a third or a half to begin with. Generations of historians, honest men but poor financiers, have exclaimed in horror at such a policy, but it was a necessary surgery since there seemed no possibility of turning the *Caisse Legendre* into a national bank because the liquid assets indispensable from such an operation (several hundred millions) could not be raised either by exchequer or by the suspicious private bankers and capitalists. No decision was reached.

This was a formidable legacy for the regency. How it very nearly brilliantly saved the situation is not part of our present subject.

THE KINGDOM

Was the kingdom's wealth strengthened by the return of peace, enough to bring about the gradual restoration of a strong economy which was the decisive remedy needed to extricate the state from the threat of financial ruin?

Historians have been in the habit of painting such a gloomy picture of 'France in 1715' that we may well ask ourselves by what miracle the age of Louis XV was subsequently able to display all the currently accepted signs of an undeniable prosperity.

There is a need for a close study of the 'poverty of France at the end of the great reign', and a number of young historians are engaged in the long and laborious effort to produce one. For the present, what must be done, by focusing the spotlight on the year 1715 alone, is to offer some important corrections to the classic picture of desolation.

It is customary to lament the depopulation of the realm as a result of the famines of 1709–10 and of 1713–14, as well as of the various epidemics which in some places were extremely serious, especially in 1701 and later on in 1719, and also in certain provinces at other times. This low demographic level (possibly the lowest, for an equivalent area of the country, since the sixteenth century) seems probable. There may, however, be other sides to the question.

For one thing, a drop in population is not necessarily a bad thing, if a country contains more mouths than it can feed or provide work for. For another, the increased death rate was largely among children and old people who were useless because they were unproductive or comparatively unproductive sections of the community, so that up to a point their disappearance might alleviate the condition of the survivors. Those among the active producers (from fifteen to fifty years) who would be most missed, were the youngest and strongest, those born between 1690 and 1700 who were comparatively few in number and who had suffered in early youth from famine, smallpox, typhoid, swine fever, and dysentery. They were not numerous and so more affected by the ever-increasing burden of taxation. On the other hand, with the return of peace and the prospect of a rapid commercial expansion and hence of readier outlets, which seemed to be on the horizon, they would probably find no shortage of land and of opportunities for industrial employment. Lastly, although the curves of baptisms and marriages show a pronounced decline between 1715 and 1720, to reach a distinct minimum, it is worth noting that this observation does not hold good everywhere, and that the following years show a marked recovery and that this concerns only certain age groups. Is it possible even that the outbreaks of disease among animals, especially cattle, in 1714, which were genuinely catastrophic, may have been a matter of much more serious concern in the majority of provinces than a temporary reduction in the burden of infants and the aged?

Suppose we save our tears not for 1709 but for 1715 and

for the wretched condition of the countryside and the wild animals? After the alarms of 1712 and 1713, regions from Picardy to Provence enjoyed good harvests again from 1714. 1715, 1716 and 1717 were all good. The price of basic food-stuffs fell almost to the low levels of 1704–7, if not to those of 1686. Only the corn merchants had some cause for complaint because they were not making any money but they, as we know, were in a minority. In Provence, the cost of wine remained reasonable, without falling too low and it was the same with olive oil. But for the continued heavy taxes, the year 1715 might have appeared, in rural districts, in fairly cheerful colours.

In fact, with the return of peace, we find farmers and tenants turning up again to cultivate the estates and farms which from 1709 to 1711 the owners had often been obliged to farm themselves or with day labourers for lack of suitable applicants. Contracts seem to have been arranged at reasonable figures and for both parties, work seems to have gone back very much to normal. All the same, one or two significant, and highly illegal little clauses were soon being slipped into these contracts to the effect that dues were to be paid in 'good gold and silver coin and not in notes ... whatever the king may do'. The countryside, more sensitive to financial hazards than it had once been, was protecting itself, in its own way, from the legislative whims of a state on the verge of bankruptcy. But at the time of the old king's death, these defensive measures had not yet begun to appear.

We have been struck by the vigorous maritime expansion which seems to mark the end of the seventeenth and the beginning of the eighteenth centuries, chiefly in periods of peace but also, with some exceptions, in time of war. The same impression has been felt, not only in Saint-Malo, but also by two historians of the younger school, fresh from their theses, Pierre Chaunu, dealing with Spain and the Atlantic, and René Baehrel, dealing with the Mediterranean coast of Provence, both of whom have discerned a swift revival of a growing maritime influence round about the turn of the century. A return to the old and admirable researches of the Swedish historian Dahlgren into the archives of French ports provides plenty of evidence in support of these views. In 1712, ten vessels sailed for the South Seas, fifteen in 1713 and twenty in 1714. The *Grand-Dauphin* out of Saint-Malo, which had sailed round the world while the war was in progress, repeated the feat between 1714 and 1717. In the year 1714 alone, a score of French ships were trading in the ports of Peru and Chile while others crossed the Pacific to trade with China. For all its risks, this was the most profitable form of trade for the economy of the realm, not only because of the returns in silver *piastres* but also because of the varied cargoes it carried out, and textiles in particular.

Other connexions were also being eagerly resumed. Historians of Marseilles have likewise shown that their great port, which had again become 'free', was strengthening its influence in the Levant. If the Government to some extent neglected the colonial sphere (although less than has been suggested), nevertheless it let François Martin pursue his able work in India, permitted the Senegal Company to push on into the interior of that country and gave Antoine Crozat (1712) trading privileges in the vast and promising territory of Louisiana. The great Atlantic ports, and Nantes in particular, were already growing rich on their connexions with the Antilles, especially with San Domingo, and were putting up sugar refineries in a number of places, especially along the Loire. More and more, merchants, officers, bourgeois and even *grand seigneurs* were venturing to entrust their money to maritime enterprises, taking shares in voyages to distant parts and acquiring plantations in the French Cape colony and in the Caribbean. From this point on, with the return of peace and the comparative security given by the new commercial treaties, a whole fresh aspect of the eighteenth century, and one which was by no means new in 1715, came increasingly to the fore.

The low cost of living, the rapid resumption of large-scale commercial enterprises, the peace and possibly a degree of inflation were all factors capable of encouraging a renaissance of the 'manufactures' (what we should call industry) which traditional historians have been so ready to depict as in hideous decline. Too little serious study has been made of this field at this period – 1715 – to allow putting forward anything more than a general impression. The wool manufactures of Picardy which had been working for the troops and for Spain seem to have at least maintained production, while the renewed prosperity of Amiens and Beauvais dates from 1725–30. For the textile trade, there is at present no reliable statistical evidence available. The remnants of Colbert's great creations, such as the Gobelins and Beauvais, having undergone a period of severe trial, were ready for a new flowering. In the field of metal-workings, the situation seems to have been less bright, especially by comparison, but there was a growing interest in coal, although even this was a good hundred years behind the English. Factories dealing with 'colonial' products were more active.

A pause, a time for taking stock of difficulties brought about by monetary problems and the redistribution of international trade, a period of decline in one place and of hopeful beginnings elsewhere but more often of stagnation: these are the impressions left by the few scholarly works on the period. What they certainly do not suggest is an atmosphere of disaster but rather a general sense of expectation.

Have we, perhaps, thrown too much light on to the traditionally gloomy picture of the last year of the reign? It is true that dukes and *parlementaires* were gathering themselves to grasp, or to recover a power of which they had been summarily bereft; true, the clergy and all 'honest men' were deeply involved in the Gallican and Jansenist controversy; Protestant churches were springing up again triumphantly despite the law, in the Midi and even in Paris itself; the financial and monetary situation, much more serious than in 1661, now seemed beyond any 'ordinary' solution; the ranks of the common people had thinned in their long suffering and there was much misery to be seen in town and country, more perhaps than in 1661; discharged soldiers, vagabonds and brigands still haunted the thickets and highways of the realm; there was little or no technical progress to be seen in fields or factories, apart from the stocking loom and one or two small machines for glazing or pressing fabrics; the country's maritime and colonial 'vocation' had been somewhat neglected by the state and that state no longer attracted the artists it had once commanded...

Yet for all that, the constant threat of rebellion which had hung over one or another region of the kingdom had lifted, except for the crushed Cevennes and a few market riots, which were speedily subdued. The troops were being gradually accommodated in barracks and no longer spread terror at the mere rumour of their approach. Even the dread bubonic plague seemed to have been overcome, and would be isolated in 1720. The king's ships might no longer rule the seas but French shipowners and merchants had many vessels at sea, both in the Mediterranean and on the high seas, and were rich and respected. Despite present threats, disputes and widespread disobedience, the kingdom had slowly acquired a more competent and better-equipped administration. The frontiers securely fastened by Vauban had been partially strengthened by the addition of one province, Franche-Comté, some lands in the north and the great bridge-city of Strasbourg. The French language, art and letters long remained a model for all the civilized world to follow. Another ten years would even see a solution to the financial crisis and, more important still, some seventeen or eighteen million Frenchmen were peacefully at work again in the fields and workshops, still using the same slow, age-old methods, still threatened by the same precarious conditions, but working with a dogged courage and craftsmanship which are beyond dispute. It was on these people that, when all was said and done, the future strength of the nation depended. For the first time now that its great potentate had gone, that nation was beginning to look for and find its own identity. Yet weary, out-dated and finally hated as he was, he left behind him at least a rather splendid image of that religion of kingship of which he had made himself the high priest.

Now it is time to ask what had been Louis' own real contribution to the slow evolution of his country – and beyond that, of Europe and the world – in those fifty-five years.

15

LOUIS XIV: THE UNIVERSAL MAN

Lucien Febvre, one of the guiding lights of French historical studies, once wrote that the historian had no business 'to pronounce judgement ... to set himself up as acting judge of the valley of Jehosaphat'. He said many times that the historian's besetting sin was the sin of anachronism, although he stated also that History was 'a child of her time' and that none of her practitioners could detach themselves from the preoccupations, currents of thought and general 'climate' of their own times. One might also maintain that a degree of passion is necessary to the historian, that it is those works which are most vibrant with personality which remain the most vivid and fertile, even if only because they provoke contradiction and are bound to produce the more important work of analysis and painstaking research inseparable from any serious study.

So let us leave to the sovereign judges, of Jehosaphat or anywhere else, the honour or ridicule of passing judgement on Mazarin's godson. In any case, whoever judges Louis-Dieudonné, judges chiefly himself. But for the would-be impartial historian, there is one question which cannot be avoided and which does seem to belong genuinely to the historian's province. That is the question of what were the precise extent and limits of King Louis' own personal acts in the course of fifty-five long years which were no more than so many seconds in the whole history of the world.

THE KING'S ACTS: HIS PERSONAL SPHERE

As early as 1661, as he declared in his *Mémoires*, Louis meant to have sole command in every sphere and claimed full responsibility, before the world and all posterity, for everything that should happen in his reign. In spite of constant hard work, he soon found he had to entrust the actual running of certain departments, such as finance or commerce, to a few colleagues, although he still reserved the right to take major decisions himself. There were, however, some aspects of his *métier de roi* to which he clung absolutely and persistently, although his persistence was not invariably absolute. Consequently, it is permissible to single out a kind of personal sphere which the king reserved to himself throughout his reign, although this sphere might vary, while the rest still remained, as it were, under his eye.

As a young man, Louis had promised himself that his own time and posterity should ring with his exploits. If this had been no more than a simple wish, and not an inner certainty, it might be said to have been largely granted.

As a hot-headed young gallant, he flouted kings by his extravagant gestures and amazed them by the brilliance of his court, his entertainments, his tournaments and his mistresses. As a new Augustus he could claim, for a time, to have been his own Maecenas. Up to the year 1672, all Europe seems to have fallen under the spell of his various exploits and his youthful fame spread even as far as the 'barbarians' of Asia. For seven or eight years after that, the armies of Le Tellier and Turenne seemed almost invincible while Colbert's youthful navy and its great admirals won glory off the coast of Sicily. Then, when Europe had pulled itself together, Louis still showed amazing powers of resistance and adaptability. Even when he seemed to be ageing, slipping into pious isolation amid his courtiers, he retained the power to astonish with the splendours of his palace at Versailles, his opposition to the Pope and the will to make himself into a 'new Constantine', and later by allying himself with Rome to 'purify' the Catholic religion. When practically on his death bed, he could still impress the English ambassador who came to protest at the building of a new French port next door to the ruins of Dunkirk.

Dead, he became a kind of symbolic puppet for everyone to take over and dress up in his chosen finery. Voltaire used him, in the name of 'his' age, as ammunition against Louis XV. On the other side, he long stood as the type of blood-thirsty warlike and intolerant despot. Even the nineteenth-century Bourbons preferred to celebrate their descent from 'good king Henri' with his white cockade, or from the 'martyr' of 21 January. The great school of historians which flourished from 1850 until 1915 did not spare him, but studied his entourage and his reign most carefully. In the twentieth century, the royalist academicians Bertrand, with superb naïvety, and Gaxotte, with more talent and disingenuousness, have made him a symbol of order and greatness, of Patriotism and even of Virtue. At the same time, the teaching of Lavisse which, although hostile, also shows great subtlety and unrivalled scholarship, still dominates the field in the scholarly academic tradition. Finally, there are the young historians, strongly influenced by philosophers, sociologists and certain economists, who pass over the king's personality and entourage – to be left to the purveyors of historical gossip and romance – in favour of concentrating on those problems of institutions, attitudes of mind, religious observances, social strata and the great movements of fundamental economic forces which, in their view, transcend mere individuals and events. While all this is going on, the general public is subjected to diatribes on 'classicism', which is an illusion, on Versailles and its 'significance', the Man in the Iron Mask, the Affair of the Poisons, on the king's mistresses, successive or contemporaneous, and on the 'policy of greatness'.

For precisely three centuries, Louis XIV has continued to dominate, fascinate and haunt men's minds. 'The universe and all time' have certainly remembered him, although not always in the way he would have wished. From this point of view, Louis' personal deeds have been a great success. Unfortunately, his memory has attracted a cloud of hatred and contempt as enduring as that which rises from the incense of his worshippers or the pious imitations of a later age.

In his personal desire to enlarge his kingdom, the king was successful. The lands in the north, Strasbourg, Franche-Comté and the 'iron belt' are clear evidence of success. In this way Paris was better protected from invasion. But all these gains had been made by 1681 and later events served only to confirm, rescue or reduce them. It has even been maintained that considering his strong position in 1661, surrounded by so many kings who were young, unsure of their thrones or simply incompetent, Louis might have hoped for greater things. He might have aimed at the annexation of the Spanish Netherlands, although Holland and England would always have managed to prevent him. Lorraine was vulnerable and Louis was less powerful there in 1715 than in 1661, while with a little shrewdness or cunning, there were Savoy and Nice to be had, to say nothing of the colonies which he tended to disregard, leaving them to traders, adventurers, priests and a few of his colleagues. He was satisfied with losing one West Indian island and the gateway to Canada while a handful of brave men were striving to win him an empire in America and another in India.

As absolute head of his diplomatic service and his armies, from beginning to end, he was well served while he relied on men who had been singled out by Mazarin or Richelieu but he often made a fool of himself by selecting unworthy successors. He was no great warrior. His father and his grandfather had revelled in the reek of the camp and the heady excitement of battle. His preference was always for impressive manoeuvres, parades and good safe sieges rather than the smoke of battle, and as age grew on him he retreated to desk strategy. Patient, secretive and subtle in constructing alliances, weaving intrigues and undoing coalitions, he marred all these gifts by ill-timed displays of arrogance, brutality and unprovoked aggression. In the last analysis, this born aggressor showed his greatness less in triumph than in adversity but there was never any doubt about his effect on his contemporaries whose feelings towards him were invariably violent and uncompromising. He was admired, feared, hated and secretly envied.

If, as a good libertine and a poor theologian, he began by taking little interest in the matter of religion, this became, from his fortieth year onwards, one of his favourite 'personal spheres'. But here he met with total lack of success. In his conflict with the great authoritarian and pro-Jansenist Pope, Innocent XI, he was forced to give way and, from a passionate Gallican became ultramontane to the point of embarrassing later popes. Against the Jansenists as a matter of policy rather than of doctrine, he only succeeded, despite repeated acts of violence, in strengthening the sect and uniting it with Gallicans in the *Parlement* and the Sorbonne and with the *richériste* priests suppressed by the edict of 1695. Whatever may be claimed, the extirpation of the 'Calvinist heresy' resulted in the weakening of the kingdom, the strengthening of her neighbours and a formidable amount of hatred, national and European, whether real or assumed. In the end, not many *religionnaires* were converted. They recanted, resisted, revolted or appealed to the enemy, and calmly rebuilt their churches in the Midi, while in Paris, the great Huguenot businessmen were generally tolerated because they were indispensable. The Catholic counter-reformation undoubtedly made great strides during the reign owing to the missions, the seminaries which were finally established, and the admirable Jansenist parish priests, but the basic foundations had in fact been laid long before 1661.

For some fifteen or twenty years, it was Louis' ambition to gather around his person the cream of artists and writers. In this field Colbert, who had learned his trade from Mazarin, was able to help him considerably while he had the power and the money. After 1773, money grew short and from 1689 downright scarce, while in the ill-fated year of 1694 even such a magnificent undertaking as the Gobelins very nearly failed. On the other hand, Louis very early began concentrating his efforts on his works at Versailles and later at Marly, and neglecting the rest. After 1680, patronage as a whole slipped away from the monarchy. Ideas became freer and more diversified and the main themes of the eighteenth century began to appear while the critical and scientific spirit progressed rapidly, shaking the old dogmatic ideas, and by that time Louis had largely lost interest in intellectual matters unless it was a case of checking some dangerous 'innovation'. But for fifteen years, there was a happy meeting of talents which shed, as it were, a lustre on the finest period of the reign. The young king had given proof of taste and even of daring. There was in him a very great *'honnête homme'*, in the sense of the period, capable of appreciating, singling out and making others appreciate (even Molière), and sometimes showing great tolerance. As time went on and he was burdened with other cares, less ably supported and in any case he was growing set in his ways, turning his back on changes in manners and ideas, he became obstinate or frankly gave up. The so-called *'grand siècle'*, with the 'Great King' as its patron was a brilliant firework display which lasted no more than fifteen years.

Louis was a child of the Fronde and although its detailed execution was left to the small fry among his servants, the humbling of all the great 'Corps and Estates' of the realm remained his constant concern. The officers' companies were debased, humiliated and taxed out of existence, the *parlements*, States, communes and consulates annihilated, the arrogant nobility reduced to begging for his favours where they had once been conspirators and instigators of provincial revolts. Most of the clergy were turned into courtiers, and all the ancient nobility tamed and barred from his councils, while the new were treated with contempt for all the cheapness of their titles. Last of all the Béarnais, Catalans, Cévenols, Bordelais, Poitevins and, above all the Bretons, with any others who persisted in untimely uprisings were massacred outright. Such repressive measures were bound, by their very violence, to lead to passionate reactions. The new regency and the new century were certainly to give striking occasion for them.

As the head of a dynasty which he could trace back to Charlemagne and which was, it went without saying, the first in the world, Louis maintained the interests and dignity of his whole family with great arrogance. It was, in the last resort, for his grandson's sake that he embarked on and pursued the war of the Spanish succession. Once Philip V's future was assured, he turned his attention to his own survival through his remaining legitimate and illegitimate descendants by means of the will of 1714 which he altered in 1715, only to have it broken as soon as he was dead, a will of which we may well ask ourselves whether it was the work of a stubborn, a benighted or a desperate man.

Everlasting glory, territorial aggrandisement, and dominion abroad; at home mastery of all political and administrative life, of religion, society and thought, and the protection of the dynasty and the succession : these were the vast spheres which, for all or part of the time, Louis dared to reserve for his own sole jurisdiction. The results of his actions varied from dazzling success, through partial or temporary success to semi-failure and absolute disaster.

For all his bravery and diligence, his frequent opportunism and his sense of greatness, he was after all, no more than a man with a varied and honourable mixture of virtues and weaknesses. His ministers, also, varied in quality, his executives often lacked means of persuasion and he was surrounded on all sides by forces which opposed his will and his glory. It remains to take a look at the actions of the men who served him and at the forces with which he had to contend.

THE KING'S RESPONSIBILITIES: THE SPHERES OF HIS AGENTS

More often than not, and permanently in some cases, administrative details and the complete running of certain sectors of the administration were left to agents appointed by the king and responsible to him. Louis rarely resorted to the cowardly expedient of laying the blame for failure on his subordinates. Not until the end of his life, and notably in the case of the bishops, did he indulge in such pettiness. Everything that was done during his reign was done in his name and Louis' indirect responsibility in matters he had delegated was the same as his direct responsibility in his own personal spheres. Moreover, the two sectors could not help but be closely connected.

A policy of greatness and prestige demanded an efficient and effective administration as well as adequate resources, both military and financial. We have followed the various endeavours undertaken in this field down the years. Now it is time to add up the reckoning.

In order to disseminate the king's commands over great distances and combat the complex host of local authorities, a network of thirty intendants had been established over the country. These were the king's men, dispatched by the king's councils and assisted by correspondents, agents and *subdélégués* who by 1715 were numerous and well organized. By this time the system was well-established and more or less accepted (even in Brittany). It met with reasonable respect and sometimes obedience. Sometimes, not always, since we only have to read the intendants' correspondence to be disabused swiftly of any illusions fostered by old-fashioned textbooks or history notes. The difficulties of communications, the traditions of provincial independence, inalienable rights and privileges and the sheer force of inertia, all died hard. Lavisse used to say this was a period of absolutism tempered by disobedience. In the depths of the country and the remote provinces, the formula might almost be reversed. Nevertheless, there is no denying that a step forward had been made and that the germ of the splendid administrative systems of Louis XV and of Napoleon was already present in the progress made between 1661 and 1715. Some of the great administrative bodies which subsequently set the tone and example for others, such as the registry office, the postal service, the highway department were even then in existence, although it must be admitted that the first of these was introduced as a purely fiscal measure, the second farmed out and the third in an embryonic state.

In one adjacent but vital field, ministers and jurists laboured valiantly to reach a unified code of French law, giving the king's laws priority over local custom and simplifying the enormous tangled mass of statute law. Colbert's codes and two or three great collections of law and practice, such as those of Ricard, Domat and Savary, will serve as examples. But how did all these excellent works fit in with the spirit of the time and with the daily march of justice? Every tiny province still persisted in judging cases according to its own local custom, fixed and written down in the sixteenth century with a mass of later glosses added. The king's law was only one law among many. It had to be ratified by the sovereign courts which, since they could not reject it, had become most skilful in the arts of delay and prevarication. Moreover, royal decrees, even the Revocation of the Edict of Nantes, seldom applied to the whole kingdom. Ordinances regulating the maximum rate of interest (the *denier*), for example, varied from one province to the next and were easily circumvented. As for the monetary ordinances, every man turned them to his own advantage: the merchants had their own rates and *équivalences* and the time was not far off when ordinary farm contracts would be coolly inscribed 'actions of the prince notwithstanding' in stipulating means of payment. As for the notorious regulations put out by Colbert and his successors, we have already seen, in passing, the extent to which they could be ignored and flouted daily in one city, Beauvais, which was less than eighty kilometres from Paris. Too much interest, routine, privilege and sheer habit stood in the way for royal legislation to be properly applied. The great efforts towards centralization and unification which were made were only partially successful but they did pave the way for the great legislators and unifiers of the eighteenth century and still more for those of the Revolution and the Empire.

Of the means to the achievement of power and glory, one, diplomacy, was in the hands of individuals rather than institutions. Long before the 'great reign' a great tradition had existed which is called to mind in the mere mention of such names as Servien, de Lionne, d'Avaux, not to mention the two formidable cardinal-diplomats. They, their colleagues, their successors and their children continued the tradition. In their different ways, Louis XIV's diplomats were among the best in Europe but they were up against brilliant adversaries in the Dutch, the British and the Romans. Two novelties, perhaps, were a degree of 'institutionalizing' and a 'career in diplomacy' and, more important, the emergence of a much higher level of negotiation of men like Mesnager of Rouen, the great merchants of the realm, whose activities had previously been cloaked in a certain obscurity.

The navy, rescued from virtual oblivion by Colbert who gave it arsenals, shipwrights, gunners, talented designers, its finest captains and fresh personnel obtained by means of seaboard conscription, distinguished itself particularly from 1672 to 1690. After that, it declined for lack of resources and any real interest on the part of a king who was a landsman at heart and private enterprise took the lead once more. Even then, Louis and the excellent staff of his navy office did not fail to encourage and make use of the fleets belonging to the shipowners and merchants of the great ports, the capitalists who backed them and the bold captains who brought them both glory and profit.

The greatest of all the king's great servants were those who helped him to build up an army, which in size and striking force was for the most part equal to all the other armies of Europe put together. They were first Le Tellier and Turenne and later, Louvois and Vauban. Many others of less fame, such as Chamlay, Martinet, Fourilles and Clerville would also deserve a place in this unusually lengthy roll of honour if the historian's job were the awarding of laurels, especially military ones. The fighting strength was increased at least fourfold, discipline was improved, among generals as well as officers and men, and a civil administration superimposed, not without a struggle, on the quarrelsome, short-sighted and in many cases incompetent and dishonest military one. New ranks and new corps were introduced; among them the artillery and the engineers, as well as such new weapons as the flintlock and the fixed bayonet, and a new military architect, Vauban, all helped to make the army more efficient. Most important of all, the army at last possessed a real *Intendance* with its own arsenals, magazines, and regular staging posts. Uniforms became more or less general, providing employment for thousands of workers. The first barracks were an attempt to put an end to the notorious custom of billeting troops on civilian households. The Hôtel des Invalides was built, on a grand scale. The instrument which these invaluble servants placed at their master's disposal was almost without parallel in their time, a genuine royal army, growing ever larger and more diversified, modern and disciplined.

Naturally, the people of the realm were not always bursting with pride in it. The army was very expensive. It still went in for billeting and foraging, even within the borders of the kingdom, and still, like the navy with its 'press gang' in the ports, claimed far too many young men who would have preferred to stay at home in their own villages. Too much conscription and to an even greater extent the militia were the cause of much of the king's unpopularity in his old age.

To please his trusted servant Colbert, the king, while a young man, did try for a time to study his finances and to keep simple accounts of his private income and expenditure, but he always believed in his heart of hearts that such occupations were beneath his royal dignity. This book has already shown in some detail how Colbert's work was endangered by the first coalition (1673) and ruined by the two which followed. Quite obviously, it was not the king's building programme, his court, his 'favours' or his petty cash which wrecked the kingdom's finances once they had been put in order by a good finance minister. The one and only reason was the length of the wars and the ever-broadening fronts on which they were fought.

Louis' finance ministers, remarkable both for honesty and ingenuity, did what they could to provide for the constantly renewed wars. They acquiesced in or invented measures which, with more courage and determination, might have been real and radical reforms: the capitation tax, the *dixième*, the *Caisse des Emprunts* and even the introduction of paper money. But all in all, they could not do more than scrape the utmost from a financial, social and administrative system so petrified that it rejected even the slightest attempt at reform. The richest went on paying ludicrously little, or nothing at all. The state failed to maintain its credit or to set up a national bank, while England was managing to do so in spite of all her difficulties. The *Ancien Régime* under Louis XIV was an accumulation of old forms, old habits and old ideas, the more deeply respected the older they were, which proved incapable of reshaping or even of reforming its financial system. To do so would have meant denying its very nature, tearing down the antiquated edifice which had been shored up a score of times although it still presented a glittering façade to the world, and daring to face up to the march of time and the nature of things. The old house stood for another seventy-five years. No one in 1715 could have foreseen how comparatively imminent was its collapse.

For all this, successes, good intentions, failures, inadequacies and refusals, Louis XIV remains, through his ministers, ultimately responsible.

Responsible, that is, if it can be truly said that any man, even a king and a great king, has the power to act effectively against the great political, demographic, economic and intellectual forces which may, after all, finally command the overall development of a kingdom which is not alone in the world. Among these forces were some which, whether the king knew it or not, were acting directly against him. Others, working more slowly and obscurely and almost invariably unknown to the king, had nonetheless a powerful long-term effect which some historians have regarded as crucial.

THE OPPOSING FORCES

An ambition to astonish the world with magnificence and great armies is all very well so long as the world is prepared to be astonished.

At the beginning of his reign, when Louis surveyed the rest of Europe, he saw nothing but weakness and decline. Some of his observations, as regards Spain and Italy, were perfectly correct. In others, he was mistaken. He stupidly underestimated the United Provinces, as though a small, bourgeois and Calvinist population were an inevitable sign of weakness. Yet another observation was swiftly belied by the changes which occurred in two highly dissimilar entities; England and the Empire.

Louis XIV found himself baulked at every turn by the diplomacy and dogged courage, as well as by the seapower and the immense wealth of the United Provinces. It is no longer fashionable to believe that the 'Golden Age' of the Dutch was over in 1661. For a long time after that, their Bank, their Stock Exchange, their India Company, their fleets and their florins remained as powerful as ever. The invasion of 1672 weakened them only temporarily and even in 1715, whatever may be said to the contrary, the Dutch sent as many or even more ships than before to the Baltic, to Japan (where they were the only nation to trade), to Batavia, to Asia and all over the high seas. Their wealth, currency and bankers remained powerful and respected and often decisive. Their policy was not yet tied directly to England's. It was simply that they no longer enjoyed undivided supremacy: another nation's economy had reached the same level and was about to overtake them.

Louis XIV always did his best to ignore economic factors but they would not be denied and they took their revenge. In addition, Louis' aggression in 1672 had a miraculous effect upon the patriotic feelings of the Dutch and brought about the revolution which carried William of Orange to the leadership of the Republic. The last quarter of the seventeenth century belongs, in fact, as much to William as to Louis. Stubborn, clever, with the whole wealth of the Republic behind him, William was a determined enemy, in spite of his bad luck in the field, and he was the soul and the financier of all the coalitions. No sooner was he dead than his place was taken by a Dutchman of no less greatness who had already seconded him on the Continent, Heinsius.

With masterly ineptitude, the King of France, having made William master of the United Provinces, went on to help make him King of England. For a long time, Louis XIV believed he had England at his mercy because he thought himself sure of both Charles II, who was in his pay, and the papist James II, and also because he was convinced that the island kingdom must have been greatly weakened by a revolution and by Cromwell. This was to reckon without the English constitutional traditions, without the deeply anti-Catholic religious feelings of most Englishmen and without the fleet, the London Merchants and the pound sterling. Louis XIV's English policy from 1685 to 1712 was one long series of mistakes and almost continual provocations. During that time, the power of Parliament, of trade, of seapower and of the Bank of England were growing and reaching out across the seas to lay the firm foundations of a strong empire, which would ultimately devour the French empire and was, indeed, already nibbling at it. The final quarter of the seventeenth century was marked by the rise of Britain, spectacularly endorsed by the treaties of 1713, much more than by the dominance of France.

Even the Empire, for which Louis had nothing but contempt, though impotent and enfeebled by the treaties of Westphalia, was ruled by a monarch who, despite his initial youth, nervousness and timidity, succeeded gradually in making an unexpected recovery and emerging as the leader of a crusade against the Turks. He had good advisers and with the support of the Pope, the majority of the German princes and kings like Sobieski, more Catholic than politic, he succeeded in halting the infidel advance for the first time in three hundred years and then in driving them back to their Balkan fastnesses. By liberating Vienna, Hungary and Transylvania, he enlarged his domains much more than Louis had extended his and relieved Europe of the Ottoman pressure once and for all. As a result he became, in his own lands, the great emperor who had succeeded where all others had failed. Artists and writers sang his praises and for all good Germans this end of the century was the time, not of Louis the Devastator but of Leopold the Victorious.

Louis XIV, for his part, put off such German sympathizers as he possessed in 1661, offending them by his ravages and his measures against the Protestants and no longer able to attract them with his impoverished treasury which was powerless in competition with the florins and the sterling which could now purchase new allegiances across the Rhine. It may be that the absence of any French contingent from the great Catholic victory of Kahlenberg in 1683 was considered shameful. It was undoubtedly a mistake, which was more serious. Violent propaganda began to issue from certain quarters in the Empire, lambasting the errors of the King of France and the sanguinary excesses of his troops. In this way, Louis XIV made his own contribution to the birth of German national feeling. Not even Leopold's death in 1705 released him for he had earned the undying hatred of his successors. By an additional irony, Prince Eugène, who had at first asked nothing better than to be allowed to serve France, outlived Leopold as Heinsius and Marlborough had outlived William.

What of the suggestion that, as a kind of compensation, French language, art and letters were making a peaceful conquest of the Europe of the coalition? It is true that every

ruler and every petty princeling was, or soon would be longing to have his own Versailles and his own Maintenon and
set about reproducing them with varying success, but even
so, we incorrigibly patriotic Frenchmen should not be in too
great a hurry to proclaim a triumph of the French spirit. To
do so would be, firstly, to ignore the real character of
baroque art, with its strong Austrian and Spanish elements.
And then, what of Locke and Leibniz, to mention only two,
whose influence was by no means negligible? And were the
prodigious advances in the scientific field a purely French
affair? And finally, if it did become fashionable in certain
foreign circles to adopt French airs and graces, how many
eminent Frenchmen from Descartes onward also went
abroad, to Holland and still more to England, to find a
breath of freedom?

Louis found other forces of opposition within the borders
of his kingdom. We have seen how he dealt with the most
obvious and persistent and there is no need for a repetition.
We have also seen that they, or others like them, appeared
again at the end of his reign, while some waited until the
despot was dead before bursting into the full light of day.
And we have seen, lastly, those which would not be put
down: the small, determined flock of Christians who did
not follow Rome, the proud, intelligent and tenacious little
group of Jansenists and the Gallicans with whom they ultimately joined.

But is there, in fact, no more to be said? There is one
thing: to try to convey some idea of the ancient, traditional
and heavily calculated weight of inertia possessed by that
collection of 'nations', *pays, seigneuries*, fiefs and parishes
which together made up the kingdom of France. Each of
these entities was accustomed to living independently, with
its own customs, privileges and even language, snug in its
own fields and within sound of its own bells. The king con-

secrated at Rheims was a priest-king to be revered and almost worshipped, but from afar. When someone sent by him turned up in the village accompanied by an escort of armed or black-clad men, or merely bearing an order in writing, he was met, on principle, with suspicion or even open hostility. What 'newfangled idea' had he brought with him? A blow struck at local custom? Or a levy of money, horses or men? There is no end to the amount which might be written about this sequestered existence with its local patriotism, its deep-rooted horror of all novelty, its fears and terrors which made up the very texture of life in France under the *Ancien Régime*. Making the king's voice heard in the depths of the countryside was easier said than done when the curé, who was the only means of spreading it, garbled, scamped or merely forgot a task which was clearly no part of his duties; when courts of law were far off, costly, unreliable and even less respected, the forces of law and order never there, the intendant a mystery and his assistants powerless. We have only to look at poor Colbert, trying to establish his manufactures, his tentative regulations and his companies. No one wanted them because all had their own traditions, habits and interests and clung fiercely to their own independence. We have only to look at every administrator, religious or secular, striving to apply contradictory instructions regarding the 'so-called reformed church' to his own particular province. We have only to look at the books of the forestry department and the papers concerned with the *gabelle*, to see the incredible number and variety of infringements which appeared whenever the well-armed dared to set foot in a region to put them down. We have only to stress, in addition, the rash of desertion prevalent in the regular army and still more in the militia (where it may have been as high as 50 per cent) at a time when parishes and even whole provinces were ready to condone, hide and feed the deserters.

If, dazzled by the splendours of Versailles, we let ourselves forget the constant presence of these seething under-
currents, we will have understood nothing of the France of
Louis XIV and of the impossible task which the king and
his ministers had set themselves, or of the massive inertia
which made it so difficult. Moreover, we have said nothing
of the inertia of the clergy and of the nobility and their
refusal to make any contribution to progress in the kingdom
beyond a few prayers and rapier thrusts and some small,
grudging alms, when they might have placed all their
power, wealth and talent at the service of these grand
designs. But was it even asked of them? They remained the
first and second orders, and the only service which they
owed was by prayer and the sword. This was yet another
instance of the inertia, the rejection of all change and progress towards efficiency, in a regime whose end no one
could as yet foresee.

THE FORGOTTEN FORCES

The inherent inertia of that great, tradition-ridden body
which was the monarchy of the *Ancien Régime*, the growing antagonism of the major European states, the forces,
vague or precise, foreseen or unforeseen, of which Louis
XIV was more or less consciously aware, were all ultimately
and undeniably in strong opposition to his designs. But were
there no other forces at work, more mysterious and perhaps
more powerful but for which no allowance was made in
state affairs and which may not even have occurred to the
minds of those who ruled it? These, surely, were the forces
which ultimately controlled the very life of the kingdom,
reducing the activities of one small king of one small country
to nothing more than the meaningless gesticulations of insects in relation to the universe.

For some years now, younger historians of a certain school

have tended to ignore the bustle of individuals and events in favour of what they call revealing, measuring, defining and illustrating the great, dominant rhythms which move world history as a whole. These rhythms emerge as largely economic. The method may have a certain rashness and temerity but it bears fruit. Suppose we give way to it for a moment.

Setting aside the gesticulations of the human insects, the economic, social and political life of France and half the world may well have been dictated by the pace of extracting, transporting and circulating the 'fabulous metal'. The discovery of the 'Indies', and the mines of Mexico and Peru, which poured ever-increasing amounts of precious metals into Europe, goes a long way to explain the prosperity, brilliance, ostentation and sheer wealth of the seventeenth century, just as, later on, Brazilian gold was behind the mounting prosperity of the eighteenth century and Californian gold gave rise to the *belle époque* of Badinguet. But from 1600 onwards, the quantities of silver reaching Spain from America grew less and less until by 1650 the imports were only a fifth of what they had been in 1600. A probable revival of the mines of central Europe was insufficient to make up the deficit. First gold, and then silver, grew scarce, giving rise to hoarding. Copper from Sweden or Japan (via Holland) tended to take their place but it was a poor substitute. The whole age of Louis XIV was an age that Marc Bloch has called 'monetary famine'. The king had difficulty in paying the English for Dunkirk. Ministers and private citizens complained of 'shortage of cash' and 'hoarding' and everyone paid their debts in *rentes* which meant pledges on the future. We have laid some stress on the way in which this situation might explain some aspects of Colbert's work and their lack of success as well as some continuous problems of government and also a certain style of opposition. But money was not the only thing.

Historians and economists have long been aware that the seventeenth century as a whole and the period from 1650–90 in particular, or even 1650–1730, was marked by a noticeable drop in the cost of basic foodstuffs as well as of a great many other things – a drop quite separate from annual 'accidents'. Landed incomes, offices and possibly moneylending, all seem to have been affected by the same general reduction. François Simiand and later Ernest Labrousse, collating and studying these observations in the 1930s, came to the conclusion that in between the great phases of economic expansion which occurred between the sixteenth and eighteenth centuries, the seventeenth, and particularly the time of Louis XIV, was a period bearing all the signs of, at best, stagnation and at worst economic recession and depression. They were followed by other historians who carried the idea further, sometimes to the point of crude exaggeration. Huguette and Pierre Chaunu, following the same general lines and supported by a remarkable statistical analysis of relations between Spain and America, drew a sweeping cross through the whole of the seventeenth century from a maritime angle from 1600 onwards, although still recognizing that elsewhere, in the north and on the Continent, the natural rhythm of growth persisted longer, an observation confirmed by others. The same authors, again supported by impressive documentary evidence, go on to describe a new linking up of circumstances favourable to maritime development round about 1700, a move towards a new expansion which spread slowly inland from the great ports. Similar observations have been made for Provence, Dauphiné and the region of Beauvais.

René Baehrel, on the other hand, argues fiercely against this cross which seems to stand by the name of the 'sad seventeenth century', although admittedly he argues only on behalf of the rural south of Provence, where he sees economic growth continuing, while at the same time agreeing that the rate of this growth slowed down considerably between 1655 and 1690. But rural southern Provence is not representative either of France or of western Europe. It is a corner of the Mediterranean, and the man who studies it a born controversialist.

Setting aside these scholarly arguments, what was the real overall bearing of the great movements of the economic conjuncture, movements rarely perceived at the time unless in some vague way by one or two exceptional minds? Do they, to echo Chaunu, reveal the 'deep breathing of History'?

There remains a strong impression that the period of Louis' reign was one of economic difficulties, suffering both from sudden, violent crises and from phases of stagnation and of deep depression. It is not easy to govern under such conditions especially when, like the king and most of his councillors, one is unaware of them. But what they tried to do and sometimes, despite such obstacles, achieved, remains nonetheless worthy of interest and even of admiration.

It is possible, therefore, that France under Louis XIV may have been unconsciously subject to powerful economic forces which are still much disputed and not fully understood. Social, demographic, mental and other factors, wholly or partly incomprehensible to the rulers, may have played their part also. How and within what limits would they have affected the nation's course?

In a century which possessed no mass media of communication, Louis and his champions of scholasticism fought a pale rearguard action against the irresistible advances of science and of the spirit of criticism. But Descartes, Harvey, Newton and Bayle were not to be gainsaid, and neither was the swing which was to follow the apogee of the Roman Catholic faith with a compensating downward trend. If the seventeenth century was 'the age of saints' (and the

Church certainly needed such champions), its last decades, as we have seen, looked forward to the age of enlightenment, when Voltaire was king. Bossuet died defeated, like Louis XIV, by his confessors and his dragoons. There is no going against nature.

About the great mass of French society and its slow, ponderous development we know almost nothing, only a few glimmers here and there. How did it happen? Louis XIV seems to have thought the existing social structures all very well so long as he was in control, and he was ruthless in his determination to remain so. But apart from such superficial movement, the society of the *Ancien Régime* seems to have petrified more than it evolved. The nobility, in its anxiety to remain pure and predominant, may have made some efforts to confirm its position but continued to live in the same spendthrift fashion, drawing wealthy bourgeois into its ranks, hunting their fortunes and their daughters. At the end of the reign, social life seemed dominated by the great businessmen, bankers, merchants, tax-farmers, shipowners and tradesmen of Paris, Lyons and the other great ports with their great fortunes, often made almost over night, their credit and their patronage, but had things been so very different at the end of the preceding reign, in the time of Mazarin, with the triumph of Fouquet and the Italian or German banks?

And yet, in the manufacturing towns, the small, independent tradesmen seemed to be disappearing, social distinctions becoming more clear cut and relations between bosses and workers hardening. A tendency to concentration? The growth of a proletariat? Perhaps, but all we know at present concerns Beauvais and Amiens. In the heart of the country, around Paris and still much further north, but also in Languedoc, some elements of a similar process seem to have been found: the small, independent peasant-farmers grew fewer and less influential, there was a vast number of

impoverished day labourers and a sudden increase of powerful middlemen, a kind of rural bourgeoisie in close touch
with the great landowners, whether noble or otherwise,
clerical or secular. In the same regions, it has been possible to
distinguish the early signs (1660–70) of some kind of seigneurial (or feudal) reaction, characterized by a renewed interest in landed property, more scrupulous collection of tithes
and dues, revival of old rights and fresh encroachments on
to common lands. But here too, René Baehrel has stated,
and perhaps proved conclusively, that nothing had changed
in southern Provence and there remain any number of provinces in the south-west, the centre and the west still un-
explored. All that can be said for certain is that the acts of
the king and his administration, wherever we find them,
tended to preserve and maintain the rights of the most
powerful section of this mixed and largely landed aristocracy
which always came off best in the courts whenever its vassals
and dependents dared to plead against it.

Apart from one small, passing effort of Colbert's, the State
of Louis XIV seems to have taken little thought for any
kind of demographic policy. The general feeling was that
fertility in France was more than adequate to cope with the
ravages of plague and 'mortality' and people were convinced
that the population of the kingdom, the densest in Europe,
was in no danger of diminution. For the most part, they did
not think at all, or thought about other things, and nature
took its course. Apart from Vauban and a few others now
forgotten, no one took much interest in 'the people' except
in terms of taxation. The chief demographic victory of the
regime, the control of the plague, is largely to the credit of
the local authorities. But this did not stop the unknown
masses from suffering, all through the reign, from the individual and collective miseries of shortages and epidemics.
Except among the very small ruling class, the demographic
characteristics of the kingdom changed very little, or if they

did, these changes have not yet emerged. The numbers in each age group varied wildly, but the population as a whole (within fixed limits) may have grown from time to time, in Brittany and one or two other places. More often than not, it certainly decreased or possibly remained static. Within this population, the cycles of poverty and ease, the many christenings and hasty interments went on, very much as they had done in biblical times. There was no apparent sign of change and hardly anyone expected it.

The court, the kingdom and the collection of princes which, for Louis, constituted the chief of the old Continent, these were the accustomed limits of his royal horizon. Far, far beyond them, Muscovy, Asia, the Americas and the whole world continued to exist for all that, and to develop. A new Caesar arose in Russia but his peculiarities were of interest only to the court and to the city. Only a few missionaries and traders concerned themselves with China, at the other end of the world, or had any inkling of her incomparable civilization. Only the Dutch had access to one small hostile Japanese island, and they reaped huge profits from it. War was soon to break out in India but Louis took little notice of such pagan empires. Africa provided Negro slaves and some other merchandise but two or three poorly protected trading posts were his only interest there. The English, while making thrifty investments in the Spanish Main, were moving further north and beginning to win a decisive battle which did not interest the Great King who cared little for Canada or Louisiana. Brought up by Mazarin in a world of court intrigues, dynastic squabbles and problems of successions and of frontiers, Louis rarely looked beyond his own lands and almost never to the world at large. Twenty nuns at Port-Royal-des-Champs, a few buildings at Marly and two or three strongholds seemed to him worthier objects of glory.

It is true that Louis XIV, like most men who grew up between 1640 and 1660, was incapable of rising beyond the limits of his education, let alone of taking in, at one glance, the whole of the planet on which he lived, to say nothing of infinite space. A king to the depths of his being, and a dedicated king, he had a concept of greatness which was that of his generation: military greatness, dynastic greatness, territorial greatness and political greatness which expressed itself in unity of faith, the illusion of obedience and magnificent surroundings. He left behind him an image of the monarchy, admirable in its way, but already cracking if not outworn at the time of his death. Like most men, and many kings, he had grown stiff and sclerotic with old age.

By inclination a man of taste, and a politician by nature, education and desire, he always despised those material accidents called economy and finance. Such commonplace things were merely appendages to his great plane. It never occurred to him that they could one day topple the throne of the next king but one. For him, all social upheavals and ideals were lumped together as 'uprisings' and 'cabals' to be forcibly suppressed.

Isolated at Versailles at an early stage by his own pride, the machinations of a woman and a few priests and courtiers, he neither knew nor cared that his age was becoming the Age of Reason, of Science and of Liberty. From first to last, he refused to recognize the power of Holland, the nature of England or the birth of an embryo German nation. He gave Colbert little support in his courageous maritime and colonial policies and failed to pursue them seriously. He was always more excited by one fortress in Flanders or the Palatinate than by all of India, Canada and Louisiana put together.

And yet he and his colleagues left behind them a France that was territorially larger, militarily better defended, with a more effective administration and to a large extent pacified.

And although he neglected it and often fought against it, there was a time when he built up and maintained what was to be, for a long time to come, the real greatness and glory of France. The Age of Enlightenment was dominated, at least in part, by the language and the culture of France.

Like many another King of France, he went to his grave amid general dislike and the particular execration of Parisians. His dead body had already become a symbol. Louis was turning into the stuffed mummy singled out for future deification by the nostalgic and for supreme contempt by his passionate enemies.

All we have tried to do is to understand Louis XIV against the background of his own time without attempting to idolize him.

APPENDIX I

INTEREST RATES

These were given in *denier* (from the Latin *denarius* a penny); 50 *denier* meant interest at a rate of 1 in 50, 14 *denier* meant at a rate of 1 in 14 etc. This table gives percentage equivalents to the commoner figures.

Denier	Approx. equivalent as a percentage	Denier	Approx. equivalent as a percentage
50	2	9	11·i̇
40	2·5	8	12·5
30	3·3	7	14·69
20	5	6	16·6̇
19	5·26	5	20
18	5·5	4	25
17	5·8	3	33·3̇
16	6·25	2	50
15	6·6̇		
14	7·14		
13	7·69		
12	8·3̇		
11	9·09		
10	10		

GLOSSARY OF TECHNICAL TERMS

Aides: indirect taxes on consumer goods.

Bailliages: legal entities which might include a number of villages and one major town. The town would be the seat of the court for the area.

Cédules: I.O.U.S.

Champarts: dues levied by some seigneurs in kind or. the produce of certain lands. Champarts tended to be high and unpopular.

Cherté: a sudden massive increase in the price of principal foodstuffs, especially of cereals, often productive of economic and demographic crisis.

Commis aux finances: staff assisting the Finance Minister.

Corvées: obligatory manual labour imposed by the seigneurs upon a large portion of the peasantry.

Dévôts: Catholics with a reputation for great piety, frequently grouped together to promote particular religious and non-religious causes.

Dixième: new tax introduced in 1710, and supposed to constitute one tenth of the subject's annual income. It was abolished several times and reintroduced in an altered form after the death of Louis XIV.

Don gratuit: the voluntary contribution made by the clergy in return for general exemption from all fiscal impositions.

Dragonnades: (dragons = dragoons) repressive forces employed by the Government to terrorize and intimidate the Huguenots, before 1685.

Édit du Toisé: royal measure aimed at raising a new tax on certain Parisian houses. It was one of the causes of the Fronde (1648–52).

Equivalent: tax peculiar to the province of Languedoc.

Faux nobles: roturiers attempting to pass themselves off as belonging to the nobility.

Fermes unies: specific and highly complicated method of indirect taxation.

Gabeleurs: 1. tax-collectors specializing in the distribution of the salt quota.

2. pejorative epithet in the popular vocabulary for any official seeking to impose indirect taxation of any kind.

Gabelle: usually a tax on salt which varied from one province to another. Pejoratively, any unpopular indirect taxation.

Gages: 1. The salary assigned to royal officials which in practice represented the interest on the purchase price of the office they bought.

2. In the case of a private employee or domestic servant, simply the annual salary in cash.

Intendance: the region assigned to an intendant, synonymous with *généralité* and occasionally, province.

Intendants: representatives of the king's authority. They endeavoured to control the administration of an entire province or *généralité*.

Leges privatae: privileged legal regime governing certain elements of society. Contrary: law.

Livre tournois: The *livre* (pound) was the monetary unit: that of Tours, or *tournois* superseded the *livre parisis* (of Paris) in the sixteenth century. As in contemporary England: 1 *livre* = 20 *sols* or *sous* (abbr. *s.*); 1 *sol* = 12 *deniers* (abbr. *d.*)

Manufactures: all forms of industry, whether isolated or concentrated.

Manufactures privilégiées: private industry in receipt of a Government monopoly of manufacture or sale, and certain other advantages.

Manufactures royales: industries set up, controlled and financed by the Government.

Maréchaussée: military forces at the disposition of the civil authorities to maintain order, particularly in the countryside and on the main roads.

Mestiers: (old Fr.) artisans organized in guilds or professional groups.

Métairies: a share-cropping system of agricultural exploitation characteristic of large segments of France in which profits are divided between tenant and landowner.

Miquelets: name used both for the militia of Roussillon and for the local rebel groups.

Noblesse d'épée: hereditary nobility originally destined for military vocation.

Noblesse de robe: generally, junior members of the nobility whose position derived from the judicial offices they possessed or exercised.

Parlement: unlike the English Parliament, this is a tribunal, acting as an appeal court for major civil and criminal cases. The most famous *parlements* were in Paris, Rouen, Rennes, Bordeaux, Toulouse and Aix. In addition, the *parlements* ratified the king's decrees (which then became law) and opposed weak kings by means of remonstrances concerning the decrees put before them.

Parlementaires: judges of the *parlements* of the kingdom, generally rich and noble.

Petites milices: troops raised by various provinces such as the Boulonnais (*milices boulonoises*) or Roussillon (*miquelets*, q.v.).

Reitre: (cf. German *reiter*) professional, usually mounted soldier, brutal and highly unpopular.

Rentes: interest-bearing bonds or annuity in return for capital investment or loan, paid by an institution or an individual.

Rentiers: persons in receipt of *rentes* and whose numbers and influence gave them important rights and position in society.

Réunions: legal dodge thought up by Louis XIV's advisers after 1678 for reincorporating into France such towns or regions as might previously have belonged to her.

Richérisme: a democratizing movement within the lower clergy inspired by the pro-Jansenist writings of Edmond Richer and fostered by the particular social and economic grievances of the silent branch of the First Estate.

Roturiers: all those not belonging to the nobility.

Seigneur: title of distinction, frequently of nobility, very often presupposing ownership of land and a certain fiscal, judicial and political authority.

Subdélégués: intendants' deputies placed in the chief towns of a *généralité* in order to execute legislation and collect information.

Taille: except in the Midi, direct taxation payable by roturiers to the king in proportion to their income. In the Midi, the taille was based on ownership of land and the nobles paid.

Trois Evêchés: the episcopal cities of Toul, Metz and Verdun, joined to France in the sixteenth century, together with their surrounding territories.

A SHORT BIBLIOGRAPHY TO THE
ENGLISH EDITION

THE preceding essay is not intended for scholars but for the educated public in general and students of history in particular. I have merely tried to offer a general guide to current work and at the same time to put forward some less widespread theories and ideas.

A complete bibliography would require not one but a dozen volumes and may be gleaned by those readers who are interested from the works mentioned below which represent a useful, basic and in many cases stimulating selection.

I. BASIC TEXTBOOKS

In French:

Lavisse, Ernest. *Louis XIV*. Vol. 3 of his *Histoire de France (1905–1906)*. Still the recognized authority on French and international history of the period of Louis XIV.

Sagnac, Ph. and Saint-Léger A. de. *Louis XIV*. Vol. 10 in the series *Peuples et Civilisations* (Paris, P.U.F., 3rd ed. 1949). A useful conscientious chronological account.

Mousnier, R. *Les XVIe et XVIIe siècles*. Vol. 4 of *L'Histoire générale des civilisations* (Paris, P.U.F., 1st ed. 1954). For the seventeenth-century 'crisis'.

Mandrou, R. *La France aux XVIIe et XVIIIe siècles*. No. 33 in the series *Nouvelle Clio* (Paris, P.U.F., 1967). First-rate.

Lebrun, F. *Le XVIIe siècle*. Collection U. Paris. A. Colin, 1967. General but extremely accurate and up-to-date.

Goubert, P. *La France d'Ancien Régime*. Vol. 1. *La Société*. Collection U. Paris. A. Colin, 1968.

Methivier, H. *L'Ancien Régime*. (Paris, P.U.F., Collection *Que Sais-je?* No. 426).
Methivier, H. *Louis XIV*, in the same series. (Two admirable, brief surveys.)

In English:

Clark, G. N. *The Seventeenth Century*, Oxford, 1947.
Ogg, David. *Europe in the Seventeenth Century*, 6th ed., London, 1954.
Lough, J. *An Introduction to Seventeenth Century France*, London and New York, 1954.
Treasure, G. R. R. *Seventeenth Century France*, London and New York, 1966. (Perhaps the best and most recent textbook.)
Nussbaum, F. L. *The Triumph of Science and Reason, 1669–1685*, collection *The Making of Modern Europe* ed. W. Langer, New York, 1953.
Wolf, John B. *The Emergence of the Great Powers, 1685–1715*, New York, 1951, same series.
Carsten, F. L. *The Ascendancy of France, 1648–1688* in The New Cambridge Modern History, vol. V. 1961.
   (Boulenger, *The Seventeenth Century in France*, as well as Bertrand, *Louis XIV* and Belloc, *Louis XIV* can be ignored as tendencious and inaccurate works.)
Ogg, David. *Louis XIV*, 1st ed., London, 1933, and many later eds.
Ashley, M. H. *The Splendid Century: some aspects of French Life in the Reign of Louis XIV*, London, 1953.
Judge, H. G. *Louis XIV (Problems and Perspectives in History . . .*), London, 1965.
Church, W. F. *The Greatness of Louis XIV, Myth or Reality?*, 1959.

II. SOURCES

The public as a whole remains generally unaware of the overwhelming mass of sources for the present and future study of France under Louis XIV. The eight volumes of *Sources de l'Histoire de France, XVIIe siècle* by Bourgeois and André are by no means exhaustive.

Memoirs and other literary sources, though lively and interesting, tend to be accepted too readily, without regard to the bias produced by the individual prejudices and abilities or to the narrow social horizons of their authors.

There are a great many French editions of the *Mémoires* of Louis XIV (these cover a period of five years and are brief and indispensable). The Letters of the Princess Palatine and the *Mémoires* of Saint-Simon are the most readable. The following may be obtained in English translation:

Fléchier, *The Clermont Assizes of 1665*, trans. W. W. Comfort, Philadelphia, 1937.

Tallement des Réaux, *Portraits and Anecdotes*, trans. H. Miles, New York and Oxford, 1965.

Sévigné, *Letters of Madame de Sévigné*, ed. R. Aldington, 2 vols., 1925.

Saint-Simon, *Memoirs of the duc de Saint-Simon*, ed. W. H. Lewis, trans. St. John. Rev. ed. New York, MacMillan, 1964. (A further ed. trans. S. de Gramont, Putnam, 1963.)

Voltaire, *The Age of Louis XIV*, trans. and abridged by J. H. Brumfit, New York, Washington Square Press, 1963.

Locke, *Locke's Travels in France*, ed. J. Lough, Cambridge, 1953.

Recommended for readers with a knowledge of French are the excellent eighteenth-century dictionaries which may be found in any good library and provide much invaluable information.

Bourdot de Richebourg, *Nouveau Coutumier général*, 1724, (provincial law).

Delamare, *Traité de la Police* (including administration as a whole), 3 vols. 1722–9, (admirable and too little known, even among historians).

Guyot and Merlin, *Répertoire universal de jurisprudence*, 1775–81. (A massive and reliable record of law and society in the *Ancien Régime*.)

Savary des Bruslons, *Dictionnaire du Commerce*, 1st ed. 1723. (All aspects of French economic life, at home and abroad.)

For those really interested there are the countless records of local administration (parish registers, minutes, cadastral surveys in the south of France) and also of departmental capitals (which are frequently richer sources than the public records in Paris), archives of hospitals and institutions, estates, law offices etc. There are old papers by the ton awaiting the historian's attention.

III. SPECIALIZED WORKS

Government and administration

Pages, G. *La Monarchie d'Ancien Régime en France*, Paris, Colin, 1928.

Marion, M. *Dictionnaire des Institutions de la France aux XVIIe et XVIIIe siècles*, Paris, Picard, 1923, (new ed. 1968). *Serviteurs du Roi*, no. 42 in the review '*XVIIe siècle*' Paris, 1959.

Brissaud, J. B. *A History of French Public Law*, trans. J. W. Garner, Boston, 1915.

Stankiewicz, W. J. *Politics and Religion in Seventeenth-Century France*, Berkeley, Univ. of California Press, 1960.

Rothkrug, Lionel. *Opposition to Louis XIV*, Princeton U.P., 1965.

Cole, C. W. *Colbert and a Century of French Mercantilism*, 2 vols. New York, 1939, (the best of all books on Colbert).

Cole C. W. *French Mercantilism*, 1683–1700, N.Y., 1943.

Religious History

In French:

Vols. 18 and 19 of Fliche and Martin's *L'histoire de l'Église*, by E. Preclin (strongly Catholic viewpoint).

Latreille and Delaruelle, *Histoire du catholicisme en France*, vol. 2 (similar).

Leonard, E. G. *Histoire du Protestantisme*, Paris, P.U.F. (Protestant).

Orcibal, J. Numerous works on Jansenism and religious questions, among the best of which are *Louis XIV contre Innocent XI* (1949) and *Louis XIV et les protestants* (1951).

Cognet, J. *Le Jansénisme* (*coll. Que sais-je?* no. 960) Paris, P.U.F., 1961.

XVIIe siècle review, many issues. i.e. no. 25 (1955).

Adam, A. *Du mysticisme à la révolte, les jansénistes au XVIIe siècle,* Paris, Fayard, 1968.

In English:

Grand, A. J. *The Huguenots,* London, 1934.

Scoville, Warren C. *The Persecution of the Huguenots and French Economic Development, 1680–1720,* Berkeley, Univ. of California, 1960.

Abercrombie, Nigel. *The Origins of Jansenism,* London, 1936.

Dodge, G. H. *The Political Theories of the Huguenots of the Dispersion,* 1947.

Thought, culture and civilization

The four most important books are

Brunot, F. *Histoire de la Langue Française,* (new ed. in prep. A. Colin)

Duby and Mandrou, *History of French Civilisation,* New York, Random House, 1965. (1st pub. Paris, 1958.)

Hazard, P. *The European Mind: the critical years* (trans. from French), New York 1953.*

Adam, *Histoire de la Littérature française au XVIIe siècle,* Paris, Domat, 5 vols.

And many others, including:

Mandrou, R. *De la culture populaire en France aux XVIII et XVIIIe siècles,* Stock, 1964.

Mandrou, R. *Magistrats et sorciers en France au XVIIe siècle,* Paris, Plon, 1968.

Foucault, Michel. *Histoire de la folie à l'âge classique,* Paris, Plon, 1961.

Tapié, V. L. *The Age of Grandeur,* 1960 (trans. from French).

Taton, R. *Histoire générale des Sciences,* Paris P.U.F., vol. 2.

Howarth, W. D. *Life and Letters in France,* vol. 1, 1965.

* Also published in Pelican books as *The European Mind: 1680–1715,* trans. J. Lewis May.

Ornstein, M. *The Role of Scientific Societies in the Seventeenth Century*, Chicago, 1928.

Brown, H. *Scientific Organisations in Seventeenth Century France, 1620–1680*, Baltimore, 1924.

Wolf, A. *The History of Science, Technology and Philosophy in the 16th and 17th Centuries*, London, 1935.

Willey, B. *The Seventeenth Century Background. Studies in the thought of the Age in relation to poetry and religion*, New York, 1953.

Spink, J. S. *French Free-Thought from Gassendi to Voltaire*, London, 1960.

Gillispie, C. C. *The Edge of Objectivity*. Princeton U.P., 1963.

Moore, W. G. *Molière, a new criticism*, Oxford, 1957.

Lough, J. *Paris Theatre Audiences in the Seventeenth and Eighteenth Centuries*, London, 1957.

Nolhac, P. de, *Versailles and the Trianon*, 1966 (English trans.).

Blunt, Sir Anthony, *Atr and Architecture in France 1500–1700*, (1953).

Bukofyer, M. F. *Music in the Baroque Era*, New York, 1947.

History of population

Reinhard, Armengaud, Dupaquier, *Histoire générale de la population mondiale*, Paris, Montchretien, 3rd ed., 1968.

Glass and Eversley (ed.) *Population in History*, London, 1965.

Daedalus, issue of Spring 1968, (Demographic problems).

Annales de Démographie Historique, Paris, Sirey 1964–8, 5 vols. out.

Aries, P. *Centuries of Childhood, A Social History of Family Life*, (trans. Baldick) New York, 1965. London, Cape, 1962.

Economic and social history

Labrousse, Léon, Goubert et al., *Histoire économique et sociale de la France moderne*, Vol. 2. 1660–1789, coming 1970, P.U.F., Paris. (Will reopen the whole question.)

Aspects de l'économie française au XVIIe siècle, No. 70–71 of the review *XVIIe siècle*, 1966.

Luthy, H. *La banque protestante de la Révocation de l'Édit de Nantes à la Révolution*, Vol. 1, Paris, 1961.

Usher, A. P. *The History of the Grain Trade in France*, Harvard U.P., 1913.

André, L. *Michel Le Tellier et Louvois*, Paris, 1942.

Clark, G. N. *The Dutch Alliance and the War against French Trade*, 1688–1697, London and N.Y., 1923.

Lossky, A. *Louis XIV, William III and the Baltic Crisis of 1683*, Berkeley, Univ. of California, 1954.

Bromley, J. S. *The French Privateering War, 1702–1713*, (in *Historical Essays presented to David Ogg*, London, 1963).

Crouse, N. M. *The French Struggle for the West Indies, 1665–1713*, 1943.

Bamford, P. *Forests and French Sea Power 1600–1789*, Toronto, 1956.

Asher, E. L. *The Resistance to the Maritime Classes: the Survival of Feudalism in the France of Colbert*, Berkeley, 1960.

Memain, R. *La Marine de guerre sous Louis XIV, le matériel*, Paris, 1937.

Corvisier, A. *L'armée française de la fin du XVIIe siècle au ministère de Choiseul*, Paris, P.U.F., 2 vols. 1964.

IV. THE 'ECOLE DES ANNALES' AND THE REVIVAL OF FRENCH SEVENTEENTH-CENTURY STUDIES

Founded in 1929 by two of the best French historians, Marc Bloch and Lucien Febvre, the *Annales d'histoire économique et sociale* (the title of which has since changed but is generally referred to simply as *Les Annales*) have exercised a decisive influence, for better or worse, upon a whole generation of historians, in and out of France. This review has been the determining factor in many historical careers. A kind of 'school' has grown up loosely around the *Annales*. The general trend is against pure scholarship, slack chronology, and traditional political and military history, and towards the primacy of the intellectual, social and economic aspects of comparative and inter-disciplinary studies, strong reliance on statistics, economic 'patterns', recent sociological work, ethnology, linguistics, symptomatic studies and so forth. It is apt to encourage a certain deliberate originality and provocativeness of style and subject matter. Apart from the review itself, the principal works of this 'school', or rather of this 'trend' are or will be published by section VI of the *École Pratique des Hautes Études* in Paris.

At the same time, although not always in full agreement with those responsible for the *Annales*, a great many, particularly among the younger historians, have come to realize that the only real advances to be made in the field of French social history lie in the intensive regional studies begun in the course of the last century.

The conjunction of these two tendencies has produced a number of recent works, many of them little known outside a narrow circle, whose regional character should not be allowed to obscure their general utility. Among these are:

Agulhon, M. *Pénitents et francs-maçons de l'ancienne Provence*, Paris, Fayard, 1968.

Baehrel, R. *Une croissance: la Basse-Provence rurale, fin du XVIe s.–1789*, Paris, 1961.

Chaunu, P. *La civilisation de l'Europe classique*, Paris, 1965.

Delumeau, Jean, *L'alun de Rome, XVe–XIXe siècle*, Paris, 1962.

Delumeau, Jean, *La civilisation de la Renaissance*, Paris, 1967.

Deyon, P. *Amiens, capitale provinciale, étude sur la société urbaine au XVIIe siècle*, Paris and the Hague, 1967.

Dion, R. *Histoire de la vigne et du vin en France des origines au XIXe siècle*, Paris, 1959.

Goubert, P. *Beauvais et les Beauvaisis de 1600 à 1730*, Paris, 1960.

Le Roy Ladurie, E. *Les Paysans de Languedoc*, Paris, 1966.

Mandrou, R. (works already mentioned, in the tradition of Lucien Febvre.)

Merle, Dr L. *La métairie et l'évolution agraire de la Gâtine poitevine de la fin du Moyen-Age à la Révolution*, Paris, 1958.

Meyer, J., *La noblesse bretonne au XVIIIe siècle*, Paris, 1966.

Poitrineau, A. *La vie rurale en Basse-Auvergne au XVIIIe siècle*, Paris, 1965.

Saint Jacob, P. de, *Les paysans de la Bourgogne du Nord au dernier siècle de l'Ancien Régime*, Paris, 1960.

There are many valuable short articles in the review *Annales Economies, Sociétés, Civilisation*. To take a few examples:

Billacois, F. *Pour une enquête sur la criminalité dans la France d'Ancien Régime*, March–April 1967.
Furet, F. *Pour une définition des classes inférieres à l'époque moderne*, May–June 1963.
Richet, D. *Croissance et blocages en France du XVe au XVIIIe siècle*, July–August 1968.

Further important books are due to be published shortly on Anjou (F. Lebrun), Dauphiné (S. Bonnin), Lorraine (G. Cabourdin), Haut-Languedoc (G. Frêche), Vexin (J. Dupâquier), Normandy (G. Lemarchand), the south of the Paris region (J. Jacquart), Lyon (Garden and Garrier), Marseille (C. Carrière), Bordeaux and others.

It should also be added that many advanced students from America are at present engaged in the study of French archives.

These and one or two more works will make it possible in the next few years to produce what may very well be an altogether new picture of French history in the seventeenth and eighteenth centuries.

INDEX